THE
ESTABLISHMENT
BOYS

THE
ESTABLISHMENT
BOYS

The Other Side of Kerry Packer's
Cricket Revolution

THE
ESTABLISHMENT
BOYS

BARRY
NICHOLLS

FOREWORD BY
MIKE COWARD

To the memory of

Ambrose Edward Blight (1914–1943)

and

Geoffrey Alfred Blight (1927–1974)

Australians are a friendly lot. They like you to get ahead …
just not of them.
                Kim Hughes addressing Melbourne Cricket Club, 1997

First published in 2015 by New Holland Publishers Pty Ltd
London • Sydney • Auckland

The Chandlery Unit 009 50 Westminster Bridge Road London SE1 7QY United Kingdom
1/66 Gibbes Street Chatswood NSW 2067 Australia
5/39 Woodside Ave Northcote, Auckland 0627 New Zealand

www.newhollandpublishers.com

A record of this book is held at the British Library and the National Library of Australia.

ISBN 9781742577067

Managing Director: Fiona Schultz
Publisher: Alan Whiticker
Project Editor: Susie Stevens
Cover Design: Andrew Quinlan
Text Design: Peter Guo
Proofreader: Jessica McNamara
Production Director: Olga Dementiev

10 9 8 7 6 5 4 3 2 1

Keep up with New Holland Publishers on Facebook
www.facebook.com/NewHollandPublishers

Contents

Foreword

The Establishment Boys

by Mike Coward

Collateral damage is an inevitable consequence of revolution. No uprising is immune. And so it was when the conservative fabric of an ancient game was torn asunder by the World Series Cricket movement from 1977 to 1979. After tentative even humbling beginnings the rebellion, primarily precipitated by Dennis Lillee and his disgruntled peers, transformed every aspect of a game that for so long prided itself on its solid, firmly entrenched traditions. Change was anathema. The casualties of the conflict, the collateral damage, became known as the Establishment Boys and their governors – the crusty, unbending Establishment.

World Series Cricket was bankrolled by media mogul Kerry Packer – it gave rise to the most pivotal yet painful period of the game's modern history. Cricket became a game bitterly divided. Resentment and suspicion ran deep and accusation and recrimination became the default position of the protagonists.

As new allegiances were forged old bonds were broken and friendships shattered. Sir Donald Bradman and Richie Benaud, OBE, giants of the game whose vision and energy had famously given the kiss-of-life to moribund Test cricket 17 years earlier, did not speak for two years. This sad impasse was symbolic of a country torn apart. Confused and conflicted cricket lovers took one position or another. They resented being compelled to direct their attention and affection to one of two Australian teams. Where should their loyalties lie: with those who upheld the honour and rich traditions of the fabled 'baggy green' cap or the admired and seemingly opportunistic rebels who were hell bent on propelling the game into new and unfamiliar territory?

Ultimately, the momentum for change was unstoppable and the people were seduced again by the charismatic souls whose deeds had established Australia as the powerhouse of the game in the mid 1970s. Left in the wake, dazed and disillusioned and seeking respect and recognition were the Establishment players – cricketers of considerable consequence but, with a few notable exceptions, were destined to remain at the margins of Australian cricket history.

As the 40th anniversary of the great schism looms, Barry Nicholls skillfully and sympathetically revisits this tumultuous time and allows the Establishment Boys to step out of the shadows and for once become the centre of attention.

Prologue

Men in white

It is as if the figures – all men, all in white – are performing a dance before my eyes.

It's different these days. Forty years on. They have changed. All so much older. One is no longer with us. If this is a dance, it is a dance with the shadows of time.

I am fifteen years old. Flickering shadows, the action on a new but tiny colour television in Mum's living room in her two-bedroom unit in Beulah Park, east of Adelaide. A December day, school broken up, textbooks put away. That sense of freedom. Summer holidays, when days stretch into weeks. And life revolves around cricket – playing, watching and reading about it.

Today, it's sunny outside. I've been killing time; the morning spent swinging a trusty Gray-Nicolls bat at a ball that hangs in one of Mum's stockings dangling from the garage door. The *bang, bang, bang* of the bat hitting the ball in an almost hypnotic manner now silenced; there is some respite for the neighbours. No more tinny radio spilling out pop songs like Boney M's thundering 'Ma Baker', Boz Scaggs' 'What Can I Say' and the diminutive, hip-swaying Tina Charles' 'Dance Little Lady Dance'.

Now it is just the television and me. Channel Two beams images live from The Gabba in Brisbane. Australia versus India. The First Test match of a new Australian summer. Australia's captain, a bareheaded, white-shirted Bob Simpson tosses the coin with the turbaned Bishan Bedi resplendent in a dark-blue India blazer. ABC cricket commentator Norman May's voice booms out of the box. A more gentle, calm-sounding Keith Miller is with him. While May has the excitable tone of a schoolboy at a Year Eleven formal on his first date, Miller sounds like he had just wandered down from Rydges Hotel, still waking up. Simpson has won the toss and Australia will bat despite the overcast and muggy conditions conducive to pace and swing bowling.

To the audience this is the real stuff – *Test* cricket. This is what will be recorded in the *Wisden Cricketers' Almanack*, the yellow Bible that arrives in bookshops from England just as footy season gets into full swing. A reminder of what has taken place, set as if in stone, the record of the 100-year history of international Tests, celebrated so extravagantly in the recent Centenary Test in Melbourne.

Today at The Gabba there is no Greg Chappell, no Dennis Lillee, no Rod Marsh. But this match feels just as important as any game they have graced.

Australia's openers appear through a curtain of drizzling rain. Debutant Paul Hibbert faces the first ball, which swings down the leg side. In long-sleeved jumper and baggy green, Hibbert looks the part – an Australian opening batsman. His partner – the bulky and bearded Gary Cosier appears more at ease and accustomed to the Test match atmosphere.

The first wicket falls … and then Australian batsmen come and go in a flurry, victims of a triumvirate of twirling Indian spinners, Bedi, Chandrasehkar and Prasanna, names we will know well by summer's end. Six first-time Test players are in the Australian side. Nervous faces, heavy feet trudging back to The Gabba pavilion. The game is punctuated by rain. In the fading light there is some resurgence from the tail-enders before the fragile batting side is dismissed.

Then an Indian wicket falls. The mighty Indian opener Sunil Gavaskar is out. And it's stumps. On the first day of a new form of Test cricket.

Introduction

Blackouts in a colour TV world

From 1977–78 through to the reconciliation two years later, there were two national Australian cricket teams existing seemingly in parallel universes: the glamorous, rock-star realm of World Series Cricket; and the harsh reality of traditional Test cricket, suddenly depicted as stodgy and obsolete but nevertheless hard-fought, by young, poorly paid men who represented their country in the time-honoured 'contest'.

Incredibly, four decades later we know more than ever about the characters and plot-twists of the WSC saga, thanks to a commercial media-driven fascination with magnate Kerry Packer and the household-name cricket heroes of the day. But the mid 1970s, years of the centuries old tradition of Test cricket seemed like a sideshow, the results and players largely forgotten – or simply unknown.

The story tracks from clandestine dressing-room deals during the 1977 Centenary Test – through the detective work of sports journalists leading to the explosive, divisive revelations – to the real meat of the story; the Test matches, series and tours of the 1977 to 1979 cricket seasons, in which the untried and largely unappreciated Establishment Boys carried Australia's cricketing banner. Somebody had to do it. It's time to hear *their* story.

The story of men like former opening batsman Rick Darling, plagued by mini-blackouts for over twenty years, at least partly attributed to the times he was struck in the head – a health problem that requires daily medication. Men like Ian Callen, the Victorian fast bowler whose reaction to yellow-fever vaccine left him battling forty-degree heat in his Test debut when he injured his back; he was never the same bowler again. Kim Hughes, who went on to captain Australia, doesn't like to talk about the days when he became known as the golden-haired boy of *The Establishment*. Tensions between the Establishment and WSC tore him apart, his charismatic smile replaced with a snarl and a scowl that stayed for years. Then there is Allan Border, whose WSC era of playing was a valuable pit stop on his way to becoming one of Australia's greats. But it could so easily have been otherwise.

Scholarly and introspective Queenslander David Ogilvie, tipped by Ray Lindwall to be one of the greats of the Australian game, became so despondent at not being picked in the Australian side to tour the West Indies in 1978, that when he was called up as a replacement, he wasn't sure if he wanted to go. He no longer has his baggy green caps. And it's time to tell the story of the late Paul Hibbert – over the moon when he finally got the opportunity to open the batting for Australia, but shattered when he lost it after one Test. In later years he struggled with depression and alcoholism and died young.

The survivors have differing memories of the fleeting years in which they held the nation's gaze during the tumultuous World Series Cricket era. They were thought of as the Establishment cricketers, the ones who were told they had to keep flying the banner of Test cricket.

They were told never to mention their competitor, or if they did, to cast WSC in a disparaging light. Australia's young guns had to compete with Kerry Packer's breakaway cricket competition and marketing onslaught that highlighted aggression in the cricket they would be playing.

That became a trap for 24-year-old Gary Cosier, then with nine Tests and an average in the forties, making him one of the most experienced in the side. Unlucky not to have been offered a Packer contract before the split, he lost form and was dropped from the Australian side before the two summers of the cricket war were over.

I found myself trying to play too aggressively, to compete with the WSC boys. I'd hear the song 'C'mon Aussie C'mon' and the line 'Hookesy's clearing pickets' and thought 'I'll do that as well'. I wasn't that sort of a player, so it was all to my detriment.

Peter Toohey was the hero of the home series against India in which he posted five half-centuries and three scores in the eighties. 'I was impetuous,' he says now. 'I threw away opportunities to score some hundreds.' What chills him most, in the light of the 2014 death of young Australian batsman Phillip Hughes, is a photo of Toohey spread-eagled on the pitch in the West Indies. That he then went out to bat at the fall of the eighth wicket has him retrospectively amazed.

For Western Australia's Tony Mann, the chance to play for Australia was one that he will never forget. As someone who had trouble finding a regular place in his state team, his call to Australian colours was crowned by a Test century as nightwatchman in his home city of Perth.

Graham Yallop led Australia to a 5–1 defeat at the hands of England. He scored a magnificent backs-to-the wall century at The Gabba in his first Test as captain, yet struggled to manage pace king Rodney Hogg and forever had his reputation tainted as one of the weaker Aussie captains. It's taken decades for Yallop to realise that he is a member of a distinctive club – the men who captained Australia – and for that he is immensely proud.

Only once before had such an inexperienced team of cricketers held the nation's hopes and dreams than across those two home-summers. The second Melbourne Test of 1884–85 featured nine debutantes and an entirely new side, after the First Test side refused to play on unless they were paid half the gate money. Not surprisingly, England won by ten wickets.

The legend of WSC

So much has been made of the cricket revolution that was Kerry Packer's World Series Cricket (WSC). Channel Nine has worked hard to keep the Packer legend alive and well-deservedly given Packer's achievements on behalf of Australia's cricketers of the 1970s and also for converting his father's newspaper business into a new business model of television broadcasting and magazine franchises.

A television mini-series appeared first on the ABC covering the downtrodden young Packer's relationship with his father, to the development of *Cleo* magazine. Sensing the value of aggrandising the Packer name, his network then took up the story, with *Howzat! Kerry Packer's War,* the mini-series about his role in setting up World Series Cricket. Soon followed *Paper Giants,* revealing Packer's rivalry with Rupert Murdoch, through the lens of rival magazines, *Woman's Day* and *New Idea* – myth and legend blended for an overall snapshot of Packer as a man and entrepreneur.

As the spotlight shone more on Packer and his World Series Cricket, it was as if Establishment cricket – real Test cricket – simply didn't exist, save for a few cartoonish, curmudgeonly Australian Cricket Board members mumbling and grumbling and feebly defying Packer in *Howzat.*

Test cricket in Australian was played to a cricketing backdrop never seen before in this country. While Kerry Packer's contracted players were attracting Australian cricket fans with all the thrills of cricket under lights, in coloured uniforms with white balls, the tradition of Test cricket continued, often on the other side of the country at the same time. It may not have had the fanfare or the same star-quality players, but a large group of the traditional Australian cricket fan base supported it. They longed to see Australian cricketers playing under the baggy green cap. Kerry Packer sent his sides out bush for matches, but the real heart-of-country Australia belonged to Test cricket. It had no choice – rural Australia could only see and hear the Test matches on radio and ABC TV. They couldn't receive the signal for Channel Nine's WSC broadcast.

Public perception was that there was something noble in the cause of the Australian Test cricketers, as if the TV presence in regional areas confirmed its authentic status for those who lived there. The Establishment cricketers were the ones prepared to play for their country against the odds. The reality was more complicated, but that was how many saw it.

In that first season, cricket traditionalists were clearly Establishment cricket-aligned but watched Packer on television mingling with his high-flying mates in the VIP boxes, looking out onto vast, largely empty stadiums such as Waverly in Melbourne. During these two domestic seasons of conflict, each side had a name. The Establishment was Test cricket and World Series Cricket was disparagingly called by the mainstream press, 'Packer's Circus'. Each competition played an important role, one kept Test cricket alive, the other extended the game's traditional boundaries and audience. One has been fully recognised, the other has seemingly slipped into the footnotes of cricket's past, almost as if it never happened.

One of the great ironies of this era is that the Australian Cricket Board, having been hijacked by Kerry Packer, appeared – at least initially – not to hear the message that senior players were sending by their defection. For Australia's Test cricketers, there were still nominal player managers at each ground with little support. The game belonged to the administrators. As one former player said about Test cricket, it was 'for those drinking piss behind the glass'.

It should however be remembered that the Australian Cricket Board was a non-profit entity, distributing all the money it earned. It was a shadow of what Cricket Australia is today. The Board in the Packer period, had no premises or employees, in fact the only paid full-time administrators were the state secretaries. The rest were part-time, un-paid honorary appointees.

Nobody really knew what was going to happen. Would Test cricket survive? We looked to the faces and voices on the ABC for some kind of reassurance. On television, the deep sounding, knowing tones of Keith Miller and Frank Tyson provided insights, while the cardigan and tie wearing Norman May described the play. It was familiar ground. The results may not have provided comfort to traditional cricket fans, but the voices did.

That first summer was a teenage cricket fan's dream. Wall-to-wall cricket on television. There were even *three* monthly cricket magazines, *Australian Cricket, Cricketer* and *World of Cricket*. In my home state of South Australia, international cricket was played on Adelaide Oval and at Football Park. Packer's sporting merchandise was promoted everywhere, on the radio, out of television screens and even in popular women's magazines.

A look at contemporary coverage makes for interesting reading. Initially the mainstream press largely focused on Test cricket, with many fewer column-inches devoted to WSC. Tour books were written of the 1978–79 Ashes series when a fleet of English journalists arrived. *Cricketer* magazine's editor Eric Beecher wrote *The Cricket Revolution*, after the first season; Henry Blofeld penned *The Packer Affair* while WSC's publicity agent Christopher Forsyth offered his version in *The Great Cricket Hijack*. In more recent years, Gideon Haigh's examination of the period in *The Cricket War* and Christian Ryan's Kim Hughes biography *Golden Boy* brought some of the Establishment players back to life and are wonderful resources … but now it is time for a more detailed retrospective look at the Test players of the day.

Establishment players

From 1977to1979, an unprecedented 31 players represented Australia, 23 of them for the first time. Test cricket fans greeted twelve new faces for the first summer of this new-look Test team, six in the First Test match against India at The Gabba. They were all good players. They had to be to get to this level, despite at times being dubbed the Australian second eleven, or even third eleven. As any A-grade cricketer can testify, to play A-grade District cricket you had to be competent; to play State cricket, or better still 'Test' cricket in any era, puts you in a rare league.

For a number of cricketers this one shot at the baggy green against strong national sides was a little like the plot of the 1976 movie *Rocky* – men previously thought to be on the outer of a big sport being thrown a lifeline. The Establishment Boys, as we will see, had mixed fortunes. For some, it was a chance they would relish, a springboard to significant careers. Others would spend a lifetime regretting their involvement. Some came and went like blazing comets. Only seven – Border, Dymock, Hogg, Hughes, Yardley, Wood and Higgs – would go on to play Test cricket again.

Out of this mix emerged one of Australia's greats, Allan Border who remained part of the Australian cricket scene for decades. On summer television throughout the 1980s and 90s he was seemingly always there: moustache, upright straight-legged stance, nervous tap of the bat on the turf as the bowler approached. A sun-bleached image, day-in day-out, defending Australia's pride amid numerous collapses. The sight of Border at the crease was synonymous with the sound of Richie Benaud on television – the latter the voice of World Series Cricket during the era Border debuted.

Kim Hughes, who later captained the full-strength Australian side, was tainted as being the golden-haired boy of the Establishment, not really deserving his chance to captain the Australian side ahead of more senior players like gruff Australian wicketkeeper Rod Marsh. Some senior players thought 'the kid' really didn't know what he was doing, that he only got the job because he had played for Australia during the WSC era. If there was some truth in it, there was no excuse for the undermining that Hughes later received at the hands of Dennis Lillee, Rod Marsh and Ian Chappell.

The volatile Rodney Hogg blazed onto the scene during Australia's thrashing at the hands of England with his 41 wickets at 12.85. It was Hogg who threatened to take inexperienced captain Graham Yallop out the back of the Adelaide Oval and 'deck him'. Hogg would never repeat his extraordinary Ashes performance, but went on to play an important role for Australia post-Packer.

Bruce Yardley, who reinvented himself at the age of thirty as an off-spinning batsman, regularly played for Australia during and after the split. Jeff Moss played one Test for Australia against Pakistan, finishing with the unrealistically impressive average of sixty. These players still had to battle high expectations under difficult conditions against full-strength teams without sufficient senior players to stabilise a side. By the end of the second summer they were more often than not labelled 'fill-ins' by the press, not really up to the job at hand. It was even questioned whether their matches should be counted as Test cricket when Kerry Packer's World Series Cricket's Super Tests were not granted first-class status.

All up, the Establishment Boys delivered seven Test wins against twelve losses in those two seasons between 1977 and 1979.

About the money

Money, or the lack of it, had been the catalyst for Australian cricketers to sign with Packer. For years, players had to work part time while trying to carve out international cricket careers. Some generous employers stuck by them, knowing that having an Australian Test cricketer as an employee could be good for business. Others tired of the lengthy absences.

In the end it was a loss of money for the Australian Cricket Board that saw them compromise and agree to sell the television rights to Kerry Packer and his publishing and broadcasting company.

The ACB had effectively been caught on the hop. Its members were more used to dealing in the incremental steps of a culture absorbed in minutiae and obsessed about raising enough money to cover operating costs. Strategic planning couldn't have been further from their minds. In the post-Whitlam era, social change was in the air. Players had moved from the 'short back and sides' unquestioning style of the 1960s to a more challenging approach led by Ian Chappell with his distinctive moustache, swaggering, salty-mouthed gang of the mid 1970s.

Many lessons were learned, the main one arguably that players needed to be treated and paid in a manner commensurate with their level of skill and the riches they could help deliver to the Board and commercial broadcasting networks. The era when Board Secretary Alan Barnes could utter the inflammatory words about the Australian captain that 'if his players didn't want to play for Australia, there were 500,000 other players who would' was over – at least in the players' eyes.

As both sides threw barbs at each other it was hard to work out who might win this Cricket war. The Establishment initially had the public's sympathy and bigger crowds, until WSC started to develop a culture of its own – one very different from the stodgy, traditionalism of the Establishment. The song 'C'mon Aussie C'mon' became an anthem for all cricket fans. It was the song of WSC. Without realising the irony, school children would sing it at Test matches as well. By the second season, Packer's style of cricket, the WSC, had attracted a broader and larger audience than the Establishment could even dream of. Cricket was changing. It had gone from a game for whites-wearing traditional cricket players to something that was colourful, bold and daring – and more women and young girls started to take an interest. Women knew the names of some of the players, and admired 'Hookesy' the West Indians, Michael Holding and Viv Richards, and Dennis Lillie.

Suddenly we couldn't get enough of the new excitement that was cricket; the colourful, bright outfits of the players, the speed of the game or the stream of never-ending instant replays from eight different camera angles that broadcast even the smallest detail of the game. Previously, the ABC broadcasts of Test cricket were shot from one end of the field, as though the viewer were sitting in one seat. No replays: if you missed a big moment, too bad. Packer introduced a conceptually different approach to broadcasting his game. Now instant replays were commonplace. The viewer could see close up shots of players sliding into the crease to avoid a run out. We could see shots of the crowds and of the commentators who, like the players, became stars of the game too.

This all contributed to the lack of on-field success of the official Australian team and also saw a waning of the national spirit for the Establishment side. Fans eventually wanted to see the *best* Australian side and that side was playing in the WSC.

While Packer was a tough taskmaster, he nevertheless took a personal interest in his players and did everything he could to support them. His familiarity with the players was a far cry from the Australian Cricket Board's distant paternalism. Former WSC player Gary Gilmour observed, 'He'd eat with us, drink with us, come to practice and bowl to us.' And he paid the players well.

In contrast to the new superstars of cricket, Australia's test cricket team appeared old and not very exciting. The first captain for the Establishment (after the split), Bobby Simpson, was old enough to be our dad. The second captain, Graham Yallop would really have preferred not to have had the job at all. The third captain Kim Hughes while young and keen appeared more like an annoying younger brother than a revered captain of the Australian team. The charisma of the WSC players promoted by Packer was missing.

So who won the war between the Establishment and Packer's WSC? The ACB called the cricket war a draw, but we all knew that Packer had won. His cricket was a slick, well-produced, widely accessible cricket series that featured the now highly paid 'stars' of Australian cricket. The WSC catered successfully to a growing audience for the one-day game and all its razzamatazz.

The season of reconciliation in 1979–80 saw a dual series in which Australia played England and the West Indies in two three-Test series and in a World Series one-day competition with three finals. By the time Test cricket was back on an even keel with the new game, only three Establishment players remained playing for Australian. Several were not even in their state sides.

Chapter One

Before the schism

Ian Chappell knew it, so did his former teammate Bob Cowper. Players were no longer content to play for the glory of the game. Both knew that things had to change for players to survive financially.

Cowper, lean and athletic, was a powerful left-hand batsman and a useful off-spin bowler. He hit the first triple century on Australian soil against England at the MCG in 1966 and retired two seasons later. His premature retirement from Test cricket, with the missed chance to captain his country, was not because he was dropped from the side; he couldn't afford to play on. It was a good decision financially as it turned out. By the mid 1970s, Cowper was a successful stockbroker and merchant banker. Still involved in cricket, he continued to point out to officials that Australian Test cricketers needed to be paid more if they wanted to field the best players.

Ian Chappell, impressed by Cowper's entrepreneurial flair (and his insistence that players should be paid more), consistently nominated his former teammate for membership on the Australian Cricket Board (ACB). Like many of Chappell's suggestions to the Board, this fell upon deaf ears. Chappell's frustration with the Board later came to a head when the Australians were asked to play an extra Test at the end of two tours: the first was a tour of India, and the second of South Africa, which Australia lost 0–4 to the Springboks in 1969–70.

The players asked for more money for these final Tests. The Board declined. Skipper Bill Lawry, furious, wrote a letter complaining to the ACB. Lawry ignored Ian Chappell's suggestion that the whole team co-sign the missive – the board surely wouldn't sack the whole team. Within a year Lawry was axed and Chappell installed in his place as skipper. 'The bastards will never get me like that', Chappell told his wife. And they didn't.

Sponsorship in sport

Despite the pay issues faced by players, sponsorship in sport generally was on the rise and by 1976, the sponsorship of cricket was also expanding. A good example is the Brut 33 (a popular brand of aftershave) campaign. Through the summer of 1975–76 Australian and West Indian players were chosen to spruik Brut 33 over the airwaves. That same year Benson and Hedges became the Australian Cricket team's official sponsor. Phil Wilkins, breaking the story in *The Australian* under the headline 'Cigarette Company offers $350,000 to sponsor our Test cricketers', wrote: 'Commercialism has been a dirty word in cricket for 100 years. Only now is the barrier being broken down.'

Old-time cricketers found the commercialisation of the game hard to take. Jack Fingleton and Bill O'Reilly declined to act as judges for Benson and Hedges match awards, O'Reilly stating, 'Sponsored money for the team winning the series is the root of all evil ... the Australian (team) has its collective eyes set on it.'

The implication that players were only interested in the money typified the conservative views about how cricket should be played: for honour, never for personal monetary gain. The Benson and Hedges sponsorship deal was a significant shift away from the Australian Cricket Board's resistance to change. The ACB was conservative by nature, and largely consisted of middle-aged, grey haired men in suits from an amateur era. For them the idea of playing cricket on a professional level was an anathema. They had served Australian cricket for years with little or no financial remuneration and stuck to a philosophy of 'if it ain't broke, don't fix it.'

However, at the same time, while the ACB began expanding sponsorships, players themselves were also being approached about sponsorship deals. Queensland fast bowler, Jeff Thomson's $633,000 contract with Brisbane radio station 4IP, struck by manager David Lord, is a notable example of the changes that were to come.

Why Packer? And why then?

The Board's move toward commercialisation meant much more money for the game, but not so much more for the players; certainly nowhere near the amount that came in to the ACB from sponsorship and gate takings. For example, the gate takings of the 1975–76 Boxing Day Test were $310,230. More than 85,000 people attended the first day's play. The players' match fees were $400 plus $75 for incidentals. That summer, Australia won most of the $46,000 in prize money; the players received only an extra $400 a test.

Player frustration about the lack of financial recognition would neatly intersect with multi-millionaire, business magnate Kerry Packer's need for cheap content for his television network. Cricket, as Packer knew, provided just that – cheap, local sporting content with the bonus of convenient advertising breaks built in. Packer could also see the potential for one-day cricket as a TV sporting spectacle.

The history of one-day cricket indicates why Packer was convinced that it was the way of the future. One-day, limited-over version cricket was introduced in England in 1962 to bolster the coffers of ailing county clubs. Individual one-day games in the four-team Midlands knockout competition were played between Leicestershire, Derbyshire, Northamptonshire and Nottinghamshire. It quickly morphed into the Gillette Cup the following season, a 65–over competition that included all seventeen first-class English county clubs. One-day cricket was seen to be the game to bring the crowds back to watch county cricket, after attendances halved in the decade following WWII and continued to dwindle. The new form of the game was an immediate success for county clubs, with the 1963 Gillette Cup final played before a sell-out crowd at Lord's where Ted Dexter's Sussex side delivered his county their first title.

Different forms of limited-over cricket were soon being played in other cricket-loving nations. In 1968–69, sixteen of the world's greatest players from Australia, England, South Africa and New Zealand opposed each other in a one-off, double-wicket, two-man team competition competing for $25,000 prize money. Despite this build up, 'international' one-day cricket only came about by accident. During the summer of the 1970–71 Ashes series, the Third (Melbourne) Test was cancelled because of rain. From then on, occasional one- day fixtures were programmed, including three one-dayers between Australia and England in 1972. It proved a winner with over 19,000 attending a Boxing Day one-dayer during the Ashes series of 1974–75, and almost as many fans attending the one-day game between Australia and the West Indies in 1975–76 in Adelaide. The limited over game gained much greater credibility after the successful staging of the first ever World Cup in England in 1975. A riveting final between Australia and the West Indies at Lord's, ended at twilight on a June summer's eve heralding the arrival of a game that had potential for mass appeal.

Several years earlier, Richie Benaud, later a consultant to Packer, had seen the writing on the wall for Australian cricket. He devised a blueprint to bring in larger crowds, which included shorter tours with a combination of Test matches and one-day knockout games. Benaud's strategy for taking the game to the masses and Packer's desire to gain broadcasting rights to improve his TV ratings were about to merge.

In early 1976, well before the secret signings, Packer had tried to buy the exclusive rights to televise Test cricket in Australia in his Channel Nine stations and affiliates. He told the Australian Cricket Board's Chair Bob Parish that he was prepared to pay half a million dollars per year for the rights once the ABC contract expired – ten times what the national broadcaster were paying. When that failed he decided to sign up the best players in the world in part to use as a bargaining tool. The concept of World Series Cricket by then was merely a fall back concept with little formality.

Historically, the commercial networks were able to bid for rights but few did as the Board always stipulated that the winning network would have to share the rights with the ABC. The commercial networks knew that viewers would choose to watch Test cricket uninterrupted on the ABC over the advert-soaked commercial coverage.

Even after the news of the dramatic signings broke in May 1977 during the Australian team's tour of England, Packer was convinced that the International Cricket Conference (ICC) would agree to his proposition that Packer control the WSC Super Tests, with the world's fifty leading players, in return for the ICC's pledge not to take retaliatory action against 'his' players. He also insisted the deal include that the ICC award him exclusive coverage of Australian Test cricket. They declined.

The cricket administrators' unwillingness to move was the catalyst for Packer to change tact and to defiantly start his own competition. With player unrest over their low remuneration, it was a perfect storm waiting to happen. The biggest Test match in the one hundred year history of the game – the Centenary Test – was to play a significant part in his plan. Not unusual for the 1970s, it was proving to be a time of dramatic change in cricket.

Living in the seventies

This era of revision in Australian cricket can be seen in the context of the wider social shifts occurring in Australia and around the world. By the 1970s, change was in the air, and it was coming from a much broader base than a bat-and-ball game.

Mark Juddery in *1975 – Australia's Greatest Year* noted that Australia was becoming a more questioning society aware of its rights.

> *Change was the key word in the early 1970s as the new Labor government foisted numerous changes on the parliament in a rush, including a lowering of the voting age, introduction of maternity leave, an increase in the minimum wage and the abolishment of university fees. Whitlam had ridden into government on the*

'It's Time' slogan, although there was barely enough time for the new
government to institute all its changes.

There was general consensus that it was indeed time to challenge authority, to demand basic rights and to protest to force change. The 1968 moratorium against the Vietnam War was an example of mass protest that saw millions of people joining forces in the streets around the world. People everywhere were protesting against the status quo. Apart from the anti-war protests, the two big movements at the time were for equal rights for women and civil rights for Black Americans in the United States.

By the mid 1970s, Cricket had proven to be no exception. Australian captain Ian Chappell had just about had enough of the status quo.

Chappell's career had straddled the 1960s and 1970s. When he started his first-class cricket career for South Australia in 1962, Australia was a conservative nation under the leadership of Liberal Prime Minister Robert Menzies. By the time he took over the captaincy of Australia in 1971, he had seen his share of cricket officials and was spoiling for a fight that he could not have hoped to win a decade earlier. Chappell had seen his players struggle under the burden of trying to combine a cricket career and finding enough money to support a family. Many players sought endorsements from commercial interests. Ian Chappell reflected on the times.

Players were becoming so heavily committed to their personal
promotional pursuits that it wasn't uncommon to see half of the team
race off on the eve of a Test to engage in this type of activity to the
extent of tasting ice creams and pumping petrol.

Chappell may have been overstating the case here, but the financial pressure on players was real. The honour of playing for Australia did little to help pay the bills. Pay had improved somewhat for Test players; but so poorly were the players paid for the domestic Gillette Cup one-day games that the promotional girls were paid more – $75 a day as opposed to $25 for players. (Jeff Thomson found this out on his first date with future wife Cheryl, following a one-day fixture.)

Cricketers were still part-time and struggled to hold down jobs of their own. Ian Redpath was an antique dealer and missed the 1975 England tour to look after his business; Paul Sheahan was a teacher ; Terry Jenner managed a sports store; Ashley Mallett was a journalist; Greg Chappell for a period was a Coke salesman and Rodney Hogg a milkman.

Despite the lack of pay for players, the early to mid 1970s was a time of growth for Australian cricket. Crowds were increasing at games. Gate takings were up. The 1974–75 Ashes series and next summer's hosting of the West Indies saw enormous crowds. But players were still not being paid well. Australian left-arm medium pacer and school teacher Geoff Dymock was relieved to receive a bonus payment of $200 after completing the 1974–75 series.

> I'd had to take seven school days off to play in the Test and go without pay. If I hadn't received the bonus I would have been financially behind, all because I played the Sixth Test match for Australia.

Dymock also bristled at the Queensland Education Department for not paying his wage during this period, saying, 'Each Saturday I'd spend hours either out on the cricket or rugby fields for no pay and I did that for years.' All this was about to change for at least some of the Australian players. The Centenary Test would be remembered for much more than who won.

The Centenary Test, March 1977

Life couldn't have been any better for Gary Cosier as he bounced onto the Melbourne Cricket Ground (MCG) that first cloud-strewn Saturday morning of the Centenary Test. He was happily combining a cricket career with a steady job at a radio station in Adelaide. This allowed him to work and fit in with his state and Australian commitments; an increasingly rare thing for players. As he strode onto the vast field at the fall of opener Ian Davis' wicket, he chose a moment to cast a glance at the Members Stand. He knew where his mum and dad were sitting; the same place they'd been when he scored a century on debut against the West Indies two summers before. This day he couldn't see them because of the size of the 61,316 strong crowd.

This ground was his. He could do anything here. Right-hander Cosier's record at the MCG in Test cricket was two matches, two hundreds. But this day would be like few others in Test cricket. Cosier was not to know that he would be one of the few outsiders who would be left out of one of the biggest shifts in Australian cricket.

The Centenary Test was to be the biggest party cricket had ever seen. It was to be a grand occasion – a celebration of one hundred years since Dave Gregory's Australians defeated James Lillywhite's Englishmen at the MCG in March, 1877. That earlier match was really a combined New South Wales and Victorian side against the commercially sponsored English tourists. That first match featured some fine players, if not the best that each country could offer, even though Australia was not yet a country. It was 1877, 24 years before the Federation of Australia in 1901 and 22 years before Australia began touring in the green and gold in 1899. However, Cricket authorities had pinpointed the 1877 match as the starting point of Test cricket history. The years immediately following Lillywhite's tour witnessed a major increase in the number of overseas tours, with 'Australian' teams visiting England every two years between 1878 and 1890. Seven English teams toured Australia from 1878–79 to 1887–88.

Now, 100 years on, the weather gods had smiled and apart from being mildly overcast on the first day, the rest of the Test was played under clear, bright, sunny skies. There was a growing sense of excitement as to what this milestone match might deliver. The marketing campaign was unprecedented in Australian sport. To celebrate her Silver Jubilee, the Queen's visit to Melbourne coincided with the match. Special postage stamps were designed. Jeweller and former Test player Ernie McCormick was asked to prepare sketches of a commemorative presentation piece for players and major cricketing bodies. Invitations were extended to every English cricketer who had played a Test in Australia as well as Australians who had umpired or played Tests against England. Ten thousand visitors came from overseas and interstate, creating the greatest influx of tourists into Melbourne since the 1956 Olympic Games. It was to be the high point of the cricket world. Even *Time* magazine featured the event as its cover story.

On a trip to see how international sport is marketed in the US and Britain, Victorian Cricket Association secretary David Richards and Tom Worrell, met with counterparts in Major League baseball and First Division soccer. They were particularly impressed with the bright uniforms and spectacle of American sporting events. As the pair celebrated Worrell's birthday at the New York Athletic Club after, Worrell pronounced after a couple of dry martinis: 'I think I'm going home to recommend we play cricket under lights in coloured clothing with a white ball.' Richards almost fell off his chair laughing. It was a joke, but one that proved to be an omen of things to come.

Finally, the day of the Centenary Test arrived. Cricket officials, delighted with the spectacle they had created, remained caught up in the bonhomie of the event, oblivious to the storm that was coming – many of their top players were about to defect.

Secrecy about the defections was paramount. The recruitment of Australia's best cricketers to Packer's troupe had been going on for some weeks, but what better symbol of defiance than to sign up many players during this historic event? Enter Packer's men, John Cornell (Strop from *The Paul Hogan Show)* and Austin Robertson, who had a willing audience with many disgruntled and prominent Test cricketers ready to break ranks. The players had become tired of sacrificing income and in some cases their employment, when touring with the national side. They loved playing for Australia but needed more than the honour of wearing the baggy green to pay their bills. They knew they were bringing the crowds into the grounds and they now wanted to be rewarded financially.

The signings had already begun. Dennis Lillee already had a contract for $105,000 over three seasons before the team left for New Zealand in February of 1977. The Centenary Test provided a ripe time for some other Australian players to be approached. Ian Davis was summoned to meet with Austin Robertson at a hotel away from the Hilton. He signed immediately after hearing Ian Chappell was one the players committed to the Packer enterprise. By the end of the game, Australia's century scoring wicket keeper Rod Marsh had signed. Rick McCosker knew his joining would be a formality but wanted to talk things through with his family. Not long after the match McCosker was on Packer's books as was Ross Edwards who had signed on for two years at $25,000 a year.

Australia's middle-order batsman, Gary Cosier, said later it was 'cool to think John and Austin were there watching the cricket'. Little did Cosier know that teammate, Doug Walters had already signed on. Australia's captain Greg Chappell, while approached in New Zealand, didn't like the idea of the Australian captain signing up being used as a lure for other players. Packer's offer to Chappell was a five-year contract starting at $50,000 and increasing to $70,000 by the fifth year. It was an obvious choice for Chappell, who at that stage thought he would bow out of cricket altogether by 1979.

It is amazing that given the size of the cricket community gathering in Melbourne, there were no leaks about the planned breakaway movement. But there had been suspicions. As early as September 1976, Melbourne Cricket Club president Ian Johnson thought something was up when the club received a letter from local television station GTV9 (part of Packer's television empire) making an application for the use of the ground for a series of cricket matches from December 1977 to February 1978. Johnson wrote back but had no further communication from the Packer group, nor any formal application to play on the MCG. There were whispers among the Australian Shield cricket community that an alternative competition was being considered by a private investor. But the details remained hazy.

When the cricketers finally started play on the first day of the Centenary Test, it was with the frenzied activity typical of players overawed by the occasion. The only change Australia made for the Centenary Test from the side that had recently played New Zealand was to drop left-hand opening bat Alan Turner who was briefly one of Chappell's band. McCosker was to open and newcomer David Hookes was included to bolster the middle order. The selectors told Turner that they wanted a chance to see what this young bloke

David Hookes could do ... Turner was also to miss out on the upcoming 1977 tour of England and never played for Australia again.

On the first day, the home side was sent in on a grassy wicket. The ball nipped around and Australia soon found itself 5 for 51 before scrambling to 138. Then England was bowled out next day for 95. It was a strange start to the match. Would the game go the distance of the five days? Thoughts turned to scheduling a one-day match to coincide with the Queen's visit on the last day of the Test. Calmer nerves and a flatter wicket saw both sides settle in the second innings. Australia, courtesy of half-centuries from Davis, Walters and Hookes as well as a hundred from Rod Marsh, set England a world record 463 to win. England almost chased the total down with the help of Derek Randall's 174.

The result was a win to Australian by 45 runs, the same outcome as 100 years before. Dennis Lillee with eleven wickets for the match was the hero, as was Marsh with a tough-as-nails undefeated 110. Debutant David Hookes left the MCG with his reputation enhanced, an innings of 56 displaying stroke-play reminiscent of Frank Woolley. England's Derek Randall, a veritable jack-in-the-box at the crease and in the field was a revelation for his batting skills and eccentricity, as he happily performed cartwheels across the field.

Australian cricketing authorities must have been overjoyed by the sheer brilliance of it all. At the end of the celebrations, they were none the wiser that 13 of their 17 Australian Cricket team had now signed (or were about to sign) to play in a breakaway competition.

Cosier and Hookes – the outsider and new kid on the block

Two players at that Centenary Test typify the schism within the team itself: Gary Cosier, who was left out of the WSC signings, and new player, David Hookes who was in.

With his easygoing manner a good social lubricant, Gary Cosier was used to being in the 'in' crowd – one of the first invited to a party. When alleged 'theatre tickets' were given out by Austin Robertson in the dressing room on the final day of the Centenary Test, Cosier missed out. He didn't know it then, but it meant he wasn't a member of Kerry Packer's World Series Cricket competition.

His mind sometimes wanders back to the vote taken under his state captain Ian Chappell as to whether the side should boycott the 'eastern states' tour in 1975. Chappell had threatened strike action with the SACA over the selection of Bob Blewett to replace the popular Rick Drewer. He'd felt slighted by the SA selectors for not consulting him on the selection of a squad to play in Sydney and Brisbane. All but two players, Cosier and Hogg, agreed to the strike action. Under duress, Chappell caved in to the SACA over the strike, and rang the players to tell them it was his problem, not theirs. Had Cosier been placed on Chappell's blacklist for opposing the strike? Or was it just coincidence?

When Chappell was asked why Cosier missed out on an offer, he replied, 'By the time I was involved in selection, I recall Coze was already aligned with the ACB.' This is at odds with the generally accepted view that Chappell handpicked the players. At the time of the signings, Cosier, Australia's number three in the Centenary Test, had been part of the Australian line-up for two full seasons. Sadly for him, the Centenary Test marked the beginning of the end of his Test career.

Gary Cosier's story of exclusion from the WSC is central to the saga of those who became known as the Establishment Boys. How Cosier arrived at this juncture in his cricket life is a story of rejection, perseverance and success. Joining the fourths at the age of eleven, still in short pants, he gradually worked his way through the grades. Future Test teammate Rod Hogg joined the Northcote Club in Melbourne a year later. Between the ages of fifteen and twenty, Cosier opened the batting for Northcote with former Australian captain Bill Lawry. In the winter, he substituted cricket whites for footy boots, playing for Fitzroy reserves in the VFL. As an eighteen-year-old cricketer, he'd played twice for Victoria, opening with Lawry in four innings, in all of which he achieved starts, but with a highest score of 34.

By the time he turned 21, with a couple of average grade seasons behind him, the door to Victorian selection (with Keith Stackpole, Ian Redpath and Paul Sheahan in the side) appeared closed. An invitation from Prospect District Club President Reg Craig was enough to lure him to South Australia. Cosier didn't take long to make an impression and debuted for South Australia, batting at number three in at match at Adelaide Oval in 1974–75 against Western Australia which was Dennis Lillee's comeback match after his crippling back injury. Cosier scored 24 and 47.

Fast forward to the excitement in the Australian dressing room after the Centenary Test. As Australian players were knocking off the tops of longneck beers with a great sense of relief, Austin Roberson was handing out envelopes each containing sign-on cheques. 'Here are your theatre tickets, fellas!', he'd say. No such tickets for Cosier but he did notice that a number of his teammates had suddenly taken an interest in the theatre.

> *I remember seeing the tickets being handed out and waiting for them to come my way. I was normally included in things like that although I did wonder why it was theatre tickets and maybe not beer tickets.*

If Cosier's non-inclusion in WSC tells a tale; so too does the story of WSC's poster boy, David Hookes.

The Centenary Test was notable for the arrival of the baby-faced South Australian batsman. During the test, Hookes hit five fours in one over from Tony Greig's off-spinners opening up a new world for him. A five-innings starburst over a few short weeks transformed Hookes from a borderline state player to a Test cricketer performing in one of the biggest matches in cricket. An invitation to join World Series Cricket followed. Hookes had everything Packer craved in a new cricket competition. He was a young, good looking cricketer, exciting to watch, photogenic with a cheeky charisma that made him stand out. While all this may have suited WSC, Hookes may well have been better off not signing. For the man who had been a Bradman medallist at nineteen, the summer of 1976–77 was the fulcrum on which the young left-hander's life turned.

In just his second season of first-class cricket, Hookes had missed South Australia's 'eastern states' tour in the second half of November, opting to repeat his matriculation as an adult student at Marryatville High School. A double failure in Perth against the Western Australian team saw him under pressure to retain his place. Lacking confidence when he arrived at the crease in an A-grade match against Prospect, he received the first of what would be a number of lucky breaks. Medium pacer Bob May dropped a dolly caught-and-bowled chance when Hookes hadn't reached double figures. He made the most of the miss and plundered a quick-fire 79.

Five centuries in six innings in seventeen days for Hookes began with 163 against Victoria, his maiden century which progressed at rapid pace including four sixes in one over. The Adelaide *Advertiser's* front page the next day showed Hookes down on one knee, old trusty bat smashing the ball over midwicket. It represented more than a cricketer in full flight. It was a statement of arrival.

A week later he smashed 185 in 191 minutes and then 105 in 101 minutes against Queensland. In the next few days, scores of 135 and 156 against New South Wales saw Hookes become the first man to achieve hundreds in each innings of consecutive games since Surrey's Tom Hayward in 1906. By the time Hookes had made 156 in the final innings of this golden run, the Australian selectors had penned his name in for the Centenary Test. Having witnessed Hookes' four breathtaking centuries in a row, Don Bradman wrote to his mate, Australian selector Sam Loxton, urging him to select Hookes for the Centenary Test. 'He's just the sort of batsman cricket needs.'

That all his runs were made at Adelaide Oval, where the wicket was true and the midwicket boundaries short, did little to detract from such an extraordinary performance. There was Hookes that night after stumps, just 21, standing with arms folded, Australia's latest selection, sweeping his longish hair back and looking a little shell-shocked, describing the run to ABC TV. 'Yeah,' said Hookes, 'I've had a bit of a purple patch. It was just one of those things that happen when you have a good run.'

It couldn't have been more understated. He was on his way to play in what was being described as the biggest cricket match in one hundred years.

When he arrived in Melbourne for the Centenary Test, Hookes soon learned that he was an easy butt of practical jokes, when roommate Gary Gilmour told him to avoid the tramlines on Wellington Parade in order to avoid getting a nasty shock from the live lines. He soon learned to show respect to senior players when Lillee refused to pick up the ball in the nets after Hookes batted it back to him. And a rushed trip back to his hotel room from an official function was called for when he had arrived not wearing a tie. When the cricket began Hookes looked the part, scoring 17 in Australia's first innings of 138, the third best score behind Greg Chappell (40) and Rod Marsh (28).

Just after England's Derek Randall was named Man of the Match receiving his gold medal and $1500 in prize money, an announcement boomed out of the loudspeakers. The match had attracted a quarter of a million spectators and a television audience in the millions. Not only was the finish of the Centenary Test spectacular, the 248,260 spectators had paid $418,019 in gate money. The event was a huge financial success. Despite his youth and naivety, David Hookes understood that the Australians' match fee of $475 and a $250 bonus paled in significance to what the Board had earned. The WSC contract must have seemed like a gold mine.

For the young left-hander, it was a matter of being careful what you wish for; the golden chariot he was riding would take him on a bumpy journey. WSC may well provide some financial security but it would do little for his development as a cricketer able to cope with the challenges of Test cricket.

Hookes felt that WSC didn't help his overall progress and later wrote:

The only disappointment I have from WSC is that maybe my cricket education didn't proceed as much as it should have … I faced a lot of quality bowlers but I never really learned how to play spin. I saw guys like Border and Hughes come back having learned an enormous amount about playing slow bowlers, experiences I didn't get the benefit of experiencing … I owe Ian (Chappell) a lot but I don't think he taught me how to best prepare myself to play cricket. There wasn't that sort of professional teaching method or proper education process.

Had Hookes not signed with Packer, he would have played two series against spin bowlers the likes of Bedi, Prasanna and Chandrasekar at home and in India. This would have enabled him to develop his technique against spinners and present a stronger case for Test selection following the reconciliation. He could play fast bowling well, which he proved when he played against the West Indians in 1975–76 and later during WSC, but his lack of footwork against spinners was well known. This inability brought an end to his stop/start Test career in the mid 1980s when he was still scoring runs at Shield level. Border's and Hughes' ability to adapt to all types of bowlers highlighted the difference.

Hookes also admitted that he struggled to come to terms with being hit in the head by Andy Roberts during a WSC Super Test, at one stage seeking a hypnotherapist to get the image out of his head. Like many players who have suffered from a serious cricket ball head injury, Hookes was never quite the same confident player again.

Hookes' career trajectory was sporadic. After playing a full Test series against England in 1977, it was five years until he did it again in 1982–83. He always believed that a strong east-coast focus by the Australian selectors did little for his chances.

> When they give out the baggy blue cap in New South Wales, they give you a baggy green in a brown paper bag as well to save making presentations.

Ian Chappell has a different take on why Hookes never fulfilled his early promise.

> I think the lure of easy runs to the short Adelaide Oval boundaries had the biggest effect on Hookesy's career and also his ability to play spin bowling. In the end he was trying to hit off-spinners around corners, a far cry from the way he played Tony Greig's [albeit gentle] off-spin in the Centenary Test, where he hit him much straighter — even through the on side.

Hookes scored one Test century against Sri Lanka at Kandy during the 1982–83 season, finishing with a Test average of 34.3 in 23 Tests. His time in the WSC spotlight proved lucrative for a short period, but Test success after the reconciliation was elusive. As Bob Simpson later wrote:

> *David Hookes ... a technically flawed batsman just needed time to get his game in order. Instead he became one of the rebels' most publicised figures and never recovered.*

Although the judgment was harsh, few would disagree.

For all the talk that Packer players would be favoured post-reconciliation, Hookes managed only two Tests in three years in the immediately following years. When he scored a pair (a duck in each innings) in Karachi in 1980, he was cast adrift and later dropped from the South Australian side. The experience of World Series Cricket must have seemed like some mad psychedelic dream that evaporated as quickly as it had appeared, robbing Hookes of his chance to excel as a Test cricketer.

The Centenary Test was significant in the future of cricket, not because it was an outstanding success for the ACB, but because it soon would be revealed that many of the first-class Australian cricketers had now joined Packer's breakaway competition. The story finally broke later in 1977 during the Australian team's Ashes tour of England.

Chapter Two

Tour of England, 1977 – the story breaks

Alan Shiell, former South Australian batsman turned journalist with the Adelaide *Advertiser,* was on a mission. In May 1977 he and *Age* reporter Peter McFarline mingled with one hundred and fifty party guests in a marquee at Tony Greig's Sussex house. They had more than free champagne on their minds. For months the pair had been chasing a story about Australian cricketers supposedly signing up for an alternative competition – one backed by a businessman. Shiell and McFarline had that very morning heard the latest in a series of denials from Australian captain Greg Chappell. There in Sussex, as corks popped and glasses tinkled, the whispers suddenly grew louder. Both knew the world of cricket and cricketers well. McFarline was the worldlier of the two, a journalist who became a cricket correspondent, but also a writer able to turn his hand to anything.

Alan Shiell knew from personal experience just how fickle cricketing life was; how limited time at the top could be. He had played twenty-three matches in three years for South Australia, experiencing the elation of an undefeated double-century against a visiting MCC side, and the shattering experience of a 'pair' in a first-class match against Victoria, playing four days for no runs. Once touted as a certain Test selection, his form evaporated, and at the age of 23, faced with the choice of a job as a cricket correspondent or battling to retain his place in the SA team, he went with the former – he was guaranteed overseas tours.

Greg Chappell was at the party. Shiell knew him well and was aware of the disquiet growing among Australia's top cricketers and how little they were earning by the mid 1970s. McFarline also had a great nose for a story and filed his copy with rich prose full of puckish humour and acerbic wit. Having listened carefully to what the journalists suggested was in the wind, Chappell replied with just a hint of a smile, 'It sounds an interesting proposition. I'd like to know more about it …'

As the night rolled on with the beers on tap and players making merry, one Australian cricketer told Shiell just enough to confirm what he and McFarline had suspected. They scurried away early from the party and filed stories of vague detail and speculation, putting together what was a broad outline of WSC without quite realising the extent of it.

Sprung, Tony Greig rang Packer and then issued a statement confirming that a massive cricket project involving the world's top players was due to start in the Australian summer. Ian Wooldridge, who had also been chasing the story for the *Daily Mail*, announced what many players had been thinking for some time, under the headline 'World's Top Cricketers Turn Pirate'.

> *The only surprise about what happened was that it was long delayed.*
> *If the game's administrators failed to see it coming, then they are low*
> *in perception.*

The cat was out of the bag. The Australian winter of 1977 introduced many young cricket fans to unfamiliar words: *schism, defectors, breakaway troupe* and *circus*, all used to describe the mercenaries who were part of the new alternative international cricket competition called World Series Cricket. The news broke like a bolt of lightning on a summer's day. In the national newspaper, *The Australian*, front-page headlines screamed of a takeover of cricket by mega rich businessman Kerry Packer.

It was a strange time to be a young fan. Loyalties were divided. Older Australian cricket fans sided with something increasingly known as

The Establishment and were affronted by the audacious manner with which Packer had made a grab for cricket's broadcasting rights. The pugnacious Packer had burst his way into heavyweight sports contention without looking anything like a cricketer. Solidly built, he looked to us more at home on the blackjack tables he loved, rather than a cricket field. Television footage showed Packer at a press cricket match in England where he walked with the lumbering gait of a dinosaur.

Packer told us he had the best interest of the players at heart but that was a hard sell. After the initial rush, news leaked slowly. We all wondered what the new competition would look like. Would we still have Test cricket? Why was Packer doing this? He had been chasing broadcasting rights for some time. After the failed negotiations with the Australian Cricket Board to buy the exclusive rights to Australian Test cricket, he now planned to set up his own competition. Traditionalists said our favourite players like Ian Chappell, Dennis Lillee and Rod Marsh had deserted Australian cricket's cause and gone to *the dark side*.

In just a matter of months, lesser-known names appeared wearing the baggy green cap. Australian cricket fans took some reassurance in the form of an elder statesman of Test cricket. At the age of 41 Bobby Simpson returned to captain his country. Slicked-back black hair, a jaunty gait, bright-eyed and a big beaming smile for the cameras, the *Daily Telegraph* pictured him on the cover peeling back his baggy green cap. Simpson was a player from a bygone era of black and white photos found in musty smelling hardback books. To younger fans, he was hardly known. Simpson was a bloke who played in the tied Test in 1960–61 against Frank Worrell's West Indians. We'd last seen him in fuzzy highlight reels still moving his feet in a dazzling manner to the Indian spinners on their 1967–68 tour. He'd once batted for three days scoring a Test triple century when they wore Brylcreem and commentary was in clipped BBC tones. Our fathers told us Simpson was lightning between the wickets. 'He and Bill Lawry really knew how to judge a run.' they'd say.

And suddenly there Simpson was again, like a movie star walking straight out of the grainy cinema screen and sitting next to you. His skin was a little more sun-flecked, his face and physique a little podgier. Here was the cricket hero riding in to save us all from the hardline approach of Packer and his mercenaries. It felt like one of those old Westerns, the good guys – Cricket Board administrators like Bob Parish and Ray Steele, facing down Packer and his cricketing villains, no longer much loved but deserving their title of *Ugly Australians*. Four decades on, it's easy to forget the animosity that existed between the Establishment and WSC and just how much each thrived on any possibility of failure of the other.

But we are ahead of ourselves. When the Australians left for the Ashes tour of England, a large portion of the side kept a very large secret. It was still largely unknown what signing with Packer meant and knowledge of who else had signed was limited. The scene was set for perfect storm to form that would cause a sense of disunity rarely before seen in an Australian touring side.

The sense of betrayal was heightened when Trevor Kennedy's article in the Packer owned Bulletin, 'The Great Cricket Story: The Inside Facts' was published. It described Packer and John Cornell as having pulled off 'the most imaginative sports promotion ever devised'. He also went on to reveal that 'the staggering coup' was carried out at least in part during the Centenary Test. For traditional cricket fans it seemed an unfathaomable that such a situation could occur let alone at the greatest cricketing event in the game's history.

A house divided against itself

The tour of England in 1977, from April to August, was most notable perhaps for all the wrong reasons. The Australian team to tour England that year was Greg Chappell, (captain) Rodney Marsh (vice-captain), Ray Bright, Gary Cosier, Ian Davis, Geoff Dymock, David Hookes, Kim Hughes, Rick McCosker, Mick Malone, Kerry O'Keeffe, Len Pascoe, Richie Robinson, Craig Serjeant, Jeff Thomson, Max Walker and Doug Walters.

Their pay had increased dramatically for this nineteen-week campaign. Chris Harte in *A History of Australian Cricket* noted that even allowing for a 115 per cent increase in the CPI since the last full tour in 1972, the players'

$10,890 fees represented a figure 83 percent higher than the average adult male weekly earnings. In 1972 it had been just forty percent higher.

However, the higher pay didn't compare with what Packer was offering. For example, David Hookes, the newcomer, was offered a six-year contract at $25,000 a year. Hookes signed on the dotted line with stars in his eyes – his sign-on cheque was $16,666.66. He felt like a millionaire.

Just before leaving Australia, John Cornell told Hookes that his good friend Gary Cosier was among the four tourists not to be signed by Packer. To complicate matters, Hookes had asked Cosier to be best man at Hookes' wedding later in the year. 'What's he going to think of me when he finds out?' Hookes wrote years later in his autobiography *Hookesy*. Hookes and Cosier endured a quieter than usual flight to Melbourne to meet up with the rest of the Australian side. During that English tour, Hookes played in all five Tests and received a good run from the selectors but later had grave doubts about the tour.

> *I never realised it properly at the time but with hindsight, it was a pretty ordinary, unpleasant tour. In retrospect, too, I think the Australian Cricket Board should have been strong enough and smart enough to have chosen a new England-tour team immediately WSC became public knowledge and we thirteen players who had signed with WSC should have been sent home.*

Perhaps, Hookes was right. Once the story broke, the ACB should have sent the defectors home. They didn't. And they seemed to ignore the lack of team discipline that was evident from the very start.

If the beer drinking competition for the 29-hour flight that left Australia on a balmy April morning was anything to go by, maturity wasn't the side's strong suit. According to O'Keeffe, it began with a senior player's question, *How many beers someone could sink between now and London?* and ended with Doug Walters winning with 44 cans closely followed by Rod Marsh with 43. The tour had begun in the way it would finish, with undisciplined behaviour. You could ask 'Where were captain Greg Chappell and team manager Len Maddocks?' But such behavior during the 1970s was not unusual. It was a different time; getting rollicking pissed on the plane on the way over was what Australian cricketers did. It was an undisciplined start to what would be a poor tour.

Former Australian wicketkeeper Maddocks took on the team manager's job completely oblivious to the ticking time bomb of World Series Cricket. Maddocks had been backup for Gil Langley, playing in only seven Tests despite having toured the West Indies (1955), England with the ill-fated 1956 team, India (1956) and New Zealand (1959–60). But nothing could have prepared him for this.

Early on he'd laid down the law banning advertising on any cricket clothes. The players agreed – it was the last time such a high level of discipline was seen on the tour. Early in the tour Maddocks was heard jokingly making the point to journalists that he was 'here for a holiday'. The fact that the press didn't pick him up on the comment shows how different journalistic attitudes at the time were to off-field matters. Overall, Maddocks was seen as out of his depth, too soft on indiscretions. When he criticised Chappell's captaincy at one meeting, it almost caused a fight. Having to effectively manage two teams in the one dressing room was not an easy task.

The touring party arrived in London to find the weather affecting all matches. They didn't complete a full game until mid May and by then the revelations of Kerry Packer's plans had been made. Not only had the non-Packer players been unaware of what was happening behind their backs, they would stumble upon the news rather than be officially informed.

When Gary Cosier walked down the steps of London's Waldorf Hotel, the first thing he noticed was that his team mates were not gathered downstairs where they would normally have been. He saw Maddocks and ABC commentator Alan McGilvray at the bar who directed him upstairs where they knew the players were meeting.

Cosier went straight to Hookes and asked what was going on. Hookes apologised, saying he didn't know if Cosier was in or not.

'In on what?' Cosier enquired.

Hookes then explained that Kerry Packer had asked some of them to play cricket when they got home. He wasn't sure if they would still be allowed to play for Australia in a separate competition.

To be included in the best seventeen by the national selectors and then not to have been asked to be part of WSC must have been galling for Cosier and the other three outsiders, Geoff Dymock, Kim Hughes and Craig Serjeant.

The Australian players who were all eventually signed by WSC and PBL marketing were Ray Bright, Greg Chappell, Ian Chappell, Trevor Chappell, Ian Davis, Ross Edwards, Gary Gilmour, David Hookes, Martin Kent, Bruce Laird, Robbie Langer, Dennis Lillee, Rick McCosker, Graham McKenzie, Ashley Mallett, Mick Malone, Rodney Marsh, Kerry O'Keeffe, Len Pascoe, Wayne Prior, Ian Redpath, Richie Robinson, Jeff Thomson, Max Walker, Doug Walters, Graeme Watson, Kepler Wessels and Dennis Yagmich.

There are few worse things for team morale than for a minority of players not feeling accepted.

Craig Serjeant, however, was simply thrilled to be in England with the Australian cricket side. In June he would experience the exhilaration and exhaustion associated with playing an innings of six hours in an intense Test match atmosphere, scoring a debut 81 in the First Test at Lord's, helping Australia to 296 as England opening bowler Bob Willis took 7 for 78. The rainy, on-again, off-again nature of the Test meant nearly a full day's play was lost in the drawn match. For Serjeant it was an experience like no other and one that left him mentally drained. Post-innings he was asked to join WSC, but declined. The offer of more than $25,000 a year for two seasons was appealing but Serjeant chose a career as a chemist over one as a professional sportman, a decision he now regrets. Serjeant initially didn't think he was good enough to play cricket on a professional basis and was influenced by his parents who didn't want him to join the breakaway group.

For the more senior player Geoff Dymock, the Packer signings came as a bit of shock, although he had been wondering what all the private meetings and whisperings were about.

'Even on the bus to the games we were playing, thirteen players would be given something and we'd be left totally out of it. It was funny as the press was uncomfortable with what they were expected to do to find a story, things like sit outside players' rooms and listen through keyholes.'

Dymock was convinced that the disruption had an effect on team unity. The sense of 'us-and-them'; and the secrecy. When he roomed with Mick Malone (who took calls from WSC contacts), the caller would ask if Malone was on his own. He would always say, 'Yeah it's just me', when Dymock was in the room all along. It reinforced the point that Dymock wasn't supposed to be privy to the conversations.

The reality of the tour was that Australia was now a team divided. As Peter McFarline put it in *A Game Divided*:

There was every reason to believe the 1977 Australian tour to England would be a successful and exciting one. That it turned out to be neither was due to a remarkable series of events, which shattered the staid and well ordered corridors of cricket like a nuclear explosion.

There were always going to be big challenges for the Australian side on this tour. The initial excitement was tempered by Dennis Lillee's absence due to stress fractures in his back. It was a significant blow. Lillee's summer of 1976–77 had been the most successful of his career. In six Test matches (against Pakistan, New Zealand and England) he'd taken 47 wickets at 21.64. With Lillee out, the selectors Phil Ridings, Neil Harvey and Sam Loxton were forced to gamble on the fitness of Jeff Thomson, who'd severely injured his shoulder on the first day of the First Test against Pakistan when he collided with teammate Alan Turner on Christmas eve 1976.

Australia's opening batsman Rick McCosker was also subject to a fitness Test after having his jaw broken by a Bob Willis bouncer in the Centenary Test. He wouldn't join the side until May 14 – almost a month after the Australians arrived in England.

Greg Chappell knew the tour was never going to be easy with thirteen of the seventeen-man squad keeping a very big secret. It proved even more difficult when the Board took the Packer news so badly. When Bob Parish flew to London to attend the International Cricket Conference, he refused to discuss anything with the Australian captain. Morale in the team was low under the constant threat that they would be sent home. Captain Greg Chappell was unimpressed with the Board's actions.

> The Australian Cricket Board reacted as only the Board can and started a campaign of divide and conquer particularly focussing on younger players like David Hookes and Ian Davis. The Board tried to undermine their confidence, which wasn't hard to do as no one really knew what was going on, so it was even more confusing for the younger players.

Kim Hughes also proved a niggling thorn in his captain's side throughout the English summer. It seemed the young, curly, blond-haired bundle of energy had enough confidence in himself for the whole side. Having toured New Zealand in 1977, he'd watched David Hookes and his State teammate Craig Serjeant leapfrog him to play Test cricket and Hughes was becoming frustrated. Hughes thought he deserved a chance to play in Test cricket. Chappell thought that with Serjeant and Hookes in the middle order, the team couldn't afford to risk another inexperienced player.

Chappell wrote in his book *Fierce Focus* about how he tried to manage the excitable Western Australian.

> He and I talked a couple of times, and I reassured him that this tour was about gaining experience. He tried to explain to me that he was a type of technician we needed in the middle order. I said I saw him as a stroke player, not ideally suited to the conditions.

Hughes managed two and three runs in the international matches, a sixty against the MCC in his first outing at Lord's, eighty against Kent, 54 at The Parks, and 95 versus Nottinghamshire.

Hughes saw things quite differently to Ian Chappell.

*The people running the team were those going to World Series Cricket;
they basically picked those going to WSC.*

One new face in the squad didn't need soothing; the 27-year-old New
South Wales firebrand Len Pascoe, born Leonard Stephen Durtanovic, of
Yugoslavian heritage and a WSC recruit. A Punchbowl High School classmate
of Jeff Thomson, Pascoe turned himself into a council arts and craft organiser,
V8 Torana driver and surfer. At 187 centimetres and a fighting weight of
around ninety kilograms, he looked like a weightlifter: thick neck, broad
shoulders and big chest. When he posed for photos it was as if he was flexing
his biceps for the audience. With his chest-on action he could be fearsome, as
could his stare from deep-set dark brown eyes and heavy brow. For him, the
tour to England and the opportunity to open the bowling in a Test with his old
Punchbowl friend Jeff was manna from heaven.

Twelve-Test player Ian Davis was one who would have benefited from
more experience around him. Dubbed 'Wiz' by Brian Taber and Doug Walters
after a comic strip at the time, Davis had debuted for Australia as a twenty-year-
old against New Zealand in 1973–74 following just five first-class matches. He
was the first kid from Shoalhaven on the New South Wales coast to wear the
baggy green.

Davis initially thought like many of his teammates that joining WSC
just meant signing on for three months of TV cricket. John Cornell had told
him Ian Chappell wanted him in the side (which begs the question why
Chappell had ignored Cosier). Still high from the events of the Centenary
Test, Davis was one of the players who received those 'theatre tickets' in the
dressing room. He'd been playing for fifty dollars a day and had in his hand a
cheque for $8,500.

But this English tour, as Kerry O'Keeffe has put it, was 'the tour so
many of us had coveted'. For O'Keeffe, Australia's whirly-gig leg-spinner, the
chance to tour England was something he thought had passed him by. He'd
gone from a casual brewery truck worker who was going to give cricket one

more year to become a Test player again. At the age of 28 after a stop/start career of 24 Tests across seven years, he'd thought about retiring. Good form in Shield cricket had led him back to Test cricket against Pakistan where success had taken him into the Centenary Test and the tour of England. Just when he thought he had achieved his lifelong dream, Kerry Packer came knocking with an offer too good to refuse.

Sadly, for most of the players, this tour would not fulfill this expectation. Early on, the Australians found themselves looking at rained-out cricket grounds more often than playing on them, providing less than the ideal preparation for a Test series. Two losses out of the first three one-day internationals, followed by a scrambled draw in the opening Test at Lord's, were ominous signs as to what lay ahead. Defeat in the Second Test at Old Trafford confirmed for David Hookes that all was not well. He later wrote:

> There didn't seem to be the overwhelming sense of team disappointment I had suspected there would be when Australia had just lost a Test match. It was an eerie feeling and … the most disappointing moment of the entire tour. There was already a sense of resignation that the tour was already finished by that stage.

Hookes made the most of the tour, playing in all five Test matches as his admiration for Greg Chappell grew, believing that his skipper 'conducted himself with great dignity throughout the tour. He held it all together as best he could, when lesser men would have failed'.

Despite Chappell's efforts, perceptions of bias in favour of WSC-signed players persisted. Even Kerry O'Keeffe and Mick Malone accused Chappell and Rod Marsh of picking their mates. The Third Test was made worse by the return of England's Geoffrey Boycott who featured, in Australia's seven-wicket loss at Nottingham. Next stop Leeds, for the Fourth Test, scene of the English opener's 100th first-class century. A loss to Australia meant England had an unassailable 3–0 lead. Australia rang some changes for the final Test at the Oval.

Kim Hughes, annoyed at having been made 'a part of the losing Australian team' was at last selected, as was Mick Malone. Hughes' score of one in 37 minutes just added to his frustration, while Malone's five-wicket haul and undefeated 46 was a memory to treasure in what would be his only appearance in Test cricket. Fellow sandgroper Craig Serjeant made a duck as twilight turned to darkness at the Oval.

Feeling increasingly ostracised as each day passed by his non-WSC status, the lowest point for Gary Cosier came in the county game against Nottinghamshire at Trent Bridge.

> *Kim Hughes and I were walking into the dressing room and everyone*
> *stopped talking. We'd gone from a friendly raucous Australian room*
> *to 'stop talking they're coming'. It was just awful and soul-destroying.*

How could it not have been, with meetings held between Packer and non-Packer players in separate hotel rooms? There was plenty of loud discussion when the team came together. Ex-captain and now Packer man, Ian Chappell, occasionally appearing on the team bus, wasn't helping. Cosier and some of his teammates thought it was strange, as Ian Chappell would never have allowed anyone else on the bus when he was captain. He remembers one incident vividly.

> *One time he got on the bus and lent over me to whisper something to*
> *Ian Davis who was sitting beside me.*

Other players say they saw Ian Chappell on the bus but he denies it.

> *Didn't happen as far as I'm concerned ... as a member of the media*
> *I wouldn't have been allowed on the team bus.*

It is of course a little different when your brother is the captain. Cosier found Chappell's presence a little unsettling. He remembered what he'd read in the January edition of *Cricketer:* Ian Chappell, picking his best squad to tour England had selected Cosier over Queenslander Martin Kent, but with little sense of generosity. Chappell had written:

> *He [Cosier] made the side virtually by default as there was no one*
> *else with enough runs. I must confess I've yet to be convinced Cosier*

*is ready for Test cricket … A question mark has arisen over his
dedication … and also over his ability to play on wickets which are
doing a bit. And he is definitely suspect outside off-stump. I'd like to
see Cosier work harder at his game. He appears to be overweight, and
I wonder how hard he is prepared to work at his batting at this stage.*

The words were as damning as one could write. Despite his
disappointments, Cosier though didn't sense a pro-Packer bias. However,
although Cosier had taken 5–18 in the second one-day international, he was
barely sighted again.

Richie Robinson with his infectious enthusiasm was one who generated
a great deal of team spirit and was considered an important part of the team
structure. The thirty-year-old had toured England in 1975 but was yet to play
Test cricket when he signed up to play WSC after a strong season with the bat
for Victoria, topping the Sheffield Shield averages with 424 runs at 85. Well-
liked by the Chappells and Rod Marsh, Robinson was a knockabout bloke
who hit hard and despite his height kept wicket with agility.

Marsh had written in *Cricketer* in April of 1977:

*Robinson is a tremendously attractive batsman. Sure his style of
batting means he'll miss out occasionally but when he clicks he really
clicks … to be honest in WA we regard him as the most difficult of all
Victorian batsmen to keep out.*

Robinson had success in the one-day internationals averaging 30
with a highest score of 70 but he failed in the Test matches. He was strong
square of the wicket but not technically equipped to deal with a moving ball.
Picked ahead of Ian Davis for the First Test as an opener having scored most
of his runs for Victoria in the middle order, he soon became a sitting duck
for English bowlers, making only 100 runs at 17 in his three Tests. Despite
modest performances in the first two tests, he was picked for the Fourth Test
of the series to bat in the middle order. A pair of twenties spelled the end of
his Test career.

The number of Tests played by 'Packer outsiders' on tour amounted to four: Serjeant three and Hughes one. Dymock and Cosier did not feature in any.

Even without the turmoil, this was perhaps a tour the Australians would have lost. Greg Chappell maintained that the tourists would have struggled against a strong English opposition even if the Packer signings weren't hanging over their heads. Craig Serjeant agrees, saying that Australia was simply outclassed by a stronger, more experienced side. The Australian press saw it differently.

Going down 3–0 against an English side that was well led by Brearley but hardly a group of world-beaters, the tour was a major disappointment. Australia won only five of its 22 first-class matches and the Test series loss was the worst since 1886. Seventeen dropped catches in five Tests didn't help and was a sure sign that the team was distracted.

The experience of the 1977 tour was enough to make an old Test opener very cranky. Jack Fingleton railed against what he saw as a lack of discipline.

> There is not the discipline in dress and behaviour that we knew and largely to blame is the prevalence of the infernal tracksuit, which in modern times seems to be the dress for all sporting occasions. I even saw one of the youngest members of the side going to the nets one day with pads over his tracksuit ... Lack of discipline off the field generally leads to lack of it on the field ... it showed in their shoddy batting and fielding.

By tour's end the future of Australia's Packer signees was still uncertain in terms of playing for Australia. On July 27, the International Cricket Conference, comprising representatives of Australia, India, New Zealand, Pakistan and the West Indies, announced that anyone contracted to Packer as of October 1 would be ineligible to play Test Matches without the express consent of the Conference. The resolution was later withdrawn after a British High Court ruling on November 25 that it represented an unreasonable restraint of trade.

The Australian Cricket Board and England's Test and County Board both got around the High Court decision by obliging players to choose between WSC and Establishment cricket. Packer's Australians were told they would only be considered to play for Australia if they gave an undertaking to be available for all scheduled Shield and Test matches. While there was some hesitation on behalf of a small number of Australians who had signed with Packer, it was only Jeff Thomson who decided to withdraw, given he'd already signed a lucrative contract with Brisbane radio station, 4IP. Nineteen current first-class players remained on Packer's books.

For Cosier, when he returned to Australia, life had changed dramatically. Not only had he missed out on an invite to join WSC, his marriage had broken up, and he had lost his job after a change of ownership at the radio station where he worked. He bumped into Sir Donald Bradman at the Adelaide Oval during this time.

'I hear you might be leaving us,' said The Don.

'Yeah, I might be going to Queensland. I need to find work and an employer who will accommodate my cricket career as well.'

Half expecting Sir Donald to try and convince him to stay, Bradman explained that he understood, and had to do the same when he was around Cosier's age.

'Yes, I had to move from New South Wales to South Australia to earn a living so I know what you are going through.'

Oh well, Cosier may have thought to himself, *Bradman doesn't seem that fussed if I go.* Jeff Thomson's offer to help Cosier get a contract at Brisbane radio station 4IP was appealing, topped up by a five-year contract with the QCA worth $5,000 a year. Within weeks he was off to play cricket for Queensland.

WSC – perhaps not such a secret

A number of players interviewed for this book consider that the great secret of the WSC signings wasn't so secretive, that in fact a number of unsigned players had an idea that some players were being signed up for an alternative competition.

During the 1976–77 season, Queensland wicket keeper John Maclean knew something was in the offing when he walked out of the WACA dressing room with Dennis Lillee.

'I might not be back,' Maclean said. Lillee responded with, 'Hang around, there's something happening.' Maclean, who had noticed Packer's middleman John Cornell at Shield matches, walked away trying to work out exactly what Lillee had meant; he knew it must have been something about money for players.

Western Australia's Kevin Wright has a similar story to tell. With Rod Marsh standing between Wright and more first-class cricket, the young keeper confided in Lillee that he was thinking about moving to South Australia.

'Don't do anything too drastic – you might want to stay here for another year to see what happens,' Lillee counselled him.

In retrospect, Wright suspects his teammate was indirectly giving him the word about World Series Cricket. The secret of what WSC represented was slowly making its way around the first-class scene, but the details were so vague it was hard to tell exactly what was looming. As Ian Chappell says, the fact that fifty cricket players were able to keep the lid on all the details of the Packer enterprise shows just how strongly they felt about the need for more pay.

A new era in Test cricket begins

At first, Bob Simpson didn't want to do it.

He had been retired from Test cricket for ten years. Yes, he had approached the ACB offering the services of his promotional company to improve the Board's image, but the initial reception to his offer was cool. But then New South Wales chairman Stan Sismey suggested Simpson return to play Shield cricket. The former Australian skipper had, after all, led the Sydney grade averages for a number of years and was still in good shape. He soon discovered he would be required for more than just Shield cricket.

Former ACB Chairman and current Board member Tim Caldwell wanted to discuss the possibility of Simpson returning to Test cricket with Don Bradman and Bob Parish, Chairman of the Australian Cricket Board In early September 1977, a meeting was convened at Sydney's Angus Steak Cave. Bradman, who had compared the idea of a Simpson comeback to his own return to Test cricket after the Second World War, noted that Simpson was in much better shape now compared to how he had been.

When The Don asked Simpson to again captain Australia, Simpson felt he had little choice but to accept. His decision was sealed after scoring a century on a very difficult wicket at the start of the 1977–78 grade summer. Simpson said of his decision:

> It was an interesting time. Don and I had been good friends for a long time. Once Bradman had asked me to come back it was pretty hard to refuse. The big advantage was that I had continued playing Sydney Grade cricket for Western Suburbs and had been playing well. So I was reasonably fit and had good form. He said to me 'Bob you should really come back. Australia is in an awkward situation. A player of your standing and prestige would be good for the game.' I told him I wasn't mad about it and he said he wasn't when he came back after the Second World War, and I realised I had a responsibility to the game that had been so good to me.

Simpson stipulated that he be appointed captain of NSW and Australia simultaneously, and that he would be the Australian captain for all five Tests against India. And so it was that Simpson was appointed to lead Australia in the summer of official Test cricket for 1977–78. The announcement was made at Cricket House on October 11 to resounding applause from the journalists.

There was something contradictory in Simpson's approach and eventual appointment. He had been one of those championing the cause of a lucrative cricket competition with more money for players. He'd set up commercially sponsored double-wicket competitions with the aim of bringing in more money to the game. Without any sense of irony he added at the time:

> *It was time for people to stand up and be counted. Cricket as we have known it for our entire lives is being threatened by the introduction of a private promoter.*

As Simpson explained in his book *Simmo,* his comeback involved the sacrifice of his business activities. 'Although we would lose money through my absence from the office, a different sort of reward would come from repaying the game that had been so good to me.'

The Establishment vs WSC

Money was the buzzword of the 1977–78 summer – how much the WSC players were getting for just three months' work. Figures like $30,000 were mentioned, huge sums for a cricketer, even of international standing. One of the benefits for the Establishment players was a trickle down effect. Having experienced the mass exodus from Test cricket in the wake of the Packer signings, the Board had little choice but to pay players more, money for fear of losing more players. Bob Parish in a press conference on September 7 cited the improved player payments 'Each player in each Test will receive from the Board for five days cricket a minimum of $1,852 and a maximum of $2,012 depending on whether the match is won or lost.'

It was an improvement, but paled in significance when compared with the money the WSC players were receiving for their commitments regardless of whether they were selected to play or not. Australia's Test players were required to sign a contract for home Tests binding them to the Board and sponsor Benson and Hedges. They received no signing-on fee; it was simply a condition of their selection.

To emphasise the reasoning behind the Board's resistance, Parish held the line that cricketers could not expect the rewards accruing to other big time athletes, describing the comparison between money earned by tennis and golf professionals and cricketers as ludicrous.

Parish argued that the ACB could not afford higher player payments.

The Board reaffirms that it will pay to the players the maximum it can afford after taking into consideration its responsibility to Australian cricket at all levels.

The traditional tour agreement was also changed to prevent any signatory from playing in a match not under the stewardship of the Board before March 31, 1979.

The Board was uncompromising in its view of the Packer signees, vowing to shut them out of any form of official cricket in Australia. The Establishment though copped a blow on November 25, when Justice Christopher Slade ruled in favour of World Series Cricket reversing bans on Greig, John Snow and Mike Procter, stating that the administrators' 'retaliation had strained the bounds of loyalty'.

The war between the Establishment and WSC was well and truly on. With the Packer enterprise and all it might bring still an unknown, the ACB believed it was fighting for the survival of Test cricket and began to look at how it could creatively market the game. They outlaid $70,000 to Tom Worrell of Sportsplan Marketing and David Richards of the VCA, who had with Worrell set up the arrangements for the Centenary Test, to organise *The Indians are Coming* promotional campaign.

Chapter 3

The Indian Tour of Australia, 1977–78

The summer of 1977–78 had five Test matches scheduled between Australia and the visiting Indian team. The first Test was to be held in Brisbane at The Gabba from 2–6 December, the second in Perth from 16–21 December; the third Test from 30 December to 4 January at the MCG; the fourth at the Sydney Cricket Ground from 7–12 January and the final Test at Adelaide Oval from 28 January to 3 February.

What would this new era in Test cricket bring with so much responsibility placed on the new Establishment cricket team?

First Test at The Gabba

The Australian team was to be Kim Hughes, Gary Cosier and Craig Serjeant (three of the four non-WSC tourists from England 1977), Bob Simpson, Paul Hibbert, David Ogilvie, Peter Toohey, Tony Mann, Steve Rixon, Wayne Clark, Jeff Thomson and Alan Hurst.

When the Australian twelve for the First Test was announced, Geoff Dymock looked in vain for his name.

> I thought, hold on, I was supposedly in the top seventeen players in the country before the Packer exodus and now I'm not even in the top twelve. It was baffling.

Although Simpson was not an official selector, he was consulted for his input. In December 2014, Simpson told ABC's *Grandstand* that he felt more comfortable having fellow Western Suburbs players in the side, namely Peter Toohey and Steve Rixon.

Dymock, despite taking ten first class wickets at 30.5 at the start of the 1977–78 season, missed out on a cap. It was a baffling decision given he was still only 32 years old and had toured England with a full strength Australian side just months before. The First Test was also at Dymock's home ground where he revelled in conditions that were more conducive to seam bowling. Perhaps the selectors thought his best days as a pace bowler were behind him (He had taken just eight wickets in five first class matches on the Ashes 1977 tour at an average of 28).

Another surprise omission was Graham Yallop, who didn't tour England but had played three Tests against the West Indies in 1975–76 and was a proven player against spin. Yallop also joined an exclusive club at the start of 1977–78 scoring a century in each innings against New South Wales at the Sydney Cricket Ground in November. The choice of Steve Rixon instead of more senior keeper John Maclean also seems to have been a captain's pick, although the case for 'having more youth' in the side could be argued in the New South Wales wicket keeper's defence.

Six Australians made their debut in the First Test in Brisbane: Clark, Hibbert, Mann, Ogilvie, Rixon and Toohey. Bob Simpson was by far the most experienced, with Gary Cosier the next most senior player. Opening bowler Alan Hurst was playing in his second Test and Australian speedster Jeff Thomson was there – only just having been prevented from joining WSC by his commitment as a Public Relations Executive to a Queensland radio network.

The Indian side was far more experienced, with three of the best spinners and one of the strongest batting lineups in world cricket. The team in batting order was Gavaskar, Vengsakar, Armanath, Viswanath, Patel, Mankad, Madan Lal, Kirani, Prasanna, Bedi (captain) and Chandrasekhar.

On the first morning of The Gabba Test there was a buzz of excitement in the dressing room as a number of a young Australians prepared for their first taste of Test cricket. They perhaps would have been less excited had they known the new curator at The Gabba overwatered the pitch, giving the Indian spinners an ideal surface.

The seasoned Simpson's presence was welcome, but even he felt a little tighter in the stomach than usual – it was after all almost a decade since he had last played for Australia (although in his last Test in 1968 he played against Bedi and Prasanna). Simpson's message to his players was 'enjoy the occasion and take advantage of your good fortune; many second choice sports people have gone on to great things.'

One young Australian batsman never short of confidence was West Australian Kim Hughes. In his second year of first-class cricket Hughes had already frustrated some of his state teammates. His first season was consistent in its inconsistency. He scored two centuries but in between wasted many opportunities that saw him average just 32.

In an often-repeated story, senior player Ian Brayshaw encouraged Hughes to be more patient in his batting. A meeting was called in an Adelaide hotel room where it was stressed that it was more important to occupy the crease for long periods that try to play one dashing stroke after another. Hughes finally got the message that he would need to set himself to bat for four hours each time he went to the crease. Asked *and how many runs will you have after those four hours?* Hughes replied: 'About eight hundred.'

Hughes, after scoring a dazzling 99 for Western Australia in the tour match against India had been tipped as a certainty to play in the First Test at The Gabba. Maybe the rush of blood that had sent him scampering down the pitch trying to hit Prasanna out of the WACA over long on had something to do with it. Perhaps it was also because Hughes had shown little remorse about the dismissal, writing it off more as trying to provide entertaining cricket for the public.

On the morning of the match, despite expectation that he would play, Hughes was named as Twelfth Man. Simpson still needed some convincing when it came to Hughes' ability to knuckle down and play a long innings.

Tony Mann remembers Kim Hughes in the dressing room 'carrying on like a pork chop, just typical Kim Hughes'. His disappointment didn't keep Hughes down for long. The series was a long one and he was sure his path to greatness lay just around the corner.

Peter Toohey was one of the few relaxed players at breakfast. The day before he had been told he was to be Twelfth Man, a decision he didn't so much mind as he tucked into that morning's serve of bacon and eggs. An hour before play as the Australians practised in the nets Simpson sidled up to his club and state teammate and told him he was batting at number five.

Toohey suddenly felt heavier in the stomach. His mind wandered back to a little over a week before when he first heard that he had been selected for Australia. That day Toohey was working as a labourer at the Flemington Markets when one of his workmates heard the team announced on the radio. Over the general hubbub of the workplace he heard 'Hey Toohey, you're in the Test side!'

For Toohey, then a freshly-minted food technologist, the announcement wasn't a complete surprise. Selector Neil Harvey had tapped him on the shoulder the season before and told him if he kept scoring runs he was a chance to tour England. When the news of World Series broke with so many top players signing with the WSC, he knew he was a good chance of wearing the baggy green that summer.

Suddenly it seemed all the hard work on the concrete backyard half-pitch at his parents' property at Barry in the New South Wales central west was worth it. The thrill of having an Australian cap, blazer and jumper was hard to match.

Toohey had grown up playing in the local under-14 hard-wicket competition as an eight-year-old – many Saturdays were spent on blistering ovals. Word soon spread around the area that the kid had an eye like a fish and watch out if you bowled anything short to him. At sixteen he toured New Zealand with an under-23 side drawn from Bathurst, Orange, Mudgee, Lithgow and other towns around the district. He boarded at St Stanislaus College where he came to Bob Simpson's attention at the Western Suburbs club. At eighteen, Toohey graduated from the second eleven to batting at number seven as Wests won the first-grade premiership in his first season. An appearance for the Rest of the World Eleven against Australia at Drummoyne followed, where he batted briefly with a 43-year-old Fred Trueman, before being bowled by Max Walker for a duck.

More than 1,100 runs in his second A-grade season saw Toohey picked for New South Wales at the age of nineteen. A first ball duck against Queensland, courtesy of former Australian opening bowler Tony Dell, reminded him of the leap he had just made at the start of the 1975–76 season. Following his century in Perth early the next summer, Toohey began to feel like he belonged in first-class and even Test company. He was soon to find out.

Told he was playing that morning of the First Test, Toohey contemplated the challenges ahead. He felt like he did the morning of a match against Bankstown when the dynamic duo of Jeff Thomson and Len Pascoe were terrorising the local Grade fraternity – it wasn't the fear of getting hurt, but the sense of occasion. As he walked out to look at the pitch before play he wondered what Thommo might do on it. It looked moister than the usual 'Gabba strip, with a tinge of green'. The pitch was known to be conducive to swing and seam bowling on the first day, but with the added moisture. The bounce was more pronounced, helping not only the pacemen, but also the spin bowlers.

Thirty minutes later when Toohey looked up from the dressing room, Simpson was signalling that Australia would bat, having won the toss.

A wet pitch and three twirling spinners greeted the Australians at The Gabba. Patrons arrived to some light drizzle and a Test match program replete with the image of Jeff Thomson, the local boy and Test cricket star who had not signed with Packer. Thomson's image on the official program represented a message of 'up yours' from the ACB to Kerry Packer and providing evidence that Test cricket was the main game in town.

Those looking though the program would have noticed the dominance of cigarette sponsorship proclaiming Benson and Hedges' *Golden Era of Cricket Sponsorship* complete with a photo of the Gold Player-of-the-Match cricket medallion. Chairman of the Board, Bob Parish was featured wishing all the players good luck. Cricket fans may have noticed a reference by Parish to what he referred to as 'exhibition cricket'. It was a derogatory comment about WSC inferring the cricket played was 'just for show' and not the competitive struggle you would see at a test match.

The Boards' Treasurer Ray Steele summed up Parish's attitude to WSC,

I don't believe exhibition cricket will maintain sufficient interest for it to be an economic proposition, but it could damage the structure of the game.

One could almost smell the hubris from the traditionalists.

It was vital, given the schism, that the ACB sell the India series as something special. One selling point was that this tour was the first time since 1967–68 that India had visited Australia and only the third time in 25 tests that the two sides had faced each other on Australian soil. Another selling point was that, in a world where sides were increasingly reliant on pace bowling, India was different – the Indians had spin wizards like Bedi, Prasanna, Venkat and Chandrasekhar. They were all idiosyncratic masters of an art that often played second fiddle to the dynamism and sheer butality of pace bowling. Most international sides might field one or two spinners but to play three and sometimes four twirlymen was unsual in the modern game.

Parish on the Indian spinners:

Bishan Bedi, with his impeccable control of line and length and such finely controlled flight … his variations had 215 victims at 27.35. The withered right arm of Bhagwat Chandrasekhar, not hindering his ability to fizz a top spinner, his five or more wickets in an innings on twelve occasions. Then there was the elder statesman at 37 Erapalli Prasanna, an off-spinner with deceptive enough flight to have already brought him 51 wickets against Australia at an average of 26. Not forgetting Srini Venkataraghavan, a quickish offie who flights the ball well and gained prodigious turn on responsive wickets …

It was enough to have any Australian batsman choking on his Weetbix. No doubt, playing on the batsmen's minds was the challenge of how to play India's world-class spinners. Australia's spin cupboard had been diluted even further by the recruitment of the likes Ashley Mallet (although he had officially retired for the first time) and Ray Bright to WSC, meaning they were even fewer quailty spinners playing at Shield level. It meant the step from Shield to Test cricket usually a large one became a yawning chasm.

Meanwhile, inside the '*other*' Australian dressing room at VFL Park in Melbourne, players were clustered around a television set, engrossed.

'What time does the Indian telecast begin?' one player asked.

'Should be on now … No wait a minute, there isn't daylight saving up there. We'll have to wait until twelve.'

An audible sigh of disappointment went around the room. A little later Dennis Lillee had taken a front row seat in front of the colour TV. 'Beauty!' he said. 'We're batting!'

But Lillee wasn't talking about his own team. He was talking about the Establishment side at The Gabba. The whole dressing room was silent, even the World Series players weren't going to miss the Test cricket. John Cornell and Austin Robertson were glued to the TV too. Kerry Packer wasn't. He was sitting in the largely empty stands of Waverly Park, beside the Governor of Victoria, Sir Henry Winneke. Things weren't going so well out on the field for the Australian World Series team. Greg Chappell and Hookes had gone quickly, victims of Holding's sheer pace. They were in trouble at 4–39.

Back at The Gabba, play is about to begin. Australia's opener, the mustachioed Paul Hibbert, comes on to the field looking like a real *Test* cricketer as if to stress the point that he's now playing international cricket: baggy cap and long-sleeved jumper – a throwback to the 1930s. His batting partner Gary Cosier appears the total opposite. Red hair, ginger beard, no cap (he walked to the middle wearing his baggy green, but gave it to the umpire to hang onto during his innings), open-neck shirt down to the second button revealing a gold chain – a symbol of the Chappell era.

The Australian openers start timidly. They're up against India's opening bowlers Madan Lal and Mohinder Armanath. The kids in the crowd yell out as Hibbert appears to leg glance a ball for a run. No. Umpire Max O'Connell sends them back. Dead ball. The first run doesn't come for another fifteen minutes. Cosier plays and misses and almost plays on. Hibbert at last makes contact and glances for a single. Cosier pulls Armarnath through mid-wicket for two and then again with a short-arm jab for four. Rain interrupts play. In a move rarely seen at this stage of a match on ABC TV, a ground reporter on the sidelines interviews Bob Simpson. He says he was glad to have won the toss because the Indian spinners on the last day would have been a handful. He then adds almost as an afterthought, 'Thommo might have been interesting bowling on this wicket.'

Play resumes in the damp. Vengsakar slips on the outfield, a divot of turf goes flying. The Australian batsmen start to look more confident. Cosier is almost caught at midwicket by Armanath and then *is* caught at slip, cutting. He walks, waving his arms at the frustration of throwing away a good start. His look says he can't believe that he played that shot. It won't be the last time in the series that Cosier will wear a similar expression.

Enter homeground debutant David Ogilvie, in great form that has already seen him score three first-class hundreds before this Test. One redhead replaces another, this time one under a baggy green cap. Ogilvie looks serious, like a maths teacher who might not take kindly to humour. Straight backed and placing the bat behind his right foot closer to his ankle than most would, making his stance more closed. Like Cosier he punches the ball and is off the mark with a boundary through the on side. Madan Lal chasing the ball slides into the boundary and looks rattled as he gets caught under a Benson and Hedges banner.

An over before lunch, Bedi brings himself on to bowl. It's still drizzling as Bedi wipes his face with his forearm, glides in, the ball pitching on leg. Ogilvie stiffly edges forward, pushing at the ball, which catches the edge and is swallowed by Viswanath at slip. The Indians circle around Bedi, celebrating, and bounce off to lunch. Australia is 2 for 33.

It's slow, plodding Test cricket but this is after all the first session of a five-Test series against a full-strength Indian team, and despite the ground's light rain, a crowd of close to 12,000 has come through the gates.

For vice-captain, Craig Serjeant, the forty-minute wait to face Bedi was an uneasy one. Fresh-faced, tall, dark and quietly determined, he has built his game along the lines of classical batsmanship; straighter-than-straight bat and patient approach to batting. The tour of England showed Serjeant at his best with his 81 on debut at Lord's, but also that fragility that saw him only cobble together another fifteen runs in four innings.

Three close-in fieldsmen greet Serjeant. Barely time to take guard, Bedi strolls in. For four balls Serjeant struggles to combat Bedi's spin. He plays and misses. Commentator Keith Miller voices surprise at the vicious grip and turn that Bedi is extracting in this, the last over before lunch. As captain, Bedi brings in two more close-in fieldsmen. Serjeant fiddles with his protector.

With raised arms and strangled cries from the men in close, he feels as if he is being slowly suffocated. The release comes quickly. He tries to leave the fifth ball as it pitches outside leg stump. Deviating sharply, the ball strikes the outside edge before arriving in the safe hands of Sunil Gavaskar at second slip. Serjeant walks with the look of someone who's had his Christmas presents stolen.

Bob Simpson hustles in. With side burns and a baggy green sitting prominently on his head. Three slips, a silly point and short forward leg greet him. He turns Bedi to leg for two runs and then sweeps uppishly for four. Umpire Max O'Connell, already sweating so much that the cameras pick up the singlet beneath his white shirt, does the signaling for a boundary. Bedi's first over is complete – he has 2 for 6.

Hibbert displays some rare aggression as the sun comes out, taking two off Armanath through midwicket. The Australian batsmen seem more confident. Simpson charges Bedi … and then meekly prods and edges to second slip. The skipper arrived in a hurry and leaves in one.

Peter Toohey walks in under a big hat like a schoolboy on the first day of term. Straight-armed and legged, he appears unfazed by the scene that confronts him and pushes easily to off for his first run. 'Dasher' Hibbert goes next on unlucky thirteen, caught behind by Kirmani off Mohinder Armanath (who has the head jiggle of a Michael Holding, if not the pace). Hibbert looks back as he walks off; he missed the ball by a fair margin.

He [Hibbert] had lasted ninety minutes in the wet, wickets falling all around him. Newcomers Toohey and Tony Mann have the chance at 5–49 to steady the ship. They've seen enough of their teammates dismissed by defensive prods. Attack will be their best form of defence; anything pitched up will go. They add 41 enterprising runs in 45 minutes. By tea, three more wickets have fallen, but Toohey is still there at 8–122. He has danced down the wicket driving Bedi for six, cutting Bhagwat Chandrasekhar with ease, playing as if the risks he is taking mean little – the opposite of a battle-hardened player who could see the pitfalls at every turn.

After tea he goes for the spinners, scoring 43 of the 44 Australian runs. Australia is all out for 166, but with Toohey's valiant 82 the dressing room is abuzz and anything seems possible.

Normally a nervous starter, for Toohey, Australia's poor start had been a blessing in disguise.

> *I didn't have a chance to get nervous; we lost so many early wickets so quickly. I'd always felt comfortable against the spinners and was confident backing myself. The wicket was damp, but had settled a bit by the time I got out there. It would have been much harder against pace.*

Toohey had put into action much that he'd learned from Bob Simpson. He wasn't going to let the spinners dominate him and he looked to rotate the strike, putting some pressure on the fielding side.

His first Test innings was the start of a successful season in which he would gather momentum as a Test batsman utilising his talents to the full. Not all of the Australian batting lineup would derive the same benefit from this first experience of Test cricket.

Bad light stopped play 45 minutes early. By then India was 1–13, with ten Test century batsman Sunil Gavaskar caught in short for three. New era, day one, stumps. India's spinners had done the damage and waited to see if Australia's spin attack, which consisted of the skipper Bob Simpson and Tony Mann could do the same.

When Tony Mann came on to bowl early on day two the pitch was still spinning. Criticised for using his wrong 'un too much, Mann tried it on with Vengsakar the seventh ball he bowled in Test cricket and had him caught bat pad. His first international spell of 3–12 had him thinking Test cricket wasn't easy, but on a turning wicket he could more than hold his own.

Things were more challenging in India's second innings as India fell just sixteen runs short of the 340 needed to win. Mann's fifteen wicketless overs went for 52. He bowled three maidens but struggled to get through the Indians' defences. Gavsakar, who proved to be a thorn in Mann's side (and in most other's sides) scored the first of his three hundreds in three Tests with 113.

For Australia Serjeant had bagged a pair, thereby scoring his third Test duck in a row; Simpson had found form with 89; while Toohey backed up his first innings 82 with a fine half-century (57) as Australia made a more respectable second innings total of 327. Jeff Thomson was the standout of the Aussie bowlers with seven wickets, while Wayne Clark's eight-wicket Test debut was impressive.

Hibbert – a man out of place

Paul Hibbert was dropped after the First Test in Brisbane never to play for Australia again. Despite his valiant effort the selectors clearly thought him not up to test standard. His stodgy batting had shown little sign of blossoming into something more substantial. It didn't really matter to Paul Hibbert that Bob Simpson once said he 'reminded him so much of Bill Lawry it wasn't funny'. Not to the left-hand opening batsman from Victoria. who was philosophical, and knew the vagaries of cricket and selection very well, but never forgot the way he was dumped by the selectors.

At the time of writing, Paul Hibbert is the only one of the Establishment players who has passed away. It was a tragic end, found dead, only 56 years old, alone in his Essendon home. The autopsy showed Hibbert had suffered an internal haemorrhage related to alcoholism. Life post-cricket hadn't been easy for him. He had been helped by the Australian Cricketers' Association when his life was derailed by family and business problems as well as a reliance on alcohol. Victorian batsman and friend Jeff Moss remembered:

> *I played a lot of cricket with and against Paul Hibbert. He was one of my cricketing friends and it was sad to watch him go downhill. We sought help from the Association, however it was too late.*

Ian Callen, another teammate, worked with Hibbert at Callen's cricket bat factory. While Callen doesn't want to provide details, it sounds like it all ended on a sour note. They had gone to England together in 1976 and played cricket; Callen in the minor counties, Hibbert in the Durham competition. Callen thought his mate was a terrific cricketer who had 'an amazing ability to concentrate' and was wonderful company.

Asked if he knows what happened to him, Callen said recently:

> *He had real problems. I don't think anyone really knew him. I don't really want to get into that, it's just very sad. He was the Victorian selector who was responsible for the selection of Shane Warne; he certainly knew his cricket.*

Hibbert was ironically called 'Dasher' for his defensive style of play, although he was a clean striker of the ball. Critics said he came from the Geoffrey Boycott school of batting where shot-making was avoided and defence the key. Boundaries were not cherished the way they were for other players. In fact, Hibbert was only the second man in first-class cricketing history to make a century without hitting a boundary (the other was former Derbyshire batsman Alan Hill, who made 103 for Orange Free State versus Griqualand West in 1976–77).

Paul Hibbert had a humorous side. Journalist Greg Baum recalls having a drink with him late in the 1986–87 Shield season. Hibbert had played innings of 129 and 88 against Tasmania and then made a pair against Queensland at The Gabba the next match. Baum asked Hibbert whether scoring 217 runs in one.match and nothing in the next was some kind of record. 'The Don probably did it' was Hibbert's reply with, Baum noting, barely a twitch of his moustache.

His debut innings in the First Test of the 1977–78 series on a wet, flaky pitch saw him eke out thirteen off 77 balls. It was followed by two in the second innings. The decision to drop Hibbert was harsh and reflected the scatter-gun approach adopted by the selectors during this time – and perhaps from the influence of Simpson.

Possibly Simpson thought Hibbert had, like water, found his level during the player-depleted era of 1977–79. Typically he fielded mostly at bat pad, never claiming the senior player's privilege of fielding in the slips. Hibbert finished his first-class career having played 78 matches from 1974 through to 1987, scoring 4,790 runs at 38.62 with nine hundreds. Many have played more Test cricket with worse first-class figures.

When he died, Hibbert had sadly been estranged for nearly 20 years from his wife Bronwyn, daughter Hannah and son Daniel – a handy cricketer with the Melbourne University Club who now works for Cricket Victoria. He had been re-employed as a batting mentor at the Essendon Cricket Club (where he had ended his playing career and was once senior coach), which offered him some income and focus. The arrangement ended, but Hibbert was encouraged to spend time there especially with the younger players. Former Victorian captain Ray Bright thought it was a bit stiff that his ex-teammate played in only one Test.

He was unlucky to make his debut on a green top at The Gabba. If it had been a flat track at Adelaide, who knows how he would have gone.

Hibbert gave up drinking for a period but his demons returned and he appeared to have suffered a relapse that led to his death. Like his Test career, his life ended too soon.

A win by 16 runs – it's on to Perth

There was a buzz about traditional cricket after the First Test. Australia had won a thrilling match by sixteen runs watched by more than 32,000 over four days, compared to the 13,000 who had made their way to VFL Park at Waverly in Melbourne for the First Super Test of the summer between WSC Australians and the West Indies. Despite winning the Test, the Australian selectors rang in changes. As well as Hibbert, Alan Hurst was dropped following his 2 for 81 runs in two Brisbane innings. Australia went into the Second Test in Perth with two more Test debutants, New South Wales opener John Dyson and Western Australian left-arm medium bowler, Sam Gannon.

Gannon, 30, had struggled to maintain his place in the Western Australian side with competition from Lillee, Massie, Brayshaw, McKenzie, Malone and Alderman. His lively pace and ability to angle the ball across right-handers helped him to a debut season performance of 6 for 107 against South Australia at the WACA in 1966–67. When WSC came into being, he played five matches in a row for Western Australia, having not played for his state in the previous five years. His talent would soon be evident in the Test series against India.

John Dyson was a physical education teacher at Caringbah in NSW. Orthodox with a strong straight drive and deft cut shot, as a twenty-one-year-old the Sutherland grade cricketer Dyson scored consecutive centuries for New South Wales Colts in 1974–75. Two summers later he made a painstaking start to his Shield career with a slow 102. It may have earned him the ungenerous nickname of the 'strokeless wonder' from a Perth newspaper, but it also caught the selectors' attention. Dyson could provide some stability at the top of the order.

The Second Test side had a different look to its batting order. Kim Hughes came in from drinks waiter duties for an injured Gary Cosier and numerous players were shuffled around. In batting order the Australia side was Dyson, Serjeant, Ogilvie, Toohey, Simpson, Rixon, Hughes, Mann, Clark, Thomson and Gannon. For India, one off-spinner replaced another: Prasanna, wicketless in Brisbane, was dropped for Venkataraghavan.

Centrestage in the *West Australian's* full colour wraparound was an image of Kim Hughes. The high profile in the press however didn't match the performance. In Perth Hughes managed 28 in the first innings (dropped twice in two balls along the way) and a first-ball duck in the second, LBW to Madan Lal. The prodigal son had returned home, but with not much to show for it. His inability to string two Tests together was about to continue.

Rumours also swirled in the West about one of their own who was accused of chucking. Despite his success at The Gabba, Wayne Clark was feeling less than comfortable. The legitimacy of his bowling action was spoken about in whispers in the Indian camp in Brisbane, becoming louder in Perth. Clark read the report he'd been dreading in the *Western Australian* where it was alleged Gavaskar, dismissed twice by Clark in Perth, had doubts about Clark's action. Before long Channel Nine News cameramen were lingering outside the WACA nets filming Clark's action. It all blew over soon enough, and Clark played the entire series but he also wondered what the future might hold. Clark would find out at the start of the Ashes summer. The Establishment players had defied the reports of being second rate and beaten one of the best teams in the world in Brisbane. But how would they fare in Perth?

Tony Mann – nightwatchman at his best

Scoring a century for Australia had been a childhood dream for Western Australian leg-spinning all-rounder, Tony Mann. The idea of raising his bat in celebration of a Test ton to a home-town audience in Perth appealed. Leaning more towards bowling leg-spin in his teens, the thought was still there in the back of his mind. Now aged 32, Mann was starting to think that dream might have passed him by. Then came the summer of 1977–78. It was one to remember for the Western Australian journeyman of the first-class scene, receiving his Australian blazer, jumper and cap.

Known as 'Rocket' for his fierce throwing arm, the son of underarm bowler and vigneron Jack Mann initially learned to give the ball a decent loop on the back veranda of the Mann household. It was only 26 yards long, which ruled out fast bowling. Tony and his brothers Dorham and Bill recruited a fourth player, the Yugoslav kid from the neighbouring vineyard. Future state wicketkeeper Dennis Yagmich proved pretty useful at stopping the ball from hitting Angela's Mann's patch of prize geraniums. The boys soon outgrew the back veranda and were playing on a backyard turf wicket made from river mud down off the flats of the Swan River, complemented by six-to-eight inches of soil from the Harvey River, 100 kilometres south of Perth. Harvey soil – also used for the WACA pitch – contains a clay called Smectite which sets particularly hard.

Sometimes cricket celebrities visited. In 1960–61 the West Indian's Wes Hall and Tom Dewdney visited the house and joined the boys (or perhaps more so Jack Mann for the wines). The Manns even named their new puppy after Wes after he spent the afternoon carrying the pooch around.

As a thirteen-year-old, Tony found that his stock leg-spinner and occasional offie were a handful for players in the local competition. He took 93 wickets playing cricket in the Minor Swan and Helena Association, beating the record set by his father Jack years before. (Jack bowled underarm leg-spinners, the legacy of a shooting accident years before.)

Midland Guilford stalwarts and Western Australian sporting heroes Keith Slater and Kevin Gartrell came calling. In Tony's first A-grade match he took 6 for 29 bowling fourteen eight ball overs. Wearing short pants, Tony was sometimes mistaken as one of the sons of a player loitering around the afternoon tea table.

'Now dear, you'll have to wait until the players have finished their afternoon tea' one of the tea ladies gently admonished him. Young Mann managed around forty wickets a season in each of his first three seasons. At fifteen he was in the state squad.

Four years later he debuted for Western Australian against the 1964 Australian team on its way to England in a match over the Easter break. The visitors showed little mercy on the teenager, belting him for 72 from ten overs. Norm O'Neill, Bob Simpson and Ian Redpath were especially harsh. His batting was worse – Mann was dismissed for a pair.

His next game for WA came two seasons later. With the bat he scored 3 and 30 against South Australia; hardly auspicious, but he knew he was in the selectors' sights. He soon discovered being picked was one thing, finding a regular place in the team another. When WACA officials recruited England's left-arm orthodox bowler Tony Lock, Mann didn't mind. Lock led by example and Mann marvelled at the way the Englishman could generate such bounce, accuracy and flight.

Lock headed to the West after the English selectors shunned him after being the leading wicket-taker on the MCC tour of India and Pakistan in 1961–62. It didn't take long for Lock to adjust to the demands of Shield cricket. He became the first post-war bowler to take fifty or more Shield wickets in a season. Mann watched on as Twelfth Man when Lock skippered WA to its second Shield win in 1967–68, taking nine wickets in the match against Victoria to clinch the title.

Mann was one of four spinners vying for a second spinning spot in the WA team, the others being Terry Jenner, Ashley Mallett and Terry MacGill (father of Stuart). Mallett and Jenner may have admired Lock's ability but they knew what his recruitment meant for their prospects and moved to South Australia. Mann himself almost went to South Australia, but in the latter half of the 1966–67 season was preferred to Jenner in the WA state side. In the 1969–70 season, Mann claimed five wickets in each innings of Shield matches against NSW, Victoria and Queensland, finishing with 25 wickets at 26, but missed out on the Australian second eleven tour of New Zealand. Ultimately it was Jenner who first wore the baggy green, selected for Australia in 1970–71 against England.

Mann showed his prowess with the bat by scoring 110 against the touring MCC team in Perth in December 1970 – an attacking team that featured Bob Willis Peter Lever, Ken Shuttleworth and Ray Illingworth. It was a sign of things to come, although Mann was an infrequent member of the strong Western Australian side that had a bowling attack centred on pace who made the most out of the lightning quick WACA wicket.

By the summer of 1977–78 things had changed. Dennis Lillee and Mick Malone had signed with WSC and there was a need to supplement the pace attack with spin. At the start of the season, Mann and his state squad teammates sat in the leather chairs at the WACA's boardroom where they had been summoned to talk about what the advent of WSC might mean. They soon found out.

Mann considered Victoria's Jim Higgs his main rival for Australian selection. He knew that Higgs was a better leg-spinner with more deceptive flight, greater turn and variation than Mann's standard leggie and wrong 'un. But Higgs couldn't bat and was a liability in the field. Mann knew he was a chance to play for Australia if he played his cards right. His decisive moment arrived against NSW, demonstrating his guile to work batsmen out. His first ball to new Australian captain Bob Simpson was a wrong 'un that Simmo just kept out with a desperate late jab. The fifth ball, a wrong 'un, Simpson cut to point. The next ball was a wrong 'un that Simpson misread and shouldered arms out, LBW.

An impression had been made on the Australian captain even though Mann disagreed with the Board's decision to appoint Simpson as skipper. Like a number of his state teammates, he was convinced the honour should have gone to John Inverarity. He thought his state captain was a thinking man's cricketer, a good strategist, a man respected by his teammates.

Mann received news of his call-up to Australian colours when he was teaching at Northam High School in the WA wheatbelt. The principal ducked his head around the corner to tell him he was wanted on the phone. When Mann returned to the blackboard scattered with algebra sums, he announced to the class he was now a member of the Australian cricket team, that he would be off to play in the First Test against India. The students gave a grunt and resumed work.

And so it was that Mann found himself in Brisbane with his Australian cricket cap, two jumpers and a blazer. Despite Australia's success in the First Tetst some of the scribes were calling the Australian team a second or third eleven, it didn't bother Mann or his teammates. As Mann commented:

We thought bugger them if they want to go off and do their thing …
we still had a very good side.

With the First Test behind him, Mann had scored 19 and 29 and taken three wickets. Relatively speaking, he did pretty well for a Test debutante. He was now relishing the thought of playing on home turf.

That turning wicket Tony Mann was hoping for wasn't present in Perth; he again struggled bowling against the fleet-footed Gavaskar (127) whom Mann feared had 'worked him out'. His nineteen wicketless overs went for 112, while Bedi's 61.2 overs yielded 10 for 194. For Mann, that first spell during The Gabba Test seemed a long time ago.

When his chance arrived late on the fourth day to bat at nightwatchman, Mann jumped at the opportunity (Steve Rixon who had made fifty as nightwatchman in the first innings declined the invitation to back up again).

Only eight runs separated the two sides after the first innings. Armanath led the way for the visitors with ninety; Simpson's 176 had occupied 355 balls and consumed six-and-a-half hours, dominating Australia's total of 394. After scoring 53 in 244 minutes in the first, new Australian opener Dyson was dismissed for four in the second, leaving Australia 1–25 at stumps, requiring 339 runs on the last day.

It was now Mann's turn at the crease – fourth day, Australian needing well over 300 runs to have a chance of winning. He survived a few nervous moments before stumps on the fifth day and sensed that the Indian bowlers were having trouble turning the ball. He decided to go out the following day and play his natural game. Six not-out turned to 105 in just over three hours.

The image of Mann that burns bright is of him driving the ball, bat held high as if he had just completed a golf swing. Not much foot movement. Wearing a baggy green cap he looks totally at ease. Keeper Kirmani and slipsman Viswanath in the background, partly obscuring a Benson and Hedges banner on the boundary fence. With well-loved, taped bat and rolled sleeves, Mann is a picture of poise, grace, aggression and control.

By the time Mann was dismissed he had steered Australia towards a two-wicket victory as Jeff Thomson hit Bedi to the fence with 22 balls to spare, Australia successfully chasing down a total of 338. All up, 1,468 runs were scored in a memorable Test.

Melbourne, then Sydney – the team struggles

Despite his success with the bat, Mann knew he had to take wickets. When he arrived in Melbourne for the Third Test, he was worried at the ease with which Indian batsman, Gavaskar had played him in Perth. Seeing the sign strung across Bay 13 *'Higgs a certainty'* didn't make him feel any more comfortable. Higgs who was considered by many to be a better spinner than Mann and could have been selected for the Third Test especially given it was his home ground. His bowling figures however were against him with just seven wickets at 43 in the lead up to the Third Test. A golden opportunity to impress the Australian selectors at the MCG was missed when Victoria bundled New South Wales out twice and Higgs didn't get the chance to bowl in the enounter before the Third Test.

Australia went into the Test with one change: Hughes out, Cosier back in. India brought in Ghavri for Madan Lal and Mankad back for Venkat.

Despite losing 2–0, India recovered courtesy of a 256 run partnership between Armanath and Viswanath. When Australia batted, Cosier at last found form at his favourite ground with 67 and a score of 85 was welcome relief for Serjeant. After a rare first-innings duck, Gavaskar managed his third hundred of the series (118), all of them in second innings. India's spin bowlers, Chandrasekhar and Bedi, then ran through the home side on a turning MCG wicket and delivered India's first win in Australia by a margin of 222 runs.

In a match dominated by Indian spinners, Mann was given nine overs, taking 1–39. It was a missed opportunity to prove he could be a Test-class spinner. He wryly remembers an Allan Langoulant cartoon from Perth's *Daily News.*

> *As a weary looking Simpson strolls off and the turbaned Indians celebrate in the background, an innocent looking bloke who resembles Mann asks, 'Tell me Simmo, if Chandrasekhar was in your team would you give him a bowl?'*

It had been a spinner's wicket, and Simpson had relied on Thomson and Clark to bowl. Mann knew his number was marked. He had to get wickets in Sydney. This time it was David Ogilvie in whom the selectors lost faith. Scores of 5, 46, 27, 47, 6 and 0 had exposed his batting weakness against spin. The out-and-in-again Kim Hughes was brought back while India's lineup remained unchanged.

India repeated the dose with the help of a Sydney wicket, damp from torrential pre-match rain. Australia was dismissed for 131, the then second lowest total in a home Test against India. Prasanna's second-innings haul of four wickets helped Australia to its first consecutive home losses since Frank Tyson had run through them in 1954–55.

Mann went wicketless and going out for ducks in both innings. As he walked off the SCG, he knew he wouldn't be in the team to tour the West Indies to be announced a few days later. Mann had had opportunities but had not made the most of them. The Indian spinners were able to take wickets yet Mann struggled for impact with his spin – his standard leg-break, wrong 'un combination could only take him so far at Test level. His good friend and teammate Sam Gannon thought he had a few more Tests in him. It was wait and see if he would be selected.

The day the team was due to be announced for the Fifth Test and upcoming West Indies tour, Mann was were doing a promotion for Town and Country Bank with good friend, Sam Gannon. Suddenly they were joined by a third Australian player.

'You're in the team!' It was the ebullient Kim Hughes, talking directly to Gannon.

He continued, 'So am I!' Then, 'Sorry Rocket. You're not.'

Later that afternoon Gannon, who had gone to the pub to celebrate the news of his selection, was shattered to read the *Daily News* to discover he had in fact been dropped. For John 'Sam' Gannon it had been a rise from rags to riches and then back to rags again before he even knew it. After a seven-wicket debut only four more victims followed in the next three Tests and by the end of the season he had been packed off back to district cricket.

Mann never played for Australia again, the brief chance to play at the highest level had passed almost as if it was a dream.

The win for India in the Fourth Test in Sydney had the series tied up at two all. The Fifth Test in Adelaide would be the decider.

Craig Serjeant – Vice-captain and then …

By the end of the Fourth Test at Sydney, Craig Serjeant was in despair. In a matter of weeks he'd gone from being touted as the man to take over from Bobby Simpson to being left out of the Test side for the Fifth Test in Adelaide. The burden of being named vice-captain contributed to his pair of ducks at Brisbane and his overall modest form. The weight of expectation and an underdeveloped technique against quality spin had left him feeling exposed. He'd only made one half-century and registered double figures just four times in eight innings. Serjeant described the ease with which he surrendered his wicket, especially in the Fourth Test where he was spun out for five runs in two innings – it was an embarrassment.

> *I just wasn't able to respond to the responsibility of being a leader and adapt my game to play the Indian spinners. I think my selection on the West Indian tour was really the Board sticking by me, given that I hadn't signed with Packer.*

With WSC slowly gaining greatly credibility and with crowds having built (especially for the innovation of night cricket) as the season progressed the decision Serjeant made not to sign with Packer was one he was starting to regret:

> *My decision was based on my preconception of me being a professional person first, and a cricketer second. I made the conservative decision. In hindsight it wouldn't have any impact on my professional career and it was the wrong decision. I should have joined World Series. I think I would have been a better cricketer. As a professional cricketer you get more time to practise. Parts of*

my game would have changed. I would have spent more time doing different things.

Perhaps some of Serjeant's traits as a younger player show why he was only briefly on the Test scene. State teammate Ian Brayshaw wrote in January 1977 how Serjeant was being mentored by former Victorian and Western Australian batsman, Ken Meuleman.

There is an aura of the Meuleman correctness and all of Ken's precision and wristiness in Serjeant's stroke play. But there used to be two ingredients of the prolific Meuleman's batting which were missing from the youngster's make up. They were his dedicated concentration and his wonderful footwork against spin bowling.

Brayshaw pondered as to why a player of Serjeant's undoubted class was 25 years old before be broke into first-class ranks. Brayshaw's comments reflect those of a man who knew his younger teammate well. It was Serjeant's lack of consistency and ability to turn a good start into a significant score, as well as his failure against India's quartet of spinners, that saw his Test career fade away so dramatically.

Serjeant would soon return to his work as a pharmacist at the Perth Medical Centre on a full-time basis.

David Ogilvie – great expectations?

David Ogilvie was dismayed. Twelfth man for the Fourth Test in Sydney dropped for the Fifth and final Test against India in Adelaide and from the squad to tour the West Indies. Ogilvie had been asked to go back to Shield cricket and score runs, which he did. He was the first to admit that he had struggled against the Indian spinners and that he had built his reputation on playing well against 'the quicks'. If he were going to succeed at Test level, it would be against pace bowling.

The 1977–78 season had promised so much. In Bradmanesque form, Ogilvie had been tipped by Ray Lindwall to become one of the game's future greats. However, failing to score a fifty in six knocks at the number three position for Australia in the first three Tests was enough for the selectors to lose faith. By the end of the Indian series all he could think of was that he had let the side down by not living up to his own high standards.

Ogilvie's ascension to baggy green status had begun almost two decades earlier, playing for Caloundra in a B-grade Sunshine Coast competition before the region became trendy and densely populated. Like many country cricketers he played against men when he was ten. At such a young age, his Saturdays consisted of piling into an older player's car and being ferried to various fields around the region. Cricket was a tradition passed down by his father who had captained Queensland country and was selected to play for the Queensland first eleven during the Second World War, only to find the season cancelled along with his chance to play for his state.

The young Ogilvie boarded at Brisbane Grammar in the city from year nine. By the next summer he was part of the first eleven. Club cricket for Toombul under-17s followed as did A-grade games for Colts and later for the University of Queensland Cricket Club where he was studying to become a teacher. It was a rapid rise to State squad company, but not so to Queensland selection.

A back injury that later plagued him on the tour of the West Indies had its genesis in a game of tennis. He was out of cricket for two years in his early twenties. His back recovered and he returned to the game, immediately making grade runs. Elevated to Twelfth Man for Queensland, it was a job he couldn't seem to shake. He performed the role so many times that as soon as he saw a selector walking towards him again, he knew what to expect. *'Sorry David, you'll be carrying the drinks' he'd hear*, to which Ogilvie would sometimes add *'Again!'*

The frustration was that he was unable to get many hits in grade cricket because he was on State drinks-waiter duties. Then one night while getting a lift home with Greg Chappell, his captain gave him the good news, with the advice. 'Make the most of the opportunity'.

Sadly he didn't. An Alan Hurst out swinger sent Ogilvie packing early, for three, caught by Robinson, in Queensland's final match of the 1974–75 season. But seeing Greg Chappell bat did more than make up for any feelings of disappointment; Chappell's flawless 122 off 129 balls, as well as Jeff Thomson's 6–17 gave his side a ten wicket victory over Victoria. He'd seen the best and now he wanted to be play among them.

Queensland selection was more successful in the 1975–76 season. Batting at three, he was a player of good starts but not much more. Eighteen against New South Wales, 35 versus Victoria, 44 and 21 (WA), 55 and 13 (SA), 33 and 20 against the visiting West Indies. Just when he looked like remaining a double-figures player, a second innings of 132 against New South Wales off 180 balls confirmed, until then, hidden talent.

The following summer it looked as if he had matured as a batsman when he opened up with a century (115) against Western Australia, but then managed only one more fifty for the season. Despite this, Ogilvie knew he was more than good enough to play first-class cricket. Advice from Greg Chappell had helped bridge the gap. Having adjusted and strengthened the way he used his top hand, Ogilvie became a more versatile stroke player.

Always one to live in the present and prepare for the future, the newly-married Ogilvie's biggest concern was how he was going to earn a decent living while still playing Shield cricket. He was lucky in that he was given time off from the school where he taught senior biology and junior science, but it still wasn't a full wage.

Season 1977–78 was a whirlwind that started with 194 against Victoria at The Gabba. It was the start of a stellar summer that yielded 1,060 runs with six Shield centuries, a record at the time surpassed only by Don Bradman and Bill Ponsford. With World Series Cricket announced and the Australia selectors seeking a reliable number three, the future looked bright. He'd heard whispers about WSC before it broke and saw his chance to wear a baggy green.

Queensland State teammate Gary Cosier wasn't sure how Ogilvie would handle the step up. He believed him to be a very good player of fast bowling, well respected by his teammates, but lacking confidence in his own ability. Said Cosier:

> *Even when he was scoring all those hundreds he couldn't believe what he was achieving, or that it would keep going.*

Ogilvie may have gone into the First Test against India in Brisbane with runs behind him but the Indian spinners had him reaching for the ball with uncertainty in the first innings when he was dismissed for five. A second-innings 46 before bowled by Chandrasekhar gave him more hope that he could succeed at Test level.

As the series progressed, Ogilvie experienced more disappointment than hope. Scores of 27 and 47 in Perth were followed by a double disappointment of only six runs then a duck at Melbourne. After three Tests, despite the promise of two scores in the forties, David Ogilvie was dropped. He'd just begun to feel comfortable against the spinners and was dismissed ruing that he was unable to develop the same momentum he had with the Queensland team.

It was a tough time for a batsman with such high expectations for himself and his equally inexperienced teammates. He felt that he and his team were the custodians of Test cricket and he wanted to do well. This added to the pressure. In some ways, Ogilvie's early Test form reflected what he'd experienced at first-class level: a series of starts without converting. It would be a matter of time before Ogilvie would discover whether or not he had a future in the game at the highest level.

Four players make their debut

Four debutants made the side for the Fifth Test at Adelaide Oval – Rick Darling, Bruce Yardley, Ian Callen and Graeme Wood. Dyson, Serjeant and Hughes had been dropped and Mann, Gannon and Ogilvie were also dropped, not only for the Test but also from the fifteen-man touring party. India's only change was Gaekwad for Mankad.

Australia batted first in the final six-day Test. A score of 505 reflected Simpson's view that the selectors had given him the best balanced team of the season. One of the debutants, Darling demonstrated a strong ability to cut in his innings of 65 and 56. Wood was less successful with scores of 39 and 8 but looked capable. Australia's new number three was Graham Yallop. It had been more than a season since he had debuted for Australia but he looked immediately comfortable in the green and gold. He took to the Indian spinners with ease on a flat Adelaide Oval to score 121 while Simpson chimed in with his second century of the series. Callen scored 22 in a first innings stand of 47. Even tail-ender fast bowler, Jeff Thomson, got into the action at one stage, slogging a sweeping shot off Bedi for six.

After one and a half days in the field, the Indian top order struggled to come to terms with the pace of Thomson who removed Gavaskar and Armanath, Fellow bowler, Clark accounted for Chauhan. India was 3 for 23. Then disaster struck when Thomson pulled a hamstring. This took the wind out of Australia's sails as India steadied and Viswanath and Vengsakar put on 136 runs.

The series was decided on the final day with the visitors falling 47 runs short of the 493-run target – a record for a highest fourth innings score in a time-limited Test. The win was helped considerably by Simpson's second century (100) of the series and a half-century for good measure. Bob Simpson was described by journalist Phil Tresidder as 'like a knight in shining pads riding out of retirement to rescue Australian cricket in its hour of need'.

Having just turned 42, Bob Simpson had a spring in his step akin to that of someone half his age, rejoicing in taking the final wicket to clinch a series.

He bestowed two birthday cakes sent by Indian manager Polly Umrigar to the Adelaide Children's Hospital just as the crew from TV show, *This is Your Life* circled him to celebrate his career and life. For Simpson and his young Australian teammates this was as good as it gets.

While Simpson was riding high, some were feeling let down by the events of that summer. The dropped Ogilvie liked and admired the skipper but felt Simpson never got the best out of him. As Ogilvie said:

> *I don't think he was a particularly good manager of people … that's not to say there was no support … there was a fair age difference. On reflection, I might have wanted more from Simpson on a one-to-one basis. I'm sure Simmo wanted more from me.*

For any such criticisms of Simpson's ability to captain the team, he became a thorn in the side of the ACB with his constant ideas on how to improve the players' lot. It proved frustrating for the administrators, who tried every move they knew to put themselves in a good light.

By summer's end it was all looking up for the Australian Cricket Board. The Adelaide Test had attracted 73,978 with gate receipts totalling $95,796. It was like a kiss of life for official Australian cricket trying desperately to rebuild.

Wayne Clark, a success story

Wayne Clark was one of the successes of the summer, despite queries surrounding his bowling action early in the series. It's true that the amiable West Australian bowled with an action that sometimes looked more like he was running up to bowl in a game of backyard cricket. Although he would lope in to bowl he delivered the ball with an explosive action generating pace from a quick shoulder action. By series end doubts raised about Clark's action had been at least publically dispelled (it would later arise when England toured in 1978/79 because of an unwritten agreement between England and Australia that players with doubt over their actions would not play in an Ashes series)

By the end of the Indian series Clark had taken 28 wickets and appeared every bit a Test cricketer.

Clark began his cricketing journey inspired by his Bayswater Primary teacher Laurie Mayne, the powerfully built right-arm fast bowler just back from the 1965 tour of the West Indies.

Mayne was a schoolyard hero, taking eight wickets in the First Test at Sabina Park, Kingston, Jamaica Clark however started as a batsman, turning out for the Perth club Bedford in junior cricket. Future Australian swing bowler Bob Massie coached the side and encouraged Clark to take up bowling. It proved a handy move for the thirteen-year-old. The following year,1968 he made the WA state schoolboy team where he met teammate Kim Hughes for the first time. At fifteen, Clark made his A-grade debut in a semi-final for

Bayswater-Morley where he came up against new Nedlands recruit, batsman Bob Cowper fresh from retiring as a Test cricketer. Cowper's 150-odd secured the game for his side and Clark went away wicketless.

Clark was a good Australian Rules footballer – his preferred sport. With East Perth in 1968 , injuries and Clark seemed to go together all too well. A fractured hand, depressed fracture of the cheekbone and then a broken collarbone dampened his appetite for the game. He decided that cricket was for him and he first played for WA in a Gillette Cup semi-final in 1972 at age nineteen, opening the bowling with Graham McKenzie.

A first-class debut followed against the MCC in 1974–75, taking 2–56 and 1–41. Despite this promise, players such as Lillee, Alderman and Brayshaw made it difficult to break into the WA state side. However, for the 1976–77 season, he arrived with a bang, taking 25 wickets at a cost of 26.

He was told he was close to touring England in 1977, where he would have been well suited to the seaming wickets. Even though he missed out on that tour, when the news broke of World Series Cricket, phone calls to Clark soon followed. First it was Rod Marsh and then Ian Chappell who asked if he was interested in signing with WSC. Clark met well-known WA television executive Brian Treasure, who had joined WSC. With no secrecy involved, Treasure met Clark at the Hillcrest oval when a match was on. Clark was offered a contract of $25,000 a year to play for two seasons, although there were no guarantees as to where and for what side he would be playing. Had he signed, Clark could well have ended up in the backwaters of WSC playing for the Cavaliers side (made up of players on the fringe of selection in the official teams of Australia, West Indies and World), which played the official sides at regional venues. Given Packer was unable to reach regional audiences with his television broadcast (channel Nine only broadcast to metropolitan regions) he used the Cavaliers to have a presence in country Australia. Clark recalls:

> *I rang the Australian Cricket Board to see where I stood and was told that I was a 95% chance of getting picked for Australia that summer but they couldn't guarantee anything. I went away and thought*

about it for a bit, spoke to some people I respected and then told them
(WSC) I would stick with Establishment cricket.

It wasn't long before another offer came from WSC that allowed Clarke to play during the school holidays only — as fellow school teacher and state teammate Rob Langer had done. He declined again. Wayne Clark badly wanted to earn that Australian cap.

Rick Darling local boy makes good

South Australian hometown boy Darling was a baby-faced, blond-haired twenty-year-old who looked more surfer than cricketer, hailing from Ramco just outside the citrus town of Waikerie in South Australia's Riverland district. Most players from the era discovered they had been selected to play for their country by listening to the radio. For Darling, it was the distant shout of his father's voice. The piercing yell could be heard puncturing the air where Darling had been zigzagging through the glass-smooth river on one ski.

'You better get your arse down to Adelaide! You've just been picked to play for Australia! And get off those skis in case you injure yourself again!'

Darling's dad's Max, who had played for SA Country against visiting MCC and West Indian teams, was instrumental in his son taking up the game, knowing Rick's predilection for injury (often at inopportune moments).

Two years before Rick had suffered a fractured skull in a collision playing Australian Rules football for Ramco. A week was spent in hospital, first in Waikerie and then in the Royal Adelaide. Six months later a shotgun exploded in his face which resulted in another week in hospital as doctors searched for shrapnel scattered through his skull. Darling had also suffered heavy falls water skiing, and with a habit of hooking on the cricket field, he'd been struck on the head more than enough times by a cricket ball.

Strangely, when Darling heard his father's shouts about his selection, he wasn't sure what to think. He was glad he had earned a much cherished baggy green cap, but wanted to spend a few more days skiing. The freedom he felt out on the river was hard to beat and he didn't get nervous skiing, unlike when going out to bat. Darling was jumpy at the crease, a jittery starter. He'd often vomit before matches, even at Grade level. That was one of the reasons he had been asked to open for South Australia and move away from his middle order position in his second season. He possessed intense energy, was quick off the mark between the wickets and prowled the cover region with pace and an accurate arm.

When the news sunk in, Darling briefly thought about his journey to national selection, about his father who had first put a bat in his hands when he was a kid and reminded him of his great uncle who captained Australian. Joe Darling, the man who led Australia to winning Ashes series in 1899 and 1902, was a symbolic figure in the household representing all that could be achieved in sport.

With no school cricket in the region in the 1960s, Darling travelled the path of many country schoolboys, starting sub-fielding (when one of the team didn't show up) for his dad's side in hard-wicket cricket at the age of ten; then playing on a turf wicket and experiencing official cricket for one of the country sides in the under-17 annual school boys' carnival.

It was there he caught the eye of Salisbury coach and SACA and English coaching import, Ernie Clifton. The lightly-built Darling found he had to rely on his ability to use the pace of the ball by cutting and hooking as well as running hard between the wickets to accumulate runs. Twice a week as a teenager he made the 340-kilometre roundtrip from Waikerie in the north eastern Riverland district to Adelaide for practice and matches.

An A-grade debut followed at fifteen, which saw Darling scramble 403 runs with a fair dose of patience and discipline in his first season in a struggling side. Elevation to the State Colts was next with scores of 67 against Western Australia and 105 against Victoria. 48 not-out for the Colts against the West Indies heralded Darling's first-class debut for South Australia in the middle order at the age of seventeen.

The first time Darling saw a first-class match was when he played in one. It was also his introduction to Adelaide Oval. The opening ball he faced in first-class cricket was from Jeff Thomson. Darling remembers the umpire's words clearly just after he'd scratched out his guard, 'Right arm over, seven balls remaining'.

Despite the bowler's fearsome reputation, Darling didn't worry about facing Thomson, playing him as he saw him. He survived those first few balls but made only five run-out. Thomson took 4–60 in a match won by South Australia and dominated by spin with Mallett and Jenner talking fifteen of the twenty Queensland wickets to fall. Overall Darling found the jump to first-class cricket not as hard as he thought it might be and was thrilled to be sharing the dressing room with childhood heroes Ian Chappell, Ashley Mallet and Terry Jenner.

Modest returns of 119 runs at 19 in 1975–76 improved the following season when Darling scored a maiden first-class hundred against Victoria (107) with a bat borrowed from teammate Ian McLean on the MCG. A season aggregate of 318 runs at 24 were signs were that Darling was maturing as a player, but his potential had still not evolved into consistency. Then came the summer of 1977–78 when Darling first played Test cricket, yet it didn't appear he was on that path at the start of the season.

After an opening district score of 86, Darling struggled and found himself carrying the drinks in the tour match against the Indians. He was finally selected for South Australia in the state's fourth game of the season and this time as an opening batsmanAn even hundred in 259 minutes against WA soon followed Test selection arrived after a face-saving unbeaten century in a Gillette Cup match in Hobart. An relative unknown to Australian cricket fans at the start of the season, Darling was suddenly thrust onto the international stage for a test debut as his home ground.

Wood and Yardley – newcomers young and old

The Fifth Test at Adelaide saw the debut of not only Darling but also of his opening partner Graeme Wood. With Bruce Laird now WSC aligned, Wood had debuted the previous season for Western Australia and in only eight first-class games had struck centuries in Queensland and South Australia. Both

Wood and Darling were quick between the wickets; Sometimes too quick to adequately judge whether their batting partner would have enough time to safely make it to the crease.

Graeme Wood, from Western Australia, was an East Fremantle boy with a talent for Aussie Rules. He played fourteen matches for his home club before deciding cricket was his game. He started in A-grade for Melvillle in Perth at fifteen and impressive performances as a teenager for Fremantle (where his father Malcolm was president) saw him selected for the WA colts team.

Playing alongside Ric Charlesworth, John Inverarity and Greg Shipperd for the University of WA helped him to a maiden Pennant century in a winning final and then first-class selection. A breezy score of 37 against the visiting English side before the Centenary Test proved he could handle the step up. Wood's training as a Physical education teacher was in keeping with his wiry physique and willingness to take part in the increasing amount of physical training before matches. Disciplined in his technical approach, Wood was forever on the lookout for quick singles, even if his batting partner wasn't.

One who appeared frantic at the crease batting but was calmer in temperament when bowling was Western Australia's Bruce Yardley. He made a late entry into international cricket as one of the WA's irregular all-rounders. Initially a fast-medium swing bowler, he became an off-spinner during the mid 1970s after a series of injuries curtailed his sliding delivery stride.

Yardley showed enthusiasm for whatever he was doing on the field, whether stealing unexpected catches in the gully, wildly wielding the willow like a school kid down the order, trundling in on an angled run, jumping at shadows when bowling his tweakers. Part of his reinvention as a spinner was giving the ball more overspin than side spin with an unconventional grip reliant on bounce and trajectory. He batted like a soldier running for a medivac helicopter to escape a war zone; it was always going to be exciting, but it would be quick and may not end well. Legs wide apart in his stance, gripping the bat low, Yardley always looked ready to swish and slice the ball to whatever distant part of the field he could.

In his autobiography *Roo's Book* he described his delight at the opportunity to play for Australia in the wake of the WSC defections.

> *I was so excited when the final eleven was named for my first Test match that I raced down to the nets behind the Adelaide Oval stands to have a bowl. Ian Callen smacked one back to me and smashed the little finger on my right hand, my bowling hand. The finger had been shortened by one joint because the bone had burst through the skin at the middle joint. The team had been announced. Jeff Thomson played doctor and pulled it straight.*

'You'll be right, get it taped up, lucky it's not your spinning finger,' Thommo said.

The Indians allowed him to tape the injured finger to his spinning finger near the webbing. It turned out to be good debut despite his injury scoring 48 runs and taking four of the top six batsmen's wickets in the second innings. Yardley even left with some advice from world-class off-spinner Prasanna.

> *If you can force the batsmen to loft you over the infield in order to score runs, then you will surely take Test wickets.*

Almost a decade apart in age both Wood and Yardley approached their test debuts with a maturity rarely seen by test debutants. It proved to be an ominous sign for opponents not only in this game but also in future series.

Mad Dog Callen

Ian Callen earned the nickname Mad Dog for his determined and highly competitive approach. He says it originated from a barroom prank when he sprayed a teammate, who was working on the bar, with a beer gun. His beer-sodden mate called him a 'mad dog' and the name stuck.

Callen's bowling was anything but mad or scatterbrain. Running in from a fifteen-stride approach and delivering from the height of 187 centimetres,

Callen had a disconcerting ability to land the ball on a good length and move it away from the right-handers.

When he first heard he had been selected for the final Test of the series against India, the 22-year-old thought to himself – about bloody time.

Then again I was a cocky bastard. I just thought I had done the same as Hookesy had done [in bowling terms] as Hookesy when he was called up for the Centenary Test. I didn't feel there was anyone I couldn't bowl to.

The comparison with Hookes was fair. Hookes had made five centuries in six innings in 1976–77; Callen had taken 32 first-class wickets in just six matches, then followed it up with another 33 wickets in the 1977–78 Shield season.

Callen loved the idea of walking into the Australian dressing room and seeing the likes of Bobby Simpson and Jeff Thomson. He remembered listening to the radio as a kid and hearing about Simpson's valiant efforts on tours in England, especially in 1964 when he batted for days scoring 311. Callen would lie back, close his eyes and convert the words he was hearing to pictures in his mind. And Thomson Callen was awestruck and privileged to be sharing a dressing room with someone who could bowl as quickly as him. He could only marvel at Thomson's athleticism and slingshot action.

Callen had come a long way from first playing cricket in the small Victorian country town of Yarck (between Yea and Bonnie Doon) where he'd watch his father play in the Alexander District Cricket Association (his mum did the scoring). His grandfather would sometimes drop by as well. Cricket in the Callen clan was a family affair.

By the time he was in long pants, the family had moved to Croydon in suburban Melbourne where young Callen found a home with the Heathmont juniors before he was invited to train at Carlton, first under the guidance of Peter Bedford, then Keith Stackpole. In consecutive years he moved from third grade to second to A-grade, playing only half a season before the call to Victorian colours. He soon learnt his greatest lesson from Max Walker in the nets before the match.

Shoving a cricket ball in Callen's hands, Walker pointed to the seam.

If you land the ball anywhere but on the seam I will kick your arse!

His Shield debut came with the instruction to 'fix' Dennis Lillee up at the WACA in November 1976, as payback after Lillee had hit one of the Victorian tail-enders in a previous encounter. The opportunity never came; Callen hadn't fancied the idea much anyway.

Always one to analyse his own game, Callen knew if he could get a leg-cutter going to match his out swing, he could go anywhere in the cricketing world. By the time he was selected for Australia, the ball was coming out a treat, with late outswing and deviation off the seam.

His enthusiasm though was soon dampened. Australia was due to fly out to the West Indies just a few days after the Adelaide Test finished. It meant a trip to an Adelaide Health Clinic for all the players and a series of vaccinations for yellow fever and other exotic diseases. On the eve of the Adelaide Test, Callen reacted badly to the injections, particularly the yellow fever serum.

The Board in its wisdom thought five injections the day before the Test match was a good thing. I felt really lethargic afterwards, and right from the first day of this most important game of my life I had to force myself through the lethargy to get anything done.

Despite his adverse reaction to the injections, in his Test debut Callen was given the ball as the injured Thomson limped off the ground. He didn't feel nervous and found the step up to Test cricket not that daunting. He felt even more assured about what he could achieve, when by the end of India's innings at 269 he had taken the wickets of India's well-respected middle order. His three wickets in Test debut were via all edges to keeper Steve Rixon. The experience made him believe that a lot of first-class cricketers could make the jump to Test level.

But there was something wrong. He felt it in his body. When he returned to his hotel room that night his back ached from the exertion of working through the tiredness from the injections. Callen found he wasn't able to generate the same pace as he had during the season. As one of the new boys of the team and not wanting to appear soft, he initially kept quiet about the pain. All he wanted to do was succeed at whatever chance he was given in Test cricket. If that meant playing through some pain, then so be it.

On the fifth day Callen went wicketless as India made inroads towards the 493 victory target. The night before the final day's play, Callen collapsed on the stairs of the team hotel. That night he found himself on a drip with a nurse in the room to care for him.

Incredibly, he awakened refreshed, and in the second innings bowled another 33 overs to go with the 22 he had delivered in the first. He took 3 for 83 and 3 for 108 as the visitors fell 47 runs short of the run target.

Despite the sore back, Callen was ready to celebrate a Test and series win, but soon found himself in an almost empty dressing room.

> When the match ended everyone shot though. I thought they might hang around for some beers in the dressing room after the match. Don Bradman came up to me and said 'well done' and handed me one of the stumps. I was expecting us all at least to go out and have a dinner to celebrate what had been achieved.

Other players interviewed had made similar observations. During this time, the team was friendly but not overly so. It was as if the competition was so tight players didn't really know where they stood. They were wary of creating too much team harmony and would rarely ask each other for advice.

A season later, Allan Border noticed blokes continually looking over their shoulders for fear they would lose their place. It was only when the WSC players returned in 1979–80 that Border and others felt more comfortable within the team environment.

The lessons of 1977–78

By the end of the season, the ACB was not only claiming the high moral ground against Packer but also the high cricketing ground. This was despite the public response being much weaker than that of the previous season against Pakistan – but even this was stronger than the response to World Series Super Tests.

Each side took pleasure in the failures of the other. The actual difference between Establishment and WSC was less than it seemed – and less than the ACB wanted the public to think.

In 1977–78, WSC had the handicap of playing on non-cricket grounds; that would change in the second season. There was an improving trend toward the end of the first season with almost 60,000 attending the four mid-week night matches. Cricket had added itself to the list of the increasingly popular after-hours entertainment such as trotting and greyhounds – crowds were decreasing for football and horse racing. There had been six Super Tests and numerous one-day matches for both *The International Cup* and in rural areas *The Country Cup Championship*. Packer's infiltration into the regions also meant proper cricket was played there, not just a one-day match against a touring team. The ACB took notice and announced that some Shield matches might well be relocated to country centres, successfully following it up in NSW where one game per season in Newcastle proved financially successful.

It was clear that by the end of WSC's first season, its success depended on the ability to provide a different style of cricket and attract a different breed of fan. With two competitions in operation, the ACB's take for five Tests was less than $400,000 compared to $1.13 million in 1975–76. Crowds for the 25 days of play totalled 256,594, just a few more than those who watched the five days of the Centenary Test. It could have been worse, as fourteen of those Test days had very small attendances of only four figures.

Given that the full Australian side wasn't playing Test cricket, these figures don't surprise, but the ACB also had to support grassroots cricket and all types of official cricket with meagre takings and the help of the sponsorship monies from Benson and Hedges. WSC was losing money, but that was offset by its television value and wasn't obliged to support the struggling state competition, the Sheffield Shield. There was also the effect of the International

Cricket Conference court costs. The ACB and fellow international boards had each lost $350,000 in legal costs and were facing more as they planned to appeal. Despite these factors, the end of the 1977–78 season represented the peak of the Board's confidence.

Victorian Cricket Association (VCA) Secretary David Richards described the situation at the time.

> *These blokes had made their choice; they were gone. We had to look after our own. Our attitude was that we had to repair the damage to Australian cricket. If that was how Australian cricket officials felt, you could hardly imagine the emotions the young Australian side was feeling in terms of pressure and expectation not only to win but to win in a manner that would draw in the crowds.*

The mainstream print media emphasised that Packer's Super Tests had largely played to small crowds. There was interest in day/night cricket and David Hookes' broken jaw was a reminder of the seriousness of the contest. However, Establishment cricket was riding high on the back of Australia's win in a five-Test series against a world-class Indian team decided so dramatically on the last day of the final Test.

There was an early hint that the attitude of the traditionalists toward Packer was changing with the appearance of the Queensland Sports Minister among Packer's guest at the Sixth Super Test. Packer had also offered the services of fourteen members of his Australian side to tour the West Indies, but the offer was quickly declined by the Board. Packer was showing he was willing to be more flexible by offering to 'loan' his players to the establishment for the series against a full strength West Indian side In the Caribbean.

Ian Chappell, sensing the growing strength of WSC, in an article for *Cricketer* in April 1978, '*Stop knocking, we won't just go away*', thought, despite all of the criticisms hurled its' way, the first season of WSC was rather successful. He described WSC as the best standard of cricket he had ever played in over a full season and noted that the introduction of the white ball and with it night cricket were perhaps the best of the innovations.

The thirty-yard circles to limit the number of players on the boundary during parts of the match made the game 'a real art' in Chappell's words. He thought the feelings of a lot of people towards WSC had changed, even if it was only to the extent that they were now saying that it *'just wouldn't go away'*.

Head injuries and helmets

When David Hookes had his jaw broken in a match at Sydney Showground in the first season of WSC, it shocked the cricketing community. After being struck, Hookes staggered like a drunken man for a few paces before falling onto his knees, grabbing his head. He spat blood as he was helped off the ground all before a live television audience. Hookes' injury was replayed from various angles to show the impact. The incident also made it very clear how dangerous cricket could be.

The injury might have Hookes drinking through a straw for six weeks and set his career back somewhat, but there were positive outcomes for cricket. One was that it proved once and for all to the cricketing audience that World Series Cricket was serious, not just exhibition cricket as had been suggested the ACB. It also pressed home the need for batsmen to start wearing helmets. Some listened more carefully than others.

Until then, despite the prevalence of fast bowlers and tendency to use the bouncer with impunity, batsmen still viewed the wearing of helmets to protect their head unnecessary.

Occasionally players wore padded caps but never a full helmet. Then Dennis Amiss, Tony Greig and Alan Knott decided to bat wearing motorcycle helmets. The sight of a Dennis Lillee delivery cannoning straight into the back of Tony Greig's helmeted head and the batsman's response, a mere wiggle of his head and a smile at Lillee, seemed enough evidence to suggest the wearing of helmets had value.

Six or so weeks after the broken jaw, David Hookes returned now wearing a motorbike lid, which gave him some confidence to hook again. A relieved Hookes was shown on TV pulling up his visor and smiling after he'd just pulled Andy Roberts for a six. It became one of the defining images of the summer.

Unfortunately, the schism between the Establishment and WSC continued with a level of antagonism in the worst possible way. Adelaide District cricket administrators voted against an injured David Hookes being allowed to wear a helmet – because it had WSC connotations. On a positive note, within 24 hours of Hookes' injury, Packer had already sought the name of Dennis Amiss' helmet maker and ordered a batch from Birmingham. When Tony Henson, the owner of a company called Coonan and Denlay (specialising in equestrian caps), heard about Hookes' injury, his ears pricked up. Henson asked his colleagues at C&D to get in touch with WSC. Wallace reported back after a meeting with Marsh and Robertson that they had their work cut out. What was needed was a helmet that could withstand half a house brick hitting a helmet at one hundred miles an hour.

Henson though was aware that most head blows were glancing and that a helmet needed really only to deflect impact rather than absorb it. They also needed something to maintain the aesthetic of it, at least looking like the batsman was playing cricket and not about to go on a moon walk.

As Gideon Haigh noted in *Cricket War,* Henson later met Marsh in the foyer of Sydney's Chateau Commodore in February 1978. C&D's engineer had also arrived with his first batch of new fibreglass helmets. The meeting soon became an all-in, with other players trying on the headgear.

A *Truth* journalist sidled up to Marsh, asking: 'Are you going to wear one?' 'Naah,' Marsh replied, all the while winking to Henson.

Making the helmets was one thing but convincing players to wear one was another, but gradually the attitude that *'tough men don't wear helmets'* was changing.

England's captain Mike Brearley had come in for considerable criticism for wearing his skullcap. When Western Australians John Inverarity and Ric Charlesworth followed suit, public perceptions softened. Just six years earlier, Graeme Watson was seriously injured after being struck in the head during the Rest of the World versus Australia series. He nearly stopped breathing and had to have several blood transfusions to save his life. He played Test cricket for Australia after the injury but was never the same player.

In November 2014, the cricketing world was rocked by the death of 25-year-old Australian opening batsman Phillip Hughes after he was struck on the head by a ball in a Shield match. Given Hughes was wearing a helmet, for many, the game has changed forever. There is greater awareness of what a cricket ball can do. We had always known, but suddenly the risk is more real.

Back in 1978, the risk of injury or death from a cricket ball injury to an unhelmeted head, despite the Hookes incident, was still just sinking in. Helmets then in their most basic form were about to become more popular when the young Australian team visited the West Indies in February of 1978.

A late call-up to the Australian side for the series against India, Graham Yallop would become the first to wear one in an official Test match.

Chapter Four

Australia's Tour to the West Indies, 1978

The Australian team to tour the West Indies from February to May in 1978 had great potential but overall proved to be far too inexperienced against such a strong side.

The chosen fifteen were: Bobby Simpson (captain), Jeff Thomson (vice-captain), Ian Callen, Wayne Clark, Gary Cosier, Rick Darling, Jim Higgs, Kim Hughes, Trevor Laughlin, Steve Rixon, Craig Serjeant, Peter Toohey, Graeme Wood, Graham Yallop and Bruce Yardley (David Ogilvie would join later).

The Board selected only those players who '*made themselves available*' for Board-controlled matches in the 1978–79 season. This ruled out WSC players on the tour, but it didn't stop Jeff Thomson (who was appointed Australia's vice-captain for the tour) from defecting a few months later.

Former Test player and journalist John Benaud warned in *Australian Cricket* in February 1978 under the headline '*Torture tour for our Test tenderlings*' that the young Australian side was in for a torrid time.

> *To the tourist, the West Indies promise balmy days, hot sun and gentle sea breezes, cool blue water and coconut palms. A grass skirt and a grass hut. A long cool drink. To the touring cricketer it is shirt-drenching humidity, sun-parched open grounds, noisy but magnificently cricket-aware crowds.*

Benaud predicted 'the greatest annihilation of an Australian touring side anywhere in the world', a statement that would have given Australian administrators pause for thought.

Benaud was correct in assessing the challenge. It was the first overseas tour for eleven of the sixteen and only the captain had previously played in the Caribbean – thirteen years earlier. Two of the party, Higgs and Laughlin, hadn't played Test cricket, while eight of the squad had all made their debuts in the previous three months against India – Callen, Clark, Darling, Ogilvie, Rixon, Toohey, Wood and Yardley. And they were up against a full strength West Indian side.

The Australians at least had the experience of Simpson, who had toured the West Indies in 1965 when he made a century against Barbados, as Wes Hall and Charlie Griffith bowled 27 bouncers in the first hour.

Australia's team manager Fred Bennett was also equipped to provide a sense of calm. A personable man who was able to cool down passions and win through tact and diplomacy, he'd experienced some of the turbulence associated with Australia's 1969–70 tour of India and South Africa. Riots at Calcutta and Bombay had seen the players needing military escorts to and from the ground. By 1978, the 62-year-old Bennett, who had served in the Second World War as a troop leader in the 2–4 Armoured Regiment in New Guinea and Solomon Islands, was granted the respect that was needed for a team manager.

Bennett was experienced as a team leader. He'd soothed issues during the South African tour when Bill Lawry, protested against poor umpiring, refused to appear at a presentation with South African captain Ali Bacher at the end of the Fourth Test in Port Elizabeth. He'd also been assistant manager and treasurer of Ian Chappell's 1972 tour of England and managed the team to the 1975 World Cup and Test tour. Now for the 1978 tour of West Indies, Bennett would require all the composure he could muster as a team manager.

The problems started even before the Australian cricket team had landed in the Caribbean. The first issue was that the West Indian Cricket Board of Control, having initially gone along with the original ICC decision not to select Packer players, didn't want the international standing of West

Indian cricket to be diminished and also didn't want to stand in the way of sportsmen earning a living. While Australian WSC players were excluded from the Australian first eleven, the West Indies Cricket Board (WICB) decided not to penalise their WSC players. The West Indies team had all their very best cricketers playing – Australia did not.

The next problem was the state of mind of the West Indies under the leadership of Clive Lloyd. He had vowed never again to be humiliated in the manner they were against Lillee and Thomson in 1975–76 when they lost 5–1. In response, they had developed a policy focused on not a two-pronged but a four-pronged pace attack. Michael Holding, Andy Roberts, Joel Garner and Colin Croft ensured they had the necessary weaponry. Within a period of twelve months they had destroyed India (2–1), England (3–0) and Pakistan (2–1). Aggression and intimidation of the opposition's captain and batsmen were their weapons.

In February 1978, the Australians jetted out from Sydney and headed east to San Francisco and took in a tram tour where the popular TV series *The Streets of San Francisco was* filmed. They also enjoyed the ambience of Fisherman's Wharf and admired the Golden Gate Bridge. Then it was across to New York, only to be delayed by a pilots' strike. Fred Bennett organised a flight to Puerto Rico and there he chartered a nineteen-seat Primair Heron propeller plane to Antigua. The sight of a stack of car batteries and jump leads wheeled across the tarmac to start the engines of the plane turned a few heads. A lack of properly sealed windows and a lack of air conditioning resulting in very cold conditions did little to inspire the visitors' confidence. Despite the uncertainty, they arrived safely to the sound of a five-hundred-member steel band organised to welcome the Australians.

Vice-captain Jeff Thomson was the most experienced player apart from skipper Simpson. At first, the vice-captaincy had been given to Graham Yalllop, then to Craig Serjeant and finally to Thomson. The selectors' had initially decided to reward Yallop with the vice-captaincy job, then they changed to Serjeant before finally settling on Thomson. The move to appoint Thomson defied the tradition that fast bowlers weren't suited to leadership roles. He had also already made his opinion known about playing World Series Cricket;

he had even signed, but was obliged to renege when it was found that signing with WSC would breach his contracts with Queensland radio station 4IP.

As the Australians experienced the inevitable problems that arise on a challenging tour, the choice of Thomson proved to be a good one. Wayne Clark was impressed by Thomson's ability to reach out to players, especially the younger ones. He and others saw him as a player's player, a sounding board when needed. Thomson led by example on the field and off.

When Kim Hughes collapsed during an attack of appendicitis, Thomson was one of those who carried his stricken teammate to the ambulance. He also led the way on the field. When tail-ender Jim Higgs, a notoriously poor batsman, was peppered with bouncers in the Second Test at Barbados, Thomson returned fire in one of the most fearsome spells in Test cricket history.

The first match saw the tourists off to a good start against Leeward Islands at Warner Park, St Kitts. Wood (122) and Simpson (113) both scored centuries while leg-spinner Higgs bagged 12 wickets for the match. Australia won by 183 runs. A heavy loss in a one-day international at St John's Antigua followed, soon forgotten when Australia defeated Trinidad and Tobago by six wickets at Queen's Park; Darling's 105 and Yardley's off-spinners snaring nine wickets in the match gave the side an early confidence boost before the First Test at Trinidad. They would need it.

The First Test in Port of Spain

While setting fire to a cricket pitch in the West Indies is one way of trying to dry a wet surface, the Australians were met with a different kind of inferno at Port of Spain, Trinidad for the opening salvo of the Test series.

The Australians in batting order were: Wood, Serjeant, Yallop, Toohey, Simpson, Cosier, Rixon, Yardley, Thomson, Clark and Jim Higgs, Australia's sole debutant.

The West Indies' lineup was formidable: Greenidge, Haynes, Richards, Kallicharran, Lloyd, Austin, Murray, Parry, Roberts, Garner, Croft.

Austin, Haynes and Parry were all making their Test debuts. 22-year-old

Desmond Haynes would prove a real find, going on to play 116 Tests, most in an opening partnership with Gordon Greenidge. Haynes, himself capable of aggression, played counterpoint to Greenidge's combative stroke play. Given the fractured cricket world, it was no surprise that there was a hint of dissent in the air before the series began. WSC players Clive Lloyd and Viv Richards wore the World Series clothing and caps in the First Test at Port of Spain and Second Test at Bridgetown. The Australians also learned that practice facilities in the West Indies were a far cry from what they were used to – no practice wickets, a difficult outfield and an unusable centre pitch.

While the weather was damp and gloomy in the days leading up to the Test match, the largest and most appealing of all the Caribbean grounds at Queen's Park Oval looked magisterial in its beauty. The Australians woke to the first day of the opening match with some unsettling news: opening batsman Rick Darling had been sick all night and was unavailable. The side's dressing room had also been ransacked and equipment left splayed around the room, including the shower alcove and toilets. Serjeant, who had resigned himself to a day on the sidelines, was into the team and needed to dry his bat which had been shoved down one of the toilets.

Thinking the Trinidad and Tobago wicket would be suited to spin as it had traditionally been, Simpson and the selection panel included spinners Higgs and Yardley. The combination of the groundsman watering the evening before plus morning rain had given the pitch some life.

There had been some ominous signs for the Australians leading up to the match. Four Australian batsmen were given out to highly dubious decisions against Trinidad and Tobago, all involving WSC umpire Douglas Sang Hue. There was paranoia in the air, as Simpson noted of Sang Hue.

In this match … revealed a different temperament and seemed to be trying to exert his authority in matters which weren't his concerns.

The crowd was a microcosm of Trinidad's cosmopolitan and diverse society – full of wonderful characters. The ground itself was on the fringe of the well to do suburb of St Clair, affording amazing views of the lush northern range complete with giant saman trees. Its grandstand carried the names of some of the greats of the game: dynamic all-rounder Sir Learie Constantine; selector and administrator Jeffery Stollmeyer; at another stand, the brothers Jackie and Rolph Grant who led the West Indies in the 1930s.

Reminders of World Series were also present at this bastion of tradition. Austin Robertson and Packer's lawyer Malcolm Turnbull were in the crowd distributing T-shirts advertising WSC's tour of the Windies later that year. They also attracted some handy new Packer signees on the tour: Haynes, Austin and Croft, who had promised the WICB they wouldn't sign with Packer.

There was an atmosphere of *liming* in the audience – unwinding, sharing space with friends – but the Australians, sent in to bat one over before lunch after a delayed start, were feeling anything but relaxed.

The Andy Roberts over before lunch was revealing. The second ball removed a large divot and the third grubbed second bounce past the keeper. Australia was none for six runs at the break with four of them byes, when one ball soared over Serjeant before bouncing into the fence.

The Sunday Times' Robin Marlar described the match in his report as 'the one over Test.' It was a batsman's nightmare, especially against an attack comprising Roberts, Croft and Garner which made the conditions virtually unplayable. It was the first time the Australians had seen the gigantic Garner and lesser-known Croft, each of whom took three cheap wickets. Besides the height and searing yorker of Garner, the Australians had to cope with the six-foot-six-inch Croft, all arms and legs in a whirl, bowling wide of the crease with an intense stare. By the time the visitors had scraped their way to nine runs in eight overs, Wood, Yallop and Serjeant were out.

Australia slumped to 4–23 when Simpson was yorked by Garner. Peter Toohey and Gary Cosier began to mount a modest comeback. Then came the moment that would define the tour. Toohey had made it to fifteen feeling remarkably calm, perhaps too calm.

> *There was no one back at deep fine, all the fielders were in close,*
> *and there were slips, a leg slip and a leg gully. I thought,* Yeah I can

handle this guy (Andy Roberts). *The previous over I'd pulled him for four. Then I got a sliding bouncer and I remember getting hit and looking down at the blood and the way it stood out on the pitch's crease. I remember Viv giving me his handkerchief and having a concerned look on his face.*

The incident was a haunting reminder of the way Roberts broke Hookes' jaw during the first summer of World Series Cricket and the way Colin Cowdrey had been laid low batting for Kent against Hampshire a few years before (England's *Cricketer* magazine had caught the moment frame by frame, showing the former England captain toppling onto his stumps).

A slow bouncer to give the batsman a false sense of security, then the doozy straight at the head, twice as fast – a ball at the mind.

Toohey hadn't taken much notice of World Series Cricket – he was now wishing he had. He considered this when he was being stitched up on the wooden dressing room table with a needle that was so big it reminded him of one of those used to sew up wheat bags on the farm at Barry in NSW.

The image was plastered across Australian newspapers. Toohey on bended knee, a stream of blood tricking down his forehead, clutching a white towel, surrounded by concerned West Indian players. A capped Viv Richards cradles Toohey's head in one hand while signalling for help from the dressing room with the other, like a teacher on yard duty caring for an injured student. Viv's expression makes it appear that he wants to look anywhere but at the injured batsman. A bat lies in the foreground, flat on the ground like a reluctant observer.

Toohey missed the next two Tests, ironically not from the head injury but with a broken thumb. Gary Cosier, who would be sent home with a broken hand before the Test series ended, was at the other end. For a while his aggressive approach countered the West Indies attack before he was the last man out, with 46 including seven boundaries. Australia had batted for just short of three hours and was bowled out in 36 overs for ninety, including fourteen extras. To highlight the calamity of the performance, nine batsmen had contributed only ten runs between them.

In just over an hour before stumps, Greenidge and Haynes thrashed 79 from fourteen overs, hitting twenty off one from Jeff Thomson.

Gordon Greenidge had a wretched tour of Australia in 1975–76, making a pair at Brisbane, padding up to Lillee in the first innings then caught in the gully off Gilmour from a ball that jumped unexpectedly. He had never forgotten the taunts from The Gabba crowd or the fact that his more senior partner Roy Fredericks had made every effort to get off strike in the few overs they had to face in the Brisbane twilight. Nor had he forgotten the feeling of being dropped for the Second Test at Perth where the West Indies, propelled by Fredericks' audacious 169, won the match by an innings and 87 runs.

Greenidge felt cursed when he could only muster three runs against a rampant Lillee and Thomson at the MCG in front of more than 85,000. Followed by eight in the second innings of an eight-wicket loss. During the next three Tests in Australia, he would prowl around the net sessions wide-eyed and disappointed. He found form the following summer in the more familiar conditions of England, his place of residence since the age of fourteen.

Now, at Port of Spain, Greenidge's modest score of 43 was just a hint as to what would follow for Australian attacks in years to come. Kallicharran's 127 and Clive Lloyd's 86 helped the home side to 405.

Australia opened its second innings with only ten batsmen, but began more steadily with an opening stand of 59 between Wood and Serjeant then a gallant 81 by Graham Yallop. By the time Higgs was bowled by Roberts for a duck, Australia was 106 runs in arrears of making the West Indies bat again.

Jim Higgs – baptism of fire

While the door to Test cricket had closed for Tony Mann, it was just opening for fellow leggie Jim Higgs. Apart from Mann and previously the occasional selection of Terry Jenner, this was an era when wristspin at least in Australian sides had become almost extinct. Higgs had toured England in 1975 but was largely ignored as a bowler on the tour with the selectors plumping for the experience of off-spinner Ashley Mallett. Kerry O'Keeffe had played in two 1977 tour Tests in England.

Higgs had the inglorious record of being bowled by the only ball he faced and therefore had gone the entire tour without scoring a run. At the time, players were considered specialists in their area and not much was expected of tail-end batsmen.

Higgs was always going to be a leg-spinner, saying, 'Yeah I wouldn't lower myself to bowling offies.'

Born and raised in Kyabram in the Goulburn River Valley, he used to fill in for his Dad's Fire Brigade cricket team on malthoid pitches when he wasn't turning out for the Methodist Church team.

He began experimenting with wrist-spin when he was ten years old to see what he could do with it by changing his finger position on the ball, altering the angle of his wrist on release. It wasn't long before he realised he could make it swerve, curve, dip and deviate off the pitch, bounce higher or lower or go straight.

When he arrived at boarding school at Trinity Grammar in Melbourne, his leg-spinners were more than useful against schoolboy cricketers. But Higgs wasn't all consumed by cricket and was aware that the game was just one part of life, combining the study of engineering with playing cricket at Melbourne University. There he came under the influence of former Australian wrist-spinner George Tribe, who helped the young man develop a standard leg-break.

Higgs made his first-class debut at twenty, taking four wickets in his first match against Western Australia at the MCG in November 1970 but it would take four seasons to be given an extended run at first-class level in 1974–75. 42 wickets at 21 earned him a tour to England in 1975. There under Ian Chappell, and watching Ashley Mallett at work, he learned the subtleties of bowling on slower English wickets. He became 'two bowlers in one', learning to bowl in attacking or defensive manner when required. Although struggling with injury Higgs took 32 wickets at 35 during 1977–78 including 6 for 131 against India – and was disappointed not be called up for Test duty.

By the time Higgs toured the West Indies he was 27 and had evolved into a bowler who wasn't at all daunted by the prospect of playing Test cricket. He knew, despite the West Indians' reputation for producing fast bowlers, the pitches in the Caribbean were more suited to spinners, slow and low, and Higgs could sense a real chance to set himself up for a Test career. He just needed to be given a chance.

As expected batting in the match let him down, scoring only two runs, a victim to an Andy Robers delivery in the second innings. Despite this, Higgs had revealed himself to be a penetrating leg-spinner, taking 4–91 off 24.5 overs. His main memory of his first Test was being struck in the ribs by short balls from Joel Garner when batting with Cosier. When it came to bowling he felt more than capable, knowing the pitch was slow; the grounds being small, Higgs knew he had to bowl tight. Bowling in tandem with Bruce Yardley also helped. Playing for Victoria, Higgs was accustomed to bowling with a spinner (such as Ray Bright) at the other end.

Higgs felt confident bowling to the world class West Indian batting line up however in what was to be West Indies' only innings. Higgs knew that if he could perform under these conditions and against this opposition his future looked bright.

Morale problems

Darling had listened to the carnage from his sick bed and remembers thinking, *How are we going to cope with this?* The result was a disaster for Australia. Despite the victory over India in Australia, the Establishment's players were now being described by the press as third rate.

Concerns that Simpson had about Umpire Sang Hue only increased during the First Test. Clive Lloyd appeared to snick Wayne Clark to Steve Rixon but was given not out. Lloyd had taken his gloves off and started walking when he saw Sang Hue's decision and simply returned to the crease. More worrying for Simpson was Sang Hue's report to WICB president Jeff Stollmeyer that Clark's quicker ball and Yardley's off-spinners were more like throws than legitimate deliveries. He would call them from square leg if they bowled in the next Test. Having faced the Barbadian bowler Charlie Griffith on the 1965 tour when it was strongly suspected that the big paceman was a chucker but received favourable home town treatment, Simpson was livid. Clark and Yardley bowled from Sang Hue's end for the rest of the tour, apart from one match when Simpson had a game off – and Yardley was called.

A heavy loss can damage team morale and there were signs Australians were already wilting. Higgs says there was disgruntlement in the camp from day one. Other players suggested that divisions were developing. And much of it surrounded Bob Simpson.

The popular Peter Toohey who played under Simpson for his club and state thought him a very good captain.

> *There were factions on the tour. I couldn't say it was a harmonious team. I was a Simmo supporter but couldn't say I was in a Simmo camp. I owed Simmo a lot. He had taught me a lot about cricket, not so much the technical things but skills like running between the wickets, how to rotate the strike, how to approach different types of bowlers, things that you don't normally get taught.*

Toohey might have been a Simpson supporter; Wayne Clark wasn't.

> *He'd create stories amongst the team ... the older blokes could see through it but the younger blokes couldn't put up with it ... there was real internal conflict over his team management skills.*

Simpson was furious with some of his players just before the Second Test at Bridgetown, after he, Thomson and Cosier had returned from a wreath laying ceremony at Sir Frank Worrell's grave. Worrell, the first black man to lead the West Indies on tour (in 1960–61, a series Simpson played in) had died of leukaemia at the age of 42 and was laid to rest on the campus of the University of the West Indies, where he had served with distinction in Jamaica and Trinidad. The simple grave at Cave Hill, a few minutes' drive north of his native Bridgetown, was a shrine. The 1978 Australians paid their respects in a solemn ceremony.

Returning to the Kensington Oval for practice, Simpson was in no mood for frivolity. When he discovered the rest of the touring party lounging around in the dressing room instead of practising, he exploded. It was a blast from the captain that had the players ears ringing and got a few players' backs up, given they had already done some fielding and given up on the shoddy practice facilities. The moment probably revealed more about the unbending disciplined approach of the captain than any laxity from the players. In Simpson's defence, it's understandable given the performance of the Australian side during the First Test that he thought they should be more disciplined.

The tension between some players and Simpson also shed light on the obvious generation gap. The younger players had noticed Simpson heading off on his own to take time out from the tour rather than spending time with them. One can easily understand the 42-year-old's stance on social activities, preferring to catch up with old friends from previous trips to boozy nights out with a bunch of 20 year olds, but it probably sent the wrong message.

Simpson's idiosyncratic habit of playing the West Indian quicks, using a technique that had worked well when he last toured in 1965, raised a few eyebrows. Thirteen years later, while Simpson had the technique and cricketing nous to handle the wily spin of the Indians, facing a brutal pace attack was another thing altogether. It had worked for him in 1965 in the West Indies, it had worked for Ian Redpath in 1975–76 and to some extent had worked for Don Bradman during the 1932–33 Bodyline series. Cosier says the players didn't understand what Simpson was doing in terms of technique.

It was effective but it looked bloody awful, especially when we were under pressure. It looked like he wasn't prepared to get in behind the line of the ball, like he was jumping out the way.

Queenslander, David Ogilvie was called up to fill in for a sick Kim Hughes who had appendicitis. Ogilvie's family holiday suddenly interrupted, he arrived after a 35hour flight and was rushed into the tour match against

Barbados. Overlooked originally, Ogilvie considered not accepting the Board's invite to join the side on tour, but after conversations with state officials decided he had better go, having been told in no uncertain terms that if he refused this time, the invite may never come again.

Ogilvie's attitude reveals a lot about him and the way he perceived cricket. He enjoyed it but unlike some of his teammates, it wasn't at the centre of his life. In fact, he wasn't much like his teammates at all. He was popular but more introspective. Not so easygoing and eager to enjoy the festivities of a tour like the others would. It wasn't a happy tour for Ogilvie. He found the touring party too divided for his liking. When pressed to comment further he declined.

> *I felt I never really settled in. It wasn't a happy tour for me. I don't want to reveal to you what happened over there but it was a bit cliquey. There wasn't great team camaraderie.*

The Australian side's morale was going downhill rapidly. No doubt the thought of a depressing domination at the hands of the West Indies and ruination of some of their test careers lingered in players' minds. The captain Bob Simpson, who had carried all before him in the home series against India, was losing the faith of players and must have been wondering why he had agreed to return to Test cricket – winning can mask many faults and a few more were shortly to be found.

The Second Test in Barbados

As Mike Coward observed in his book, *Caribbean Odyssey,* Barbados, home to the small Kensington Oval, is the most easterly of the Caribbean islands, with an inescapable Englishness having been British territory from 1626 until 1966. Only once you move beyond the small stone cottages, which open to narrow winding lanes to architecture of Bridgetown, to the palm-fringed beaches of the western coastline and onto the country that features sugar cane, do you find the Caribbean identity.

A tiny country of just 426 square kilometres, Barbados has produced quality players such as Sir Frank Worrell, Sir Garry Sobers, Everton Weekes and Clyde Walcott, all of whom have grandstands in their honour. The Australians would encounter some future greats on their own ground, in the form of Greenidge, Haynes and Garner.

Prior to the Test, the Australians played a first class match against Barbados. While the match was a draw, there were some good signs for Australia. Serjeant (114) and Simpson (102) continued their good match form. Ogilvie played against Barbados but, unable to get into a batting rhythm, was not considered for the Second Test. The drawn match also saw Darling well and truly off his sick bed and hitting a confident 62.

For the second Test, Darling replaced injured Peter Toohey; the West Indian side remained the same. The Test was historic, with Graham Yallop the first batsman to wear a helmet, albeit a motorbike one, in an official Test match. Having heard so much dressing room discussion on whether helmets should be worn, Yallop decided the time was ripe for him to try one.

When Bruce Yardley arrived for a look at the Kensington Oval a few days before the Test, it reminded him of his home ground at the WACA. It had shorter boundaries, a place where anything short would often clear the stumps, rewarding a player of Yardley's ilk, who was prone to slash anything that bounced above waist height. He later wrote:

> I loved the Windies' style of play and it suited my game also. When bowling to them I felt that at any time I would be hit out of the ground, but they in fact encouraged me to attack them, to set attacking fields and they would be up for the challenge ... I wish all cricket was played this way. When batting against Andy Roberts, Joel Garner, Colin Croft, Michael Holding and Sylvester Clark, I figured that I would attack them and get as many runs as possible before they either got me out or killed me.

Clive Lloyd won the toss and again sent Australia in to bat. Darling departed early but Australia was stabilised by the space-helmeted Graham

Yallop and the steady play of Wood. The promising start disintegrated when Wood was LBW to Croft for 69 and Yallop was caught in spectacular manner by Austin off Croft at square leg for 47. Australia had collapsed to be 7–161 half an hour before tea.

Yardley's aggressive approach certainly helped when he arrived at the crease at 6–149. He adopted the policy that anything pitched up would go straight down the ground, and if it was short he would give himself room to leg side and swing hard. He admitted to having no idea as to where the ball was going. Yardley's innings was described by Kim Hughes as 'something resembling sideshow alley at the local fair, like shooting at a moving duck not with a pop gun and corks though, but machine guns.'

The West Indies bowling quartet was getting upset at Yardley's Catherine-wheel approach. Garner bowled a beamer; Yardley just got his head back in time. The next ball was short outside off stump. Yardley cut it for six.

Non-striker Steve Rixon had a look of horror on his face 'Take it easy mate, you'll get us killed!'

Standing at short leg, Desmond Haynes checked out Yardley's bat.

'Nice blade, Bruce.'

'It's not the blade, Desie,' replied Yardley, tongue in cheek. He must have felt superhuman at this stage, belting the West Indies quicks who had given his teammates and their WSC counterparts so many challenges over the home summer. The feeling didn't last long.

The following ball struck Yardley on the point of the elbow, the next saw Yardley caught halfway through a pull shot when he realised he was in trouble. The ball hit him in the throat and down he went.

'You doin' alright,' said Viv Richards with a wry grin.

Doing well with his bat, but Yardley didn't feel too good.

'Here's your equipment, Bruce,' said Haynes, returning Yardley his bat.

Before he was yorked by Joel Garner, Yardley had scored the world's fastest fifty, off 29 balls top scoring for the side with 74 including thirteen fours and two sixes. Yardley had used a combination of death-defying strokes including a series of inside-out cover drives and a square-cut for six that had

Joel Garner rolling his eyes. Garner responded with a pinpoint precision yorker that neatly extracted Yardley's middle stump. Australia was bowled out for 250 in 65 overs.

Jeff Thomson – lethal pace attack

Any thoughts that Jeff Thomson had lost his pace were soon dispelled when the West Indians began their first innings. It was the frightening Thomson of old, as if he had been teleported from the time before his shoulder dislocation. John Benaud in his book *Matters of Choice* described the spell:

> *Each West Indian batsman may deny until the day they die that Thommo's pace, his deadly line and lift startled them, upset them and unbalanced them, but I saw it.*

A sun-bathed late afternoon had Thomson in the mood to give some hell to the host team. He'd been a little annoyed on the tour so far. It started when he was told that a blue suit he had bought especially to wear in the West Indies was not to be worn. The ACB decreed that players had to wear team issued grey slacks and Australian team blazer when they travelled as a group.

Thomson's casual and approachable attitude had his teammates loving the job he was doing as deputy leader; he was a good antidote to the old-school style of Simpson. Today he was especially annoyed. He didn't appreciate the West Indian quicks' treatment of tail-ender Higgs whose ability with the bat was at best schoolboy standard. As vice-captain he wanted to shake things up a little.

Greenidge was the first to face Thomson's lethal stock ball that seemed to have gained a yard in pace from the previous Test. Not so short, but steepling and slanting back in towards the batsmen's rib cage. Sometimes it was directed at the throat, other times the chin. And always very quick.

Standing another pitch length back, keeper Rixon was taking the ball on the up like Marsh had done when Thomson had scared the living daylights out of England's batsmen in 1974–75.

Thomson's first ball thumped into Greenidge's gloves as he arched backwards like a limbo dancer, the ball ricocheting into his shoulder before flying to Craig Serjeant in the gully. 'Not-out' was the umpire's response as Greenidge rubbed his shoulder. In Thomson's third over he repeated the dose, this time having him caught off the chest into the gully where Cosier took it.

Richards was ready for an onslaught. The first ball to Viv Richards cannoned into his left pad, leaving him hobbling around the crease. In the same over, he miscued a pull shot that hit high on the bat and went ballooning and swirling in front of square leg where Trevor Laughlin scrambled to catch but missed. It was an uncertain start for the man considered unflappable in his first season in WSC. The next from Thomson came from just short of a good length and hammered into Viv's right wrist. Off the fifth, a thick edge flying through the air for a long way before bouncing into the boundary. The next, a flat-bat pull onto the red-rimmed roof of the grandstand.

Thomson still clearly remembers the stroke:

The ball careered low and fast and hit the tin roof of the little building just over the boundary fence at square leg. I had barely finished my follow-though when it hit the roof with a loud bang and clatter. I said to him, 'Shit Viv, that's bullshit!' He looked back at me and shrugged and we both laughed.

The ninth ball of the over, another bouncer, Richards top edged, the ball looped high toward square leg. Clark and Laughlin converged, then both hesitated, fearing a collision; Clark dived full-length forward, the backs of his hands scraping on the ground, held the catch aloft in two hands like he's just received the World Cup trophy. The world's best batsman was out, Thomson had at last claimed his victim.

Thomson bowled the last over of the day. The second last ball reared at the diminutive Alvin Kallicharran like a rattlesnake after prey. Kallicharran raised his bat as if in self defence, the ball spooned to Yardley at backward square leg. It was as close to an unplayable ball as possible. By stumps, Thomson had taken 3–40 off 6.5 overs. His six wickets for 77 would be the best figures by an Aussie bowler in a Barbados Test.

But it was too good to last. Thomson's calf muscle played up the next morning. Haynes, Lloyd and Murray made hay while Thommo iced his calf. By the time Thomson was allowed back on the ground, the West Indies were 13 runs ahead with four wickets in hand. With Thomson's help, Australia was just 38 runs behind by the end of the West Indies first innings. By stumps, however the visitors were again in strife at 5–96. Simpson had again blotted his copybook in the eyes of some players, batting himself at number seven and sending in a nightwatchman, Steve Rixon, half an hour before stumps.

As Rixon emerged from the pavilion, the crowd taunted Simmo: 'Come on Simmo, come on and have a bat, man. They kill you man, they kill you'. The West Indians may have appeared at times overly blessed with rum and humour but they knew their cricket.

In the end the ploy backfired as Rixon was dismissed, as was second nightwatchman Bruce Yardley, and Simpson had to bat that night. Even Toohey, a Simpson supporter, noticed the dismay at the move, 'It cost Simmo a bit of respect in the team'.

By the time Australia had lost the Second Test by nine wickets, Simpson's contribution sat at 40 runs and 1–95.

Changing of the guard for the Windies

The Chairman of the Board Stollmeyer was apoplectic.

'I feel like a stranger in my own dressing room!' he shouted upon hearing the news. It was an unusual display of emotion from the former West Indian batsman-turned-administrator and it shocked those who knew him. What had he just heard – that West Indian players Austin, Haynes and Croft had signed with WSC.

It must have been a strange time for Stollmeyer, who had also been meeting with Kerry Packer. WSC was seeking the use of West Indian grounds for an upcoming tour. But what followed was like an earthquake around the Caribbean islands.

Austin Haynes and Deryck Murray, the secretary of the new West Indian Players Association, were not selected for the Third Test at the Bourda ground in Georgetown, Guyana. Lloyd immediately resigned as captain and his eight WSC teammates followed.

All had not been well between the West Indies Cricket Board (WICB) and the West Indian WSC players for some weeks. Packer's players were not happy with attempts to pressure them over the scheduled tour of India and Sri Lanka at the end of the year, which would clash with WSC commitments in Australia. Anticipating a need to blood new players, the WICB set a deadline of 23 March (between the Second and Third Tests) for WSC players to indicate whether or not they were available to tour India and Sri Lanka from November 1978 to February 1979. These tours conflicted with the West Indian WSC signed players' commitments in Australia. The WICB wanted to force the players into deciding whether they would side with Packer or traditional cricket when there was a conflict of fixtures.

With support from the West Indian cricket fans behind their WSC players, fans reacted badly during some of the matches especially when the West Indies lost. The second one-day international at St Lucia was an example of how things could get out of control. The game which saw Australia win by two wickets off the last ball of the match was held after the third Test on 12 April. It indicated the high level of unrest and anger of the West Indian fans. West Indian fans were passionate about their cricket and didn't like to see their team field a side that wasn't their best because of political manoeuvring by the West Indies Cricket Board.

Australia's tour almost ended here when the crowd turned on WICB's Jeff Stollmeyer who gave a speech at the end of the game. Toohey remembers the crowd 'really not liking what was in the speech but not being really sure what all the fuss was about'.

Sensing the crowd's inflamed mood, security officials told the Australian players to leave, which they did, reaching for helmets as they went. As the

Australian bus slowly crept out of the ground, the Australians had to contend with angry crowd members pounding the bus with their fists and whatever else they could get their hands on. A number of players by then had had a gutful of the tour. This was close to the final straw.

The Third Test in Georgetown

Bourda had a reputation as one of the world's wettest venues. The ground itself had a very old-world feel about it, with the wooden pavilion at fine leg an imposing structure. There was also a Ladies' stand and an unprotected area called The Mound, a home to disc jockeys pumping out music.

Georgetown in Guyana on the South American mainland was a city almost entirely constructed of wood, with once grand buildings having seen better times. On Guyana's Atlantic coast on the east bank of Demerara River estuary, Georgetown first hosted Test cricket in 1930 and was one of the lesser-known West Indian cricketing venues. Later that year Georgetown would become infamous when the mass suicide of more than 900 followers of the Jim Jones cult shocked the world.

The Australians, who were down 2–0 in the series and starting to think the tour was going to be a very long one, were at least buoyed by the news that they wouldn't be confronting a full strength West Indies side from here on.

A high-scoring draw at Georgetown ensued. Darling wiped the memory of his double failure at Barbados with 123. Cosier made 114. Yallop, batting without a helmet, made it to 118 before a Colin Croft bouncer broke his jaw. Yardley had also been hit on the head by the same bowler, prompting team manager Fred Bennett to issue a statement describing Croft's overuse of the bouncer as a 'direct contravention of both the law and tour conditions'.

Croft had felled Yardley on 37 after the Australian off-spinner had taunted him: 'Keep your arm straight you chucker!'

To call a fast bowler a chucker is the worst insult one can make. Yardley kept moving back towards square leg until Croft, with his wide-of-the-crease action, eventually nailed him. When consciousness returned, Yardley asked the short leg (and soon, new captain of the West Indies Alvin Kallicharran) what had he had done to anger Croft.

Kallicharran simply replied, 'You got what you deserved, Bruce.'

Yardley was starting to realise that his mouth was getting him into more trouble that he bargained for and decided that a quieter approach on field at least in the short term may be beneficial.

For many players the Third Test did not go well. Darling had experienced a miserable Test tour despite finding runs easy to come by in the matches against the individual islands. The excitement of leaving Australia for the first time and the chance to experience the beaches and culture of the West Indies was not matched by the thrill of Test cricket in the Caribbean. Frustration grew as Darling tried to convert his island form to the Test arena and couldn't work out why it failed:

> It was just one of those things. I was often facing the same bowlers I had scored runs off in the Island matches. It was a pity we didn't have the infrastructure around us to help. You didn't even feel comfortable asking your mates as you didn't want to give too much away because you were after each other's positions.

Substandard pitches and training facilities as well as third-world hotels made for a difficult tour. Looking back, Darling is surprised the Australian side coped as well as it did.

> When I look back I don't know how we did it. As a team of largely inexperienced players. At times we had to face the best fast bowlers in the world without the benefit of decent practice facilities or much support.

Darling had managed only four and eight in the Second Test at Barbados against an attack including Roberts, Croft and Garner, but his form against Guyana just before the Third Test hinted that he might be turning the corner.

The Georgetown Cricket Ground was a reawakening for both the West Indian and Australian sides. Only Parry and Kallicharran remained in the new look West Indies side; in batting order: Alvin Greenidge, Williams, Gomes, Kallicharran, Shillingford, David Murray, Shivnarine, Philip, Holder, Parry and Clarke with five of the side making their Test debuts.

Australia brought in Victorian all-rounder Trevor Laughlin for his debut and Ogilvie replaced the injured Yallop. Built like your local baker, Laughlin was a spasmodic then consistent performer who bowled right-arm medium pacers and hit the ball hard as a left hand middle-order bat in the manner of Gary Gilmour. Former 'King of Collingwood' and Australian Test cricketer from the 1920s Jack Ryder had encouraged Laughlin's development, leading to a successful Victorian debut in 1974 where he took 5–72 and scored a half-century against South Australia. A career-best 113 versus Western Australia the next summer encouraged him to head for England, spending two Aussie winters playing league cricket. He returned with a greater ability to move the ball off the seam, a skill he exploited when he took 5–137 against Guyana to earn his Test call up.

Australian cricket fans would soon learn about a couple of new players for the West Indies. Basil 'Shotgun' Williams was known for his strong offside play. Larry Gomes, a small and lean left-hander from Port of Spain was more of a nudger than his teammates. Gomes kept the Australians honest, taking advantage of anything slightly wide or full of length. He and Williams both made centuries. Diminutive keeper David Murray had replaced his namesake Deryck, while off-spinner Sew Shivrarnine, a surprise selection, celebrated by scoring a half-century. The West Indians were doing well without their 'star' WSC players.

Regardless, West Indian public sympathies were on the side of the WSC players; and while an armoured division of riot police escorted the teams to the ground for the start of the Test, a spectator boycott meant there were so few in the crowd that police almost outnumbered them.

The home side won the toss and went in to bat. By lunch, they were 4–84. Australia failed to make the most of their bowling success after dismissing the home side for 205. With Australia now batting, Ogilvie spooned to Phillip on four; Darling was wondering whether he had been cursed after getting a start (15) before edging a Phillip delivery to slip; Serjeant was soon out for a duck; Simpson (67) and Rixon stopped the rot (54). For the West Indians, the windmill bowling action of Norbert Philip (4–76) and the sheer force of a four-game first-class veteran Sylvester Clarke (3–57) took the majority of the spoils.

By the end of the third day it seemed Australia was about to go 0–3 in the series, needing 359 in two days – more than either side had ever scored against each other in the fourth innings of a Test. To make matters worse, strikes in Georgetown meant that their hotel, The Pegasus, had no electricity or running water. A swim in the pool wasn't worth the risk and the toilets wouldn't flush. Serjeant went to bed a little more nervous than usual the night before the run chase. He'd been playing Test cricket for less than a year and was facing a second pair of ducks.

I remember going to sleep that night thinking this is either death or glory. Fortunately for me it ended up being glory.

Australia's run chase began poorly. Clarke's bounce removed Darling and Ogilvie each for no score and Simpson was gone for four within the first forty minutes. Serjeant avoided short leg and another pair by the smallest of margins and then batted with belief in another chance at Test cricket. Both Serjeant and Wood went on to get their first Test centuries with scores of 124 and 126 respectively.

They had inveigled eighty singles in a 251–run partnership in 268 minutes. The combination of left and right-handed batsmen had confused the largely inexperienced West Indian attack. Despite his experience, Bob Simpson was so nervous about the result he could barely bring himself to watch the action. It must have made for an interesting sight with the Australian captain ever present in the dressing room but with eyes focussed on anywhere but the middle of the ground. .To be fair, the last day run chase of 69 needed with four wickets in hand would have made most captains feel a little uneasy. 'I've never known a Test to be so desperate. We had to win or the tour wasn't worthwhile,' he explained.

Laughlin was dropped on twelve but hung around long enough to score 24. When Yardley pulled a boundary, Australia had snuck home. It was a rare Test win for the Australians in the West Indies.

Success followed success for Australia only a few days later (6–8 April) when Australia won a first-class match in Guyana against the Windward Islands by 52 runs. Wayne Clark took 7–26 and 5–45 in this memorable win during a very trying tour.

Fourth Test at Port of Spain

The Australian side for the Fourth Test was: Wood, Darling, Toohey, Yallop (back for Ogilvie), Serjeant, Simpson, Rixon, Yardley, Thomson, Clark, Higgs (replacing Laughlin). The West Indies team was AE Greenidge, Williams, DA Murray, Gomes, Kallicharran, Bacchus (on debut) Shivnarine, Parry, Phillip, Holder, Jumadeen (replacing Shillingford).

Only two runs separated the sides in the first innings. It indicated that this would be a hard-fought battle for success. However, left to score 293 to level the series, Australia was sent packing for a second innings of 94.

The contrasting spin of Jumadeen and Parry accounted for eight wickets between them. Victory by 198 runs had given the home side an unbeatable 3–1 series lead, regaining the Sir Frank Worrell trophy after nine years. The new-look West Indian team had still not convinced the locals. After a crowd of 25,000 had packed into the stands for the opening day of the First Test, the largest crowd for any day of the Fourth Test at the same venue was no more than 5,000.

Bob Simpson described Australia's performance during the Test as 'the worst performance since I've been in charge … poor concentration, inconsistency and poor mental conditioning'.

Following the dismal result of the fourth Test, the Australians regained some confidence after a narrow victory against a strong Jamaican side, whose number included WSC players Austin, Holding and Rowe. The bad news was that umpire Douglas Sang Hue called Yardley twice for throwing in the first innings. Simpson let it be known that he would object if Sang Hue umpired in the final Test at Sabina Park, Kingston. Wesley Malcolm stood instead.

The Fifth Test at Kingston

Bob Simpson wanted to finish the tour with a win. A narrow series loss (3–2) would be more easily explained to the Australian selectors and public. But it wasn't to be. Australia's chances of a final Test victory would be cruelled by a crowd riot and a lack of willingness by match officials to allow some extra time to finish the match.

The Australian team was: Wood, Ogilvie, Toohey, Yallop, Serjeant, Simpson, Laughlin, Rixon, Yardley, Thomson and Higgs. The West Indies: Williams, Bacchus, Gomes, Foster, Kallicharran, Murray, Shivnarine, Parry, Phillip, Holder and Jumadeen.

Darling's low scores of 16 and 17 in the Fourth Test hadn't saved him from the selectors' axe. In a case of musical chairs for the opening pair. Ogilvie was brought back into the side, as was Laughlin for the injured Clark. Laughlin's sliding deliveries produced a first innings haul of 5–101 when he opened the bowling with Jeff Thomson, helped by some sharp catching.

In the West Indies side, local player Maurice Foster took Alvin Greenidge's place. Foster was a solid middle-order batsmen with a wristy style who had scored 125 against Ian Chappell's Australians in front of his home crowd in 1973.

Jim Higgs remembers the events leading up to and including the final Test. At centre stage was the advice from Vanburn Holder.

> *In Trinidad, three weeks before, Holder had asked a few of us to sample some of his special rum. While doing so he warned us not to do anything that might incite anybody when we played in Jamaica.*

As it turned out, it wasn't the Australians who incited the incident at the final Test; it was the dismissal of Holder.

Higgs recalls the irony of the conversation with Holder.

Holder was the one who warned us not to react and he was the one who helped spark the riot. The next bloke in was Jumadeen who had lasted about six balls in the four innings he had played against us.

Mike Coward later wrote of Kingston, Jamaica.

There is an underlying and inescapable sense of menace in Kingston. And it is so pervasive that the visitor to the Jamaican capital feels conspicuous and unsafe outside of the hotel compound and the rusted metal capsules which pass for taxis.

That was exactly how the players felt in 1978. They were warned that crime was rampant and under no circumstances to go out alone at night. 'The robbers don't just steal your ring, they chop your wrist off,' they were told.

The message got though. As the Australians checked into their hotel, a bursting balloon had them all ducking for cover. Highly organised security plans remained in place for Jamaica. When the players arrived at the grounds the sight of wire netting circling the ground, from the grandstands to the fence, gave an eerie feeling.

Most Test matches end with a final wicket or run being struck and the players shaking hands and walking off. The Fifth Test didn't. It ended on 4 May with the sight and sounds of riot police as the Australians sprinted for the pavilion.

With 38 deliveries remaining and one wicket to get, Australia was on the verge of victory when the riot began. Higgs had just dismissed Holder, caught behind for six. Holder paused a few seconds before walking off, shoulders slumped. He took his gloves off, purely in disgust at himself for getting out, and hit them against his hip.

A few overs earlier, umpire Malcolm had upheld Higgs' LBW appeal against a sweeping Kallicharran. News reports had circulated about Sang Hue's dropping from the umpiring panel because of pressure by the Australians; some in the crowd viewed Malcolm as an Aussie stooge. When he gave Holder out it was the last straw.

Peter Toohey, who tempered himself for once, scored his maiden Test century (with 122) and then 97. He didn't have long to stew on the missed opportunity of a hundred in the second innings.

The bottles started coming and didn't stop. We were in the middle of the field and there were these missiles coming from everywhere, from inside the Members Stand, even from the other side of the stands. Some of these blokes had pretty good arms. Out came the riot squad who formed a corridor for us to get off the field; someone had set fire to one of the grandstand. It was unreal.

As the crowd chanted 'We want Sang Hue', ABC commentator Alan McGilvray was heard down the phone line saying, 'I suggest, ABC, that I will phone you tonight from my bedroom and give you a report. I guess that's the safest place to be right now.' By the next morning, McGilvray, on advice from an Australian Diplomat, had left Jamaica.

It was a sad end to a disappointing tour. Simpson wanted to play a sixth day. Some of the players had had enough, but when a vote was taken the Australians agreed to continue. The game was declared a draw when umpire Ralph Gosein and third umpire John Gayle refused to stand. Simpson was not happy, adamant that the match should be allowed to conclude. Although tour conditions made no provision for six day Tests, the WICB had been willing.

Higgs wasn't that fussed. 'The pitch was dug up overnight. We couldn't have played anyway.'

The match was drawn and so ended the fourth Australian tour of the West Indies. The Australians hadn't disgraced themselves but had given some context to the sense of jubilation that surrounded the home victory against India. Test cricket had copped a blow in that the final three matches of the series were largely devoid of world-class players. Australia's test cricketers now had time to ponder how their performance would be judged in the light of an approaching Ashes series against a full strength England side in the 1978–79 season.

Lessons learned from the Caribbean

So what was learned from the tour of the West Indies? The result was better than first expected with a 3–1 win to the Windies after the disappointing Fifth Test draw under unusual circumstances. Graeme Wood had proven to be a Test-class batsman, averaging 47 from the five Tests. Peter Toohey had also demonstrated his worth with 296 runs at 59 and Graham Yallop's 317 at 45 reinforced his ability with the bat.

All-rounder Bruce Yardley's 206 runs at 20 and 15 wickets at 15 was an impressive debut tour. Higgs (15 at 25) and Clarke (15 at 30) had also performed. Jeff Thomson returned to Australia with the respectable figures of 20 wickets at 28 and his reputation as a leader enhanced. There was, however, a lingering disquiet over the sense of unity of the side.

Skipper Simpson later recalled his thoughts on the tour and in particular his relationship with Thomson.

> *Several positives should have come out of that tour for Australia, but unfortunately most of them eventually came to nought. Chief of these was the case of Jeff Thomson, who was fantastic throughout the tour. I thought we worked very well as captain and vice-captain, but not long after we returned home he wanted to join WSC … he missed the 1978–79 season. I don't think he was ever the same bowler again.*

Thomson didn't appear to feel the same way. On return from the West Indies, he had a word with his old mate Len Pascoe who then contacted WSC managing director Andrew Caro with the news that Thomson didn't like playing under Simmo much, that 'he was tired of the old bloke's tirades and lectures … [he] reckons he'd rather play with us.'

Thomson found that the much hyped $630,000 deal with radio station, 4IP over ten years in reality delivered only around $28,000 a year. Also he was still struggling with a shoulder injury sustained in 1976 when he and Alan Turner collided attempting to catch Zaheer Abbas against Pakistan at the Adelaide Oval. Despite Thomson's struggles, 4IP told him he had to tour the West Indies in 1978 as part of his contract. When Thomson returned from the tour, he was able to pull out of his contract and had no guilt associated with doing so. At this stage the lure of a WCS contract was critical financially. He was then an undischarged bankrupt with debts from his All Sports stores and a tax bill owing to the tax office of $24,000 –a large sum at the time.

For Kim Hughes, the tour to the West Indies promised to be one of the highlights of his short international career but didn't turn out that way. Hughes was one of the more dissatisfied younger players, at the lack of opportunity afforded him by the skipper.

Before the first match against the Leeward Islands, Hughes had been felled with appendicitis. As a result, he never really got going on the tour. The limited chances (which he wasted by throwing his wicket away), a frustration that a disciplinarian and tough operator like Simpson found hard to accept.

Australian opening bowler Wayne Clark says Simpson referred to Kim Hughes as 'nothing but an arsehole' on the tour.

Never to his face, always behind his back. But Simpson would bag everyone, it wasn't just Hughes.

Simpson denies that he said it. For someone as disciplined as Simpson it must have been difficult to see someone of Hughes' talent consistently batting so carelessly. By the end of the West Indies tour Simpson thought that he could nominate the ball and the shot that Hughes would get out on. Hughes' memories of the tour had nothing to do with his poor batting.

I remember sitting and listening to Lou Rawls in the back seat of a taxi, having just arrived in Grenada. The scenery was breathtaking. It's a small island and very mountainous. I'd just had appendicitis and it made me think of my wife and home.

The idea that players rarely remember the play after a tour was something that Bobby Simpson told his team. Rick Darling explains.

Simmo said to us one day that when you are on a tour you'll remember the good times you've had with your mates and the cultural experiences, rarely will you remember what went on during the actual playing time. Simmo was right. I've got vivid memories of the beautiful beaches, sailing, the water skiing and the mucking around on the beach.

Simpson's leadership on the tour was questioned by some. In Simpson's defence, taking on the role of captain leading a young inexperienced team was a difficult task. Doing it at 42 years of age, dealing with some players half his age, is even more challenging. Simpson along with team manager Fred Bennett took on the responsibility for everything. This is in stark contrast to the modern (2014) Australian structure in which coach Darren Lehman has eleven full time staff, complete with specialist coaches and medicos. Looking back, the austerity of off-field support throughout the 1970s seems primitive to the point of being irresponsible – but that's the way it was.

Simpson later reflected on the lack of ongoing success for the likes of Toohey and Serjeant and the fact that Yallop and Wood didn't achieve more in their Test careers.

In the years to come, once the WSC and the Board joined forces, none of these batsmen fulfilled the potential they showed on this tour … the truth is none of them improved much after that tour. In the case of Serjeant and Toohey, they went backwards. I often wonder if I had stayed on as captain (and as something of a coach too), their careers might have evolved differently.

Serjeant believed the tour was instrumental in the development of some of the careers of players who were to become regular Test players such as Hughes, Yardley and Wood. It also made Serjeant realise the value of practising fulltime, noting how much his fielding improved and how much better prepared he felt overall. The previous summer he had been trying to play Test cricket while working full-time as a pharmacist at a Perth Hospital.

Ian Callen found he didn't have much to take away from his tour to the West Indies besides a chronic back problem that was getting worse. As the tour progressed, Callen found he could run and jump but when it came to twisting he was limited. He found he had lost something.

> *I tried to bowl but no one knew what was going on. I just couldn't get the pace, every time I bowled it hurt. I had lost my pace and accuracy. It was incredibly disappointing.*

Callen had played only two first-class matches taking four wickets at 16. He did though have one highlight in a one-day international (ODI).

> *I'd gone to the dressing room at the fall of a wicket to change my boots. I was about to come out when we got another wicket. It meant Viv Richards was next in. I saw Viv go downstairs to get his bat from the dressing room, and so I pulled the door shut on him and locked the door from the outside. He started calling out, 'Hey man, hey man, open the door!' and eventually someone did. I took one wicket in the match and it was Viv.*
>
> *Years later when we were having a drink in one of the Lancashire League clubs, Rishton, Viv came up and tapped me on the shoulder and said, 'Hey Mad Dog, I'm your bunny.'*

It was a comforting way to remember what had been a very disappointing time for Callen.

Steve Rixon had played in all five Tests in the West Indies and despite having some success with the bat, his work behind the stumps had been inconsistent.

By the end of 1977–78, Queensland's wicketkeeper John Maclean, who had missed out on the tour to the West Indies, thought about quitting. His friend and former Test player, Graeme Watson, who was in Queensland playing club cricket encouraged him to keep going: 'Listen mate, just keep playing for another year, because you just might get a go.'

Maclean decided to give it one more tilt. He had wondered why he was never picked. There had been an approach to join World Series Cricket. He even went down to Adelaide with Ashley Mallett and Ian Chappell to look at the drop-in pitch at Football Park where he was offered a three-month contract to be a player/manager for $10,000. Maclean wondered whether Australian cricket officials had heard about the visit.

Two Test Victorian fast bowler Alan Hurst was wondering when his next chance to play for Australia might come. Injuries had restricted him to just one Test against India and now he was fielding calls from Packer's agents. He'd taken calls from Ian Chappell and Austin Robertson offering him a WSC contract. Hurst longed to play more Test cricket for Australia. There were other factors also to consider.

> I also had a teaching job that I enjoyed and there was no guaranteed future after the two-year contract with Packer. When I informed Chappell I wasn't signing on, he was totally taken aback and told me I was an idiot in a way only 'Chappelli' can!

Australian cricket fans had added a new word to their lexicon, the word 'riot'. Although there was limited coverage – no live radio or television broadcasts and limited newspaper reportage of the West Indies tour – cricket followers were shocked about the way the final test had ended. Australia's inability to defeat the second-string West Indies side would have disappointed Australian fans. It appeared that despite the fanfare of the previous home summer, Australia was not the force the ACB was selling them as.

Nonetheless there was excitement surrounding the approaching Ashes series. For some fans who were now wavering in their support for the Establishment, this would be the all-important season upon which the cricket war between the ACB and Kerry Packer's WSC would be decided.

The ACB also knew how important the financially lucrative series against the traditional rival was. With more and more questions being raised about the quality of Australian cricket, this was to be a make or break summer, for all concerned.

Chapter Five

The Ashes Tour of Australia, 1978–79

When England came to Australia in the summer of 1978–79, the tour included a six-match Test series, and five one-day internationals.

The experienced English team included Brearley, Boycott, Gooch, Randall, Taylor, Gower, Botham, Miller, Edmonds, Old and Willis. It was a world-class team captained by Mike Brearley, not a brilliant batsman himself but an excellent captain.

It was a team determined to retain the Ashes from the six Tests; the first in Brisbane (1–6 December), the second in Perth (15–20 December), the third in Melbourne (29 December – 3 January), fourth in Sydney (6–11 January), the fifth Test in Adelaide (27 January – 1 February), and the final and sixth Test back in Sydney (10–14 February).

In terms of Ashes series, England was a team on the upswing. A 3–0 victory against a full-strength Australian side in 1977 had in part made up for the 5–1 humiliation inflicted on England at the hands of Lillee and Thomson in Australia in 1974–75. Success against Australia on home soil would provide the final part of England's recovery. It would also be further vindication that the English system of picking the captain first and then the side was working (and that concerns about the quality of county cricket would be again if only temporarily put to bed). England's captain Mike Brearley would not have made the English side as a batsman (and therefore would not have been captain) had the Australian system of selecting the team first, then the captain from the selected players second been in place. He would not have been a part of the Ashes tour. But captain he was.

Simpson bows out gracefully

Though England arrived with their captain in place, the Australian captaincy was still not assured

Bob Simpson again sought a guarantee from the ACB that he would be selected in all six Tests, and the 1979 World Cup. When he was told that the captain would be named only after the side for the First Test was chosen, Simpson announced he was leaving the game. When Simpson retired he released a statement that read:

> I love the game of cricket; I love being part of this new resurgence in Australian cricket. At the same time, I have to be realistic. I believe that twelve months ago, when I was given the honour of coming back and playing for Australia, it was only on a stopgap basis, to allow Australian cricket to regroup and perhaps take the challenge up a little later on. I believe the time has come to allow a younger person, a person who is going to be with the Australian cricket team for many years, to take over.

Despite his earlier wishes, Simpson's announcement sounded as if this was the way he had always planned. Simpson's departure proved a significant loss for Australia because his leadership skills against those of England captain Mike Brearley would have added strength to the side. His batting and fielding alone, with 4,869 runs at 46, with ten Test centuries and 110 catches, would also be sorely missed.

Simpson's captaincy though had at times proved to be a double-edged sword. He was a generation apart from most of his players, creating a division that was at times hard to bridge – as it would have been for anyone.

For Bob Simpson, his comeback, after the Establishment's schism with WSC, was one of mixed feelings.

I think I did as well as I possibly could. I scored more runs in the series against India than in any other Test series I played in. We more than held our own against Packer cricket although there was no doubt the quality of players in WSC was superior … The West Indies tour was a big challenge personally for me and the side … but my reflexes weren't quite as sharp as they could have been.

Australian players were divided about Simpson's captaincy. Some were fiercely loyal, others critical. He was considered either a man who gave favours to those from New South Wales and Victoria, or he was seen as a true mentor who helped young players develop. It depended on whom you talked to. Simpson thought the teams he coached during this period were very close, although he noted the younger players were easier to manager than more senior ones, which may explain some of the selection priorities.

For Simpson, the era 1977–79 is a short but significant one in a lengthy and very successful career. That he managed to return to international cricket after ten years away from the top level of the game is an enormous tribute to him – as a cricketer and a man. Once he retired and with Australian cricket uncertain as to how long the cricket war would continue, the selectors looked to players who could lead the side for several seasons. The choices were limited. Jeff Thomson (although he was in the throes of signing with WSC) after his good work in the West Indies, and his Queensland teammate Gary Cosier must have been considered; so too 33-year-old John Inverarity, the front runner of this group.

Bernard Whimpress in *On Our Selection* wrote:

While Inverarity would never match the quality of Simpson as a player, he could well have been Australia's answer to Mike Brearley as a tactician in 1978–79 and made more runs than the English skipper.

Inverarity had already been a third selector on the tour of England in 1972. He was also a successful Shield captain for Western Australia. He was a mature and analytical cricketer and certainly would have handled Rodney Hogg, having already had to deal with headstrong players such as Lillee and Marsh.

In December 1977, Inverarity was interviewed by *Australian Cricket* after spending eighteen months in England working as a school teacher. He was an astute thinker who, if the cricket authorities had wanted, would have surely been prepared to lead Australia against India in 1977–78.

When asked whether or not the Kerry Packer 'superstars' would be 100 percent dinkum he answered, 'They cannot afford not to be.' With Hookes' broken jaw later seen as proof of how serious the competition was, his words proved telling.

Inverarity's Test career had been brief, playing just six matches between 1968 and 1972, including two tours of England, but there was a strong argument for his selection and the captaincy. He had taken WA to Shield wins in 1972–73 and 1974–75 to make it three wins in four years (later 1977–78). During the 1978–79 series, Australia could have done with the experience of Inverarity as a batsman to help stave off middle-order collapses. That season, in Shield cricket, he scored 510 runs at 51 including a career high of 187 against New South Wales at the SCG. But he would finish his Test career with an average of 17.40 from limited opportunities.

Western Australian teammate Kevin Wright, who debuted for Australia during the final Test of the Ashes series, thought himself lucky to have had Inverarity standing next to him at slip.

> *His anticipation of what was happening in the game was extraordinary. He would often say to me, 'You need to switch on, you need to switch on, something is going to happen' and invariably it did. It was as if he had a sixth sense.*

Wright described one match in which Western Australia needed one wicket to win, Victoria one run to take the honours. Inverarity gathered the players and asked bowler Wayne Clark to deliver a bouncer; for Wright to slowly take a keeping glove off as the bowler ran in; Bruce Yardley to run up to the stumps to take Wright's throw; and then signalled from his fielding position to Clark to bowl a yorker. The result was a last-ball run-out, just as Inverarity had ordained.

While many people believed that Inverarity would make a great captain and a good match up against Brearley, ultimately he missed out on the role and selection in the Australian side.

Graham Yallop: An unlikely skipper

Another in the selector's sights and one who was assured of holding his place in the Australian side as a batsman was Graham Yallop, already one of three new state captains in 1977 after the defection of Richie Robinson to WSC. He was a proven Test batsman, but perhaps most importantly a player that the Board thought they could keep in line to promote the Establishment cause.

The stylish left-hand top-order batsman had debuted for Victoria at twenty in 1972–73. His first full season in 1974–75 included a century against South Australia. Twin scores of 108 not out and 95 against New South Wales just before Christmas of 1975 thrust his name in front of the selectors. He was called up for the Fourth Test against the West Indies at Sydney, replacing popular team man Rick McCosker who had struggled in the series, making just 42 runs in six innings. Yallop batted at number three in two of the remaining three Tests of the 1975–76 series.

Was Yallop welcomed into the side? Despite reports to the contrary he was, especially by Greg Chappell. Yallop, number three for Victoria, says he felt humbled to initially bat in his first Test series in the position Chappell brothers had occupied for the preceding three years with great success. They were still in good form. Despite the challenge of facing a West Indian attack comprising of Roberts, Holding, Keith Boyce, Holder and world-record Test wicket holder Lance Gibbs, Yallop proved he belonged in such company, scoring 179 runs at 44.

Slow starts to the domestic season worked against him. Yallop had played for the full-strength Australian side against the West Indies two summers before, but had to wait until the Fifth Test of the Indian tour to Australia in 1977–78 to be called into the new side.

He was thrilled to have any opportunity to play for Australia and make every post a winner. He showed class, moving down the wicket and driving the spinners with confidence for a first-innings score of 121. Remarkably by the time he returned to wearing the baggy green for the Fifth Test in Adelaide, he had missed fifteen intervening Tests.

Yallop's love of the game was nurtured at Carey Grammar, under the tutelage of former England fast bowler Frank Tyson. Working at his father's *APY Castings* foundry in Kensington, he made slips catching cradles and then became an agent for Duncan Fearnley's Sportsgoods.

His reserved nature would prove to be his Achilles heel when it came to leading volatile men such as paceman Rodney Hogg.

When Yallop's outbound flight for Victoria from Western Australia was on the runway, the Ansett pilot's voice asked that the Victorian Sheffield Shield players please remain on the plane once it landed in Melbourne. There, VCA secretary Dave Richards appeared on the plane and announced Yallop as Australia's third-youngest Test captain.

Despite Yallop thinking that he was 'maybe a chance', he was 'floored by the announcement … you never knock back the Australian captaincy.'

Teammates Trevor Laughlin, Alan Hurst and Jim Higgs were also named in the twelve.

Ominously, former captain Bob Simpson felt sorry for the new skipper. He was, after all, well versed in what was in store.

I remember him calling me after it was revealed I was retiring, to say he hoped it wasn't true. This was hardly a man aching for the top job.

In *Lambs to the Slaughter*, his book about the 1978–79 series, Yallop wrote that he found it hard to ignore the reaction to his appointment. He was considered to have been born with a silver spoon in his mouth ... not tough enough to handle difficult situations – too much a Mr Nice Guy.

Comments such as these would have stung even the hardiest of souls let alone such a reserved man. It wasn't long before the new Australian skipper requested a silent phone number, so frequent were the calls from the media. None were forthcoming from places of authority where he hoped he might receive some advice in his new role. When they later did, Yallop soon became fed up with directives from ACB Chair Bob Parish that he condemn WSC at every opportunity.

I had very good friends in WSC and wasn't prepared to denigrate what they were doing.

His first press conference as captain of Australia was a portent of what was to come. Yallop arrived at Brisbane's Eagle Farm Airport in preparation for the First Test against England and uttered the words that would haunt him for the entire series. When asked how Australia might fare he rather flippantly retorted: '6–0'. With a lot on his mind and flanked by numerous cameras and journalists, he performed his first official role as captain. However, he spoke without really thinking. These words then took on a life of their own, a tidal wave that nothing but an Australians series victory could prevent.

If that wasn't bad enough, when Yallop arrived at The Gabba the next day to prepare for the Test he began to realise how difficult a task he was being set. He had no manager, no advisors, and a team in which no one really knew each other. His men had accumulated only 55 Tests between them.

There was really no support from the Board. I had to do everything myself, tickets, taxis to the ground, arrange for the boys' laundry, everything.

And of course he had to lead his side against a close to full-strength English side, and he had to bat well himself. Yallop was suddenly getting an insight into some of the challenges his predecessor Bob Simpson had faced.

Clark – questionable bowling action

Wayne Clark had been one of Australia's key bowlers on the West Indian Tour but when he returned from the West Indies, he was told he wouldn't be playing for Australia in the Ashes series – not by a selector but by a journalist. It was Reporter at *The Age,* Peter McFarline who informed Clark that his and Bruce Yardley's bowling actions had been reported to the ICC. Since the 1960s there had been an unofficial arrangement that players with suspect actions were not picked to tour or play in Ashes series. It was why Ian Meckiff didn't tour England in 1961, and why Tony Lock missed out on the Australian tour of 1962–63 (instead playing domestic cricket for Western Australia). McFarline informed Clark that while he would miss the Ashes series, he would be brought back to play against Pakistan.

Clark wanted some answers, to see if what McFarline had told him was correct. Hadn't he just come off a golden summer against India where he'd taken 28 wickets and then come home from the West Indies with another nineteen Test scalps from four Tests? So Clark rang ACB Treasurer and 1978 delegate to the ICC, Ray Steele, but received no answers, nor any support.

> *I was really dirty on the ACB after that. They just didn't want to know. They gave me absolutely nothing.*

When Clark took six wickets against South Australia at the time when Australia was 2–0 down in the Ashes series, McFarline asked ACB Chairman of selectors Phil Ridings if Clark would get a game. 'No, and you know why,' was the response.

Clark felt let down but vowed to change attitudes by sheer weight of wickets. He started slowly but regained confidence as the season progressed, taking 33 first-class wickets with a best of 6–47 against South Australia at Adelaide Oval. And sure enough when the side to play Pakistan was announced, Clark was in it.

Toohey and Border – get their chances

Peter Toohey was Australian cricket's poster boy at the start of the 1978-79 Ashes summer. An image of him gently turning a ball to leg, wearing Australian cap and jumper, adorned the cover of the *ABC Cricket Book* for the season. He was front and centre in Australian cricket marketers' and fans' eyes, for good reason. Not only had he been a dominant figure in eight Tests averaging 47 with a top score of 122, he looked likely to be part of the Australian Test side for the long haul. His pen portrait said:

> *A noticeable feature of his batting is the time he gives himself to make a decision to a particular shot … a touch of class in itself, and his execution of his cover and square drives leaves little to be desired.*

That touch of class, so evident the previous season, would remain elusive for Toohey over the next twelve months.

Before the season began, Toohey and Graeme Wood had been offered WSC places for 1979–80 once their ACB contracts expired. Toohey visited Consolidated Press Holdings CPH and accepted an offer in principle. Wood, after initially declining, signed a five-year offer.

Toohey recalls:

> *I was keen because the money was good and by then I would have experienced a reasonable amount of Test cricket. Back then a sign-on fee and $25,000 a year for three years was enough to set you up nicely. But I still wanted to Test myself in an Ashes series. If I was still scoring runs and they wanted me after that, then I would have signed.*

For Toohey it was mainly about playing an Ashes series. He remembered watching his mentor Bob Simpson playing Ashes cricket and wanted to become part of the folklore. Without necessarily knowing it at the time, Toohey's sense of expectation, along with the public's, was setting himself up for a fall. Despite the hype surrounding WSC, an Ashes series was the one that Australian and English players measured themselves by. If they succeeded in these contests, they would be well regarded as Test cricketers. Toohey, like his teammates, knew this and were desperate for success against the traditional enemy.

The Ashes summer of 1978–79 would turn out to be a summer of losses, but also an arrival – that of Allan Border, the pugnacious, no-nonsense, left-handed batsman with squat stance, back-lift that seemingly veered to slips before straightening at the last moment.

Tap, tap, tap … there he is, the new Rock of Gibraltar who would be the stabilising force for Australian cricket for the next fifteen years. Simpson was one of the first to understand that Allan Border had something special.

In December 1976, Border was 21 and Simpson's Western Suburbs team had hosted a match with Mosman at Pratten Park. Simpson scored a ton, Border eighty-odd. Border, then in the state squad, was given some Toohey Cup games through Simpson's promotions company. The bond that later led to Simpson coaching Australia under Border's leadership was forged.

The WSC/ACB war continues

The summer of 1978–79 was a make-or-break season for Packer's WSC; time to win or lose the cricket war. Australian cricket was fighting against the might of the WSC marketing machine as they talked about their task of promoting cricket in a crusading mood.

WSC official Bill Macartney had some early concerns. He had arrived in Perth a week before the start of the season and asked a cabbie, as *Australian Cricket Annual* reported: 'Going to the cricket are you mate?'

'Ugh,' was the reply.

'World Series, Gloucester Park … planning to get down there at all?'

'World Series? They're not coming to Perth, are they?'

A publicity assault was launched on newspaper offices, radio and TV stations, shopping centres, trotting meetings and any other place where crowds mingled.

The WSC marketing and promotions team spun into action, stealing the spotlight from the traditional Ashes Contest.

The WSC marketing machine swung into gear. It was a full-on attack. Although politically incorrect today there were T-shirts with: *Big Boys play at night* and *I'm into cricket, balls and all*. There were WSC blow-up pillows, white cricket balls (of soap) with the WSC logo, an imprinted Dennis Lillee tie, a Super Test hat and jacket, a promotion to face a Dennis Lillee ball or bowl to Rod Marsh. You could play night cricket on your dining room table with a dice, smother your bedroom walls with colour posters, or buy the recording of 'C'mon Aussie C'mon'. World Series players, when not on the park, were promoting WSC at shopping centres, inundated by multitudes of screaming kids.

Cave, took a more traditional approach. Working in a manner that left the ACB in the shade, her role included making sure VIPs we well looked after, ensuring the press were well fed and kept informed, and managing the dietary requirements of players – all was handled quickly and with the minimum of fuss.

There was great excitement and a sense of confidence the night before WSC's SCG one-day debut under lights. Packer was the first advertiser to use the hoardings on the back of taxis; *The Australian* ran a four-page advertising supplement; a balloon carrying the WSC logo floated above the city; *The World Series Cricket Story*, more commercial than documentary, narrated by John Laws, screened the night before the first day/night match in Sydney.

Even the Test was advertised with the placement of a Benson and Hedges advertisement for the Ashes beginning in three days. It was, however, totally overshadowed by the WSC commercials.

While the approach of the ACB in the lead up to the Ashes season wasn't quite *'If you can't beat them join them'*, for the Australian Cricket Board, it came close. They planned to counter Packer's marketing package with cheap children's tickets, skydivers, a brass band and a commemorative coin toss. In addition, cricket was being marketed on the ABC. The hype fell well short of what was on Channel Nine to promote Packer's one-dayers and Super Tests, but it was a start.

ABC TV's Ashes promotion included an advert under the banner, *Battle for the Ashes*. Basic compared to the glitz and glamour of WSC, it featured Ian

Botham wearing his England jumper with the four lions across his middle. The voice over began.

> *It's on again! [A voice boomed as a camera panned to a baggy-green-capped Peter Toohey] The battle for the Ashes. England has the experience. Australia has the enthusiasm. [Pan back to Botham delivering the ball and Toohey hooking] A classic battle for a classic prize, only on the ABC!*

As fundamental as the advert was, the message was clear that Test cricket is the only real cricket and to get it you had to watch the Ashes on the ABC. At the same time, there was a sniff of change from the ACB hinting at a long-term vision that would include commercial networks. The ACB had granted exclusive Gillette Cup rights to the 10 Network. The competition even mimicked WSC by agreeing to a six-ball format.

The summer of 1978–79 was to be, as journalist Peter McFarline described in his book, *A Testing Time*:

> *… a momentous season for Australian cricket. Not only because it featured the 55th Ashes series between Australia and England. Followers of the game in both countries saw it as the ultimate Test of the strength of the traditional game, in opposition to the rival World Series Cricket troupe.*

While the ACB was quick to decry Packer and his circus and rejoice in the empty stadiums for WSC matches, they privately estimated a syphoning off of around a quarter of a million dollars of money that would normally have gone to traditional cricket in 1977–78.

Perhaps the biggest blow of all to the Establishment cause occurred on the night of November 28 – a date now famous in the history of World Series Cricket as the night Packer cricket officially arrived. The match itself was a reasonably innocuous affair that ended forty minutes early with an easy win for the Australians against the West Indies. Five thousand early arrivals turned to 30,000 by tea as the lines of spectators continued to snake down Anzac

Parade toward the floodlit SCG. Packer, who had already taken the new step of admitting ladies to the Members area, agreed to a request from police to open the gates to ease the queues banked up at turnstiles that had already recorded an attendance of 44,377.

Estimates were that a crowd of more than 50,000 was packed in. Ian Chappell, who played in the match, saw the game as the night that the Australian public had voted them as the Australian side.

John Cornell uttered philosophical phrases such as 'These people have found the truth' as he sat next to his wife Delvene Delaney, Austin Robertson and Paul Hogan.

National Times Adrian McGregor wrote a fortnight later:

> *That Packer at that moment, so absolutely removed from the hoi polloi should have... achieved the proletarianisation of cricket. He had enticed fans out of pubs... transforming the subtleties of traditional cricket into the spectacular that is night cricket.*

On the eve of Establishment cricket's most important Test series against its traditional rival – the series that they hoped would derail Packer – their enemy had struck gold.

The English tourists

England's touring side was announced with few surprises; all had played Test cricket. Mike Brearley, who had led the side to Pakistan and New Zealand, was in charge of the sixteen-man squad. It looked a strong side on paper with a pace bowling quintet of Willis, Hendrick, Old, Botham and Lever; three spinners including Miller and Emburey who had experienced Australian conditions and the main tweaker Edmonds, who hadn't. Also in the team was Geoff Boycott who lost the vice-captaincy of the English side to Bob Willis.

There was some excitement about seeing the blond curly-haired, baby-faced Gower who cricket fans had seen on the television news pulling his first ball in Test cricket against Pakistan to the boundary. We'd heard that Centenary

Test hero Derek Randall had lost form and been omitted from the previous England tour. We'd watched Graham Gooch score a pair against the Aussies in England on debut in 1975 and wondered if he would ever recover.

Then there was the man with the Midas touch, Ian Botham. Botham, who'd knocked over Greg Chappell as his first Test victim and kicked on to take 64 wickets and score three Test hundreds in his first eleven matches, had played club cricket in Melbourne the summer before but with little success. Botham also hinted at a little of the turmoil that would come to haunt him, by gashing the inside of his forearm 36 hours before the team left England.

The first-class season began on Friday 3 November with a match at the Adelaide Oval. The first Test was scheduled for 1 December at The Gabba in Brisbane. However, the national focus was on the Equity Court in Sydney and the news that Jeff Thomson was going fishing. This was a major blow for Establishment cricket. Jeff Thomson had chosen to 'retire' so that he could be released from his ACB contract (which continued into March 1979). He had decided to join WSC and tour the West Indies from February to April 1979 – a decision based on the increased income he could earn with WSC. Thomson famous utterance that he would rather go fishin' than play Test cricket made it clear that we would not be playing for Australia in the Ashes summer.

It's hard to estimate what the ACB lost when the news of Thomson's 'retirement' came in September. Until then he had taken 145 wickets at 25 in 32 Tests and his leadership in the West Indies had been a revelation. Although it was clear he was no longer the force he was before his shoulder injury and that his form was wavering, his presence alone would have been an intimidating factor for the English batsmen.

While the public's sentiment had largely been behind Establishment cricket during the previous summer's series against India, English journalist Alan Lee, who was covering both the Ashes and WSC series for his tour book *A Pitch in Both Camps,* noticed a change of mood from the locals, hearing comments such as *'I only watch the best, I'll be at the Packer matches'* and predictions that in fact it would be Australia that would lose the Ashes, going down 0–6.

Predictions about whitewashes it seemed were heard on every corner. It just depended on which side of the Establishment fence you sat on as to which team you thought would be dominate. With the Ashes series about to begin, we would soon find out.

Rod Hogg – too hot to handle

Fast bowler, Rodney Hogg, was added to the Australian line up, as was other paceman, Alan Hurst. Wicketkeeper and right-hand bat, John Maclean was also included for the First Test. Only six players from Australia's final Test in the West Indies in Kingston had made it into the eleven: Yallop, Toohey, Laughlin, Yardley, Higgs and Wood. Cosier and Hughes came back into the side to make up the eleven.

Much had happened since the April riot at Jamaica. A slow start to the first-class season for former vice-captain Craig Serjeant meant he missed the selectors' nod. Kim Hughes, with some sparkling early season form, was preferred. The forewarned Wayne Clark was also missing because of his bowling action – journalist Peter MacFarline's prediction was spot on.

One name that would make an impact that summer in all manner of ways was pace bowler Rodney Hogg. He became hero and villain that summer, evolving from relative unknown plying his trade for South Australia into an international cricketing sensation. Sir Donald Bradman described Hogg to Brearley as 'slippery' , that is, a quick bowler to face. Given Bradman had played with and against some of the most distinguished fast bowlers of all time, his comments were worth noting.

Early in the tour, Hogg bounced out England's Clive Radley in the first-class match against South Australia and in the process broke Radley's skull. To counter rising concerns, the English players started referring to Hogg not by his name but 'Road' or 'Hedge' to make him seem more familiar, less of a terrifying and effective force.

Even Mike Brearley compared Hogg with former English champion opening bowler, Brian Statham:

He reminds me of Brian Statham but with more belligerence ... also has a streak of Dennis Lillee and Fred Trueman in his aggression, which makes him an even more dangerous bowler.

How true these words proved in 1978–79. As the summer progressed, questions were asked about where Hogg had been all these years. In typical manner, he was quick to reply: 'I've been around, but I haven't been selected.'

Hogg was right when he said he had been around for some time. A Victorian by birth, he debuted for Northcote as a fast bowler in the grade scene when just sixteen. Within two years he was in the Victorian squad. His reputation as being a bit wild and his habit of occasionally missing training didn't help his cause. By 1974–75, with his career at a standstill, he faced the daunting prospect of displacing established opening bowlers Max Walker and Alan Hurst from the Victorian lineup.

Friend and former Northcote teammate Gary Cosier encouraged Hogg to join the land of cricketing opportunity in South Australia. Selection for his adopted state was initially hard to come by. In his first-class debut he was relegated to carrying the drinks before playing the final match of the season. Frustration followed in 1976–77 when he wasn't selected at all. It was only the Packer intervention the following year, which had lured away South Australia's main strike bowler Wayne Prior that opened the way for selection the following season. A haul of 36 wickets in nine matches including 10–152 in the final game against Queensland after the Australian team left for the West Indies finally brought his name to the fore.

Hogg was mercurial, one day steaming in bowling genuine pace, the next deciding to take a few overs to warm up. When he ran in it was a low-to-the-ground approach gradually becoming more upright the further into his run-up. The lower the stoop, generally the quicker the ball. At times it looked as if he were running uphill. When he was really on song he would lunge forward to delivery stride, almost falling flat onto the pitch. It looked uncomfortable but it gave him rhythm and smoothness with action at the key moment when he released the ball.

When his asthma condition was playing up, he could also be effective off a short run. Although he bowled an effective bouncer, it was more his accuracy and pace that made him so successful. For captain Graham Yallop though, Hogg was a handful; this placed the skipper in an invidious position.

In his book *The Whole Hogg*, he reveals his dislike of Yallop since playing against him at school. He had a set against Yallop's wealthy private school background when playing for Northcote against Richmond.

> *I began to bowl as many short balls as possible in an effort to maim him ... I just didn't like Graham's mannerisms or his style ... it was a cultural thing ... I was probably a hard bloke to handle but I just wasn't a big fan of Yallop as captain ... I didn't think he was ready for the captaincy ... the truth was I wasn't really fit enough for Test cricket. I was a district cricketer who bowled when and if it suited me.*

Hogg's attitude would prove a niggling thorn in the side of the Australian cricket team all summer. Yallop though didn't seem to mind.

> *Hoggy was like a lot of fast bowlers who have their own ideas. I was supportive of him throughout the series.*

While the 1978–79 Ashes series proved record breaking for Hogg, it was also a triumph for Victorian fast bowler Alan Hurst. In the first innings of the First Test at The Gabba, Hurst joined Hogg opening the bowling, taking four wickets to complement Hogg's six; the successes would only continue. Alan Hurst proved the perfect fast bowling partner for Hogg

Hurst was given his first cricket bat by his father who had shaped it out of a piece of scrap timber; but it was with the ball that he would make his mark. Hurst also resisted his father's efforts to encourage him to bowl spin. Like a lot of young cricketers he wanted to bowl fast. By sixteen he was on the bus for a forty-minute journey to practice at Footscray every Tuesday and

Thursday afternoon. Selection in the Victorian Combined High School side followed. Hurst was helped by South Kingsville junior coach Bill Deller, best known in later years as a top AFL footy umpire and also a handy fast bowler.

> Bill used to pick me up at home in the mornings for Under-16 matches, take me home for lunch, and then pick me up for the afternoon seniors' game. I opened the bowling with him and really enjoyed his guidance. When Footscray Cricket Club approached me, Bill was very supportive. As Club President, some thought he should be trying to keep me at the Club, but Bill envisaged a future and fostered the move.

Former Test player Ron Gaunt was another encouraging Hurst 'not to worry about where the ball was going, to just bowl fast. Medium pacers are two bob a dozen.'

Hurst bided his time in the Footscray thirds and then seconds before establishing a place in the firsts. 1972 proved to be a landmark for Hurst. Victoria had lost Alan Connolly (retired), Graeme Watson (to WA) and Alan 'Froggy' Thomson (lost form, discarded) in the previous two seasons. The other regular pace bowlers at the time were Ross Duncan, Robert Rowan and Max Walker. Duncan decided to return to Queensland and Rowan chose to pursue his baseball career; Hurst found himself in the Victorian team to play West Australia on the MCG.

Despite nerves at playing with and against some of his mates, and only taking a wicket in each innings, Hurst felt like he belonged. Frank Tyson as Victorian coach and Max Walker were integral to Hurst's development, helping him work batsmen out and make the ball move through the air and off the seam. Hurst looked more like a movie star than a cricketer. With trendy sideburns, curly black hair and an Errol Flynn moustache, he could just as easily have been selected for the centrefold of Cleo as for *Cricketer* magazine.

He bowled right-arm fast with a powerful shoulder action. A flurry of arms and the ability to move the ball disconcertingly through the air with a damaging outswinger provided a challenge for batsmen. '*The fastest Victorian since Ernie McCormick*,' wrote Ray Robinson.

Hurst would need a few attempts to prove himself in elite company. He was first selected for Australia in his second first-class season in 1973–74. Hurst was told by reporters he had been picked for the final Test against New Zealand at Adelaide. Photographers arrived and then later the ACB called to inform him of his selection. He found wickets hard to come by in that first outing at Adelaide Oval. With only one wicket to his credit for the match, the feeling of euphoria of playing for Australia was short lived. But what happened afterwards taught Hurst a valuable lesson.

> *The selectors were in the rooms after the game, but it was actually a cricket reporter at the airport as I returned home, who gave me the news that I had been dropped for the tour of New Zealand. I know that Ian Chappell wanted me in the touring squad – he spoke to me about it later. However, there was never any contact from the selectors, nor ever any explanation why I was not included in the squad. Thankfully that regime changed with the Packer influence a few years later and relationships with and respect for players improved.*

It was a reminder that the players were the least important when came to communicating news. Subsequently picked to tour England in 1975, Hurst was more spectator than player and didn't appear in any of the Tests. The gap in Test matches was lengthy. Hurst had debuted with Geoff Dymock and Ashley Woodcock during the Third Test against New Zealand in 1973–74, but his next match wouldn't be until the first Test in Brisbane of the 1977–78 series.

The First Test – a fine toss to lose

It would have been a good toss to lose, but Graham Yallop won it and elected to bat in overcast conditions perfect for seam bowling. The unlikely opening pair of Wood and Cosier appeared in the middle together. One moved at full speed like lightning, the other was an ambler. Glad to be bowling, Brearley was rubbing his hands together, encouraging tall, lanky Bob Willis who delivered the series' first over.

Wood, having already tried one risky single off the first ball of the series, tries another, this time to Gower, who swoops in, running Cosier out for one. The echo of school kids in the crowd fades as Cosier, like a man suddenly woken from a dream, slowly departs. Wood bangs his bat on the ground, realising what he has done.

ABC TV commentator Frank Tyson has just been describing how good Australia's opening pair is at running between the wickets. He waxes lyrical on the state of the pitch – *I don't think there'll be much moisture in it* – and goes on to explain that the wicket hadn't been covered overnight and therefore hasn't sweated in the way it otherwise might have

The hero from last summers' 'Gabba Test, Peter Toohey, arrives under the weight of his baggy green and the responsibility of batting number three for Australia in an Ashes Test.

Three slips, two gullies and a point greet him, with only two onside fieldsmen. Toohey is late on the first ball from Willis, an uncertain defensive jab rather than the soft hands and composure of last year.

Wood appears guilty and nervous at the other end, playing shadow shots and kicking his feet to warm up. Toohey in straight-arm stance is beaten twice in a row by the outswing of Old, and then almost cut in half by Willis, the ball coming back into him and rearing over his leg stump.

A loose drive at a Willis delivery and he's bowled neck and crop for one. England's pace and seam bowlers have shown Toohey's technique is not attuned to the moving ball. He may have looked like a schoolboy the previous summer but he appeared to be playing like one in this brief innings.

His first innings in a much-cherished Ashes Test seems like a nightmare.

I found out that my technique wasn't good enough; maybe because I'd been around for more than one season they concentrated on certain areas. I wasn't a new ball batsman and they were good at bowling at that frustrating offside line.

Enter helmeted skipper Graham Yallop, who assuredly turns the ball behind square for two. Wood's stooped body language isn't helping the cause and he's soon caught behind off Old; Australia 3–14. Hughes in yellow sweatbands and with the hint of a moustache arrives, playing shadow forward-defensive shots all the way to the crease. Keith Miller in the commentary box states the obvious: 'It's English conditions and no one bowls better than the English in these conditions.'

Yallop plays an airy shot and is dropped by Gooch in the slips. As Gooch lunges to catch the ball, his finger-guard slips off and bounces up in the air. Hughes tries to pull a ball outside off stump from Willis out of the ground. Yallop is squared up by Willis and is caught in the slips by Gooch. Australia 4–19. Trevor Laughlin with his Beatle hairstyle pushes his first ball through the gully for two. Hughes ignores three outswingers just wide of off stump from Botham's first over and then falling forward while driving at the fourth is caught behind. Hometown favourite John Maclean with a big smile and St Peter blade drives Botham for two past mid-off, with more bottom hand than finesse.

Laughlin hooks to fine leg where substitute fielder John Lever takes the catch. In less than an hour and a half, Australia is 6–26.

The first-day crowd of 14,026, the biggest Friday attendance at The Gabba since 1946, is silent, except for school children chanting the popularised WSC theme song, 'C'mon Aussie C'mon'.

Maclean, watching on from the Australian room, can't believe his luck, both good and bad.

John Maclean: a keeper's chance

When John Maclean first heard he'd been picked as Australia's wicketkeeper, he was in the men's toilet during a Queensland Cricketers' Club lunch.

The burly Maclean looked at his shirt, examining the beads of sweat dripping down. He'd just been contemplating what he would say when asked by Adrian McGregor why Queensland had yet to win a Sheffield Shield, when his train of thought was suddenly interrupted by the person standing next to him at the urinal. 'You've just been picked in the Test team. Can you believe your luck?'

Maclean later said:

I thought to myself, 'Well I've been believing it for ten years (that he'd be picked one day). I thought, Why not?'

The following days passed in a blur. All Maclean knows is that he felt euphoric. He would say more than once, 'It's not about the arrival, it's about the journey.' His story epitomises that sentiment.

For Maclean, an engineer, the journey to a baggy green cap was long and circuitous. As a kid in short pants he was elevated to keeper status for his school side after proving himself more useful at longstop than the team's wicketkeeper. His performances in Year Four at Annerley Junction Park State School for the school's Under-11 side caught the eye of the school's grade six teacher Barry Maranta, a sometime first-grade player for (Queensland) University who later became one of the first directors of the Broncos Rugby League team. Maranta encouraged Maclean to attend the state schoolboys' trials. Cricket was lucky to have Maclean; it could easily have been soccer, rugby, rugby league, baseball or Australian rules, such was his feel for games.

Picked for Queensland schoolboys in 1959 for the Perth carnival, he skippered the side the next year when he first played against Rod Marsh. His confidence grew when a friend of his dad's arranged a visit to Wally Grout's house where the cricketing legend threw balls at Maclean and told him he had a good technique and to just keep working hard.

At fifteen, although aligned with South Brisbane, he made his A-grade debut for Colts, a team of promising youngsters. Two years later he was wicketkeeper for South Brisbane in its 1963–64 premiership, still then a diminutive figure among a bunch of burly men in the premiership photo. Maclean's soft hands, ability to move either side of the wicket with ease and reputation for not missing chances, soon had the state selectors paying close attention. The chance for a maroon cap arrived when Lew Cooper, seven years Mclean's senior, broke his thumb in a double wicket competition, standing up to England all-rounder Basil D'Oliveira. It highlighted to Maclean how chance can change a player's opportunities in cricket, especially so when you are a wicketkeeper.

> *If Lew hadn't been injured then that could have been it for my state aspirations; and then when Lew retired they could easily have opted for a younger keeper.*

Maclean debuted for Queensland as a 22 year old in the first game of the 1968–69 Shield season in October 1968. He took four catches and scored an undefeated 25 in the second innings. It was a promising debut that helped Queensland to a 255–run win over New South Wales. When Queensland played Western Australia at The Gabba a month later, Maclean watched on as Englishman Colin Milburn – the first man out in the over after tea on day one – scored 243 out of 328.

> *I can still see him three paces down the wicket to spinner Bob Paulsen, losing his footing and hitting the ball one-handed through point for four as he fell over. They declared at 6-615, but still there were no byes.*

The ease with which Maclean took to first-class cricket was aided by having the state's spearhead Peter Allan as his club bowler. By then he'd also been playing grade cricket for eight years where he'd played with and against Queensland opening bowlers Sammy Morgan and Ross Duncan. He was kept on his toes by the words of his grade captain Ian Oxenford, 'You can't afford to drop catches that Lew Cooper would have taken.' Maclean kept catching them and Cooper was relegated to grade ranks for good.

Maclean wished he had the chance to learn more from the expertise of Don Tallon, who was still playing for South Brisbane club as a leg-spinner in his mid-to-late forties, but found that the former Australian keeper was so gifted, he couldn't pass on much technical detail. The skills of wicketkeeping came so easily to Tallon that he rarely thought much about it. He therefore found it hard to explain how he did things to others.

Maclean knew from a young age that life was about more than just cricket. By the time he was playing first-class cricket he was working on an Economics degree to go with his engineering qualifications, having first started working for the Queensland Government as a coordinator general cadet.

The image cricket fans have of Maclean is that of a stockily built keeper who looked friendly enough on the field; you felt one day you could go and have a beer with him. But by the time he earned national honours, he was 32 and knew the frustration of waiting to be selected. In his more than decade-long first-class career, he'd seen a string of keepers come and go on the national stage; so many, he was wondering what he done wrong in the eyes of the national selectors.

After three summers playing for Queensland, Maclean toured New Zealand with a second eleven Australian team in 1969, before Rod Marsh had even worn the gloves for Western Australia. He remembers the shocking wickets and the ball sometimes bouncing three times before reaching him, but it taught him a lot about staying as low as possible as a keeper.

Victoria's keeper Ray 'Slug' Jordon was picked as Taber's deputy for the tour of India and South Africa in 1969–70. It was a decision that still bemuses Maclean, but he puts it down to the Queensland disadvantage of not having a national selector and more often than not finishing the season closer to the bottom of the Shield ladder than the top. Maclean's comments ring true: the preceding season, 1968–69, Queensland finished third in the Shield and had no Test representation during the home series or in the touring squad.

Rod Marsh was picked to play for Australia for the First Test of the 1970–71 Ashes. Marsh had only taken the gloves for Western Australia at the start of the previous season. After having a poor opening two Tests, he was given the unkind moniker of 'iron gloves'.

Maclean now views Marsh as the best keeper of his era, although he, Maclean, could easily have been selected before the Western Australian in the series. He thought Taber would be retained for the Ashes summer of 1970–71, but when the Chairman of selectors Sir Donald Bradman was at The

Gabba to watch Queensland ten days before the First Test, Maclean thought he was a chance. He had kept well in the drawn match, but Queensland batting twice enabled Marsh to take six victims, helped by the pace of Lillee and McKenzie, and the spin of Inverarity, Mann and Lock. Marsh also scored 39 while Maclean scored a duck; he took two catches in Western Australia's first innings of 407. On the final night of the match, Maclean had Marsh, Lillee, Inverarity and Derek Chadwick over to his house for a meal. It was when he dropped them off and started driving away and heard the shouting and screaming that he knew Marsh had been picked ahead of him to play for Australia.

When World Series Cricket broke, Maclean thought *at last, here is my chance.* The week before the side for the First Test against India was picked he had gone to play in a Toohey's Cup match in Lismore. He'd accompanied his Lismore born and bred teammate Sam Trimble. The announced Australian captain Bob Simpson was already there.

'I'll see you in Brisbane,' Simpson said, hinting that Maclean was a shoo-in to wicket keep for Australia in the First Test of the Ashes series. Maclean missed out and Steve Rixon, a player from Simpson's grade club, took the gloves.

Maclean became convinced that Simpson's retirement helped with his own elevation to Test ranks. Hence his surprise when the day before the First Ashes Test match, he read what Simpson had written in his syndicated column for the *Courier Mail* that he was 'all for John Maclean taking over as captain'. Maclean couldn't believe what he was reading.

And so at The Gabba, Maclean, Australia's new wicketkeeper, felt a combination of excitement and nervousness as he made his way to the wicket with Australia perilously placed at five wickets down for 24. soon to be 6–26 when fellow debutante Trevor Laughlin holed out to twelfth man John Lever off Bob Willis at fine leg.

I'd been sitting there talking with selector Sammy Loxton in the dressing room as the wickets tumbled.

Maclean can't remember exactly what they were talking about. Perhaps it was that decision to bat.

> *Dunno, it might have been. Whatever it was, it wasn't a very long conversation. I know I felt a bit of an adrenaline rush sitting there knowing I was playing in a Test match. I was batting and keeping as well as ever.*

Maclean hardly had time to get settled in his seat before he found himself retreating to the bowels of the dressing room to get his pads on.

He batted like he felt; overdue and ready to play Test cricket. The first ball he drove past bowler Botham for two. The aggressive approach continued as he and Rodney Hogg posted a sixty-run partnership full of short arm jabs and flourishing strokes.

It was a good start that halted the raid of wickets and gave the Australian side a glimmer of hope that all was not lost in the series. Maclean had entered Test cricket with the same aggression that he had used at Shield level for more than a decade. He was determined to take the same approach when he wicket kept – to be confident in the ability that had taken him to this level. Whether he could do so across and entire Ashes series would soon be tested.

Some hope from The Gabba

The Australian selectors and Board members must have looked on grimly. The only highlight so far was the parachutists delivering the commemorative gold coin that the captains used to toss.

Maclean and Hogg's resilient batting rescued Australia to the point that they made 116. At one stage the scribes were seeking out the lowest score ever made in an Ashes Test for fear of not missing a historic score. In the end Australia easily overtook its lowest score of 36 against England at Edgbaston in 1902.

With Australia all out for 116, England went in to bat. By stumps on that first day, they were 2–60.

Bill O'Reilly thought Australia's first innings of 116 in the conditions

Bobby Simpson from the 1960s. He would
come back after close to a decade break to
lead Australia during the schism between
the Establishment and World Series Cricket.

Paul Hibbert played just one Test for
Australia, with scores of 13 and 2 in the
First Test against India, 1977–78.

Phil Carlson, John Maclean and Gary Cosier before the First Ashes Test at The Gabba, 1978–79.

Gary Cosier clips one off his legs in his final Test innings of the Second Ashes Test at Perth, 1978–79.

Craig Serjeant cuts off the front foot during his debut Test against England at Lord's, 1977.

Nightwatchman Tony Mann at the crease in the Second Test against at Perth, 1977–78.

Englishman, Derek Randall not out again!
This time against Alan Hurst. John Maclean
(wicketkeeper) joins in the appeal.

Australia's opening bowler Alan Hurst
relaxes after taking 25 wickets against
England in the Ashes series.

A young Phil Carlson bowls one down –
a childhood prodigy who managed only two Tests.

Jeff Moss, a one-Test wonder,
finished with an average of 60.

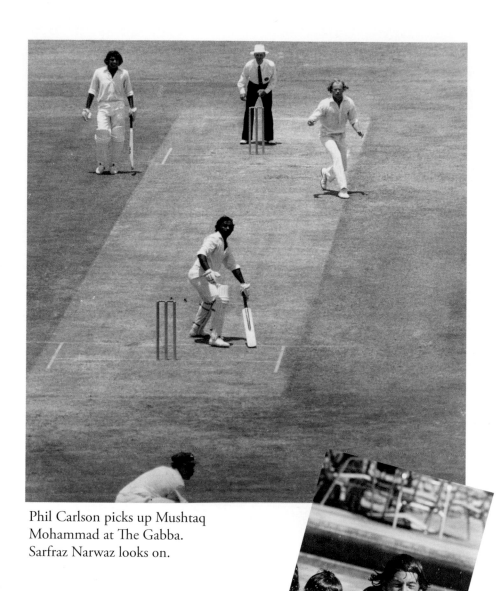

Phil Carlson picks up Mushtaq
Mohammad at The Gabba.
Sarfraz Narwaz looks on.

Australian wicketkeeper Steve
Rixon in the hotel swimming
pool on tour in the West Indies,
1978.

Bishan Bedi is caught by Kim Hughes (sub) off Wayne Clark in India's first innings of the Adelaide Test, January 1978.

Bruce Yardley with his deceptive off-spinners transformed to a player of Test class during the 1977–79 period.

Wayne Clark attracts the attention of cameramen
after whispers about his bowling action were heard
after the First Test of the 1977–78 series.

Peter Toohey and Wayne Clark sample
the grapes at the Wyndham Hill Estate
on the rest day of the Fifth Test against
India at Adelaide Oval, 1977–78.

Wayne Clark strikes, Ghavri is caught Simpson in the first innings of the Adelaide Test against India, 1978–79. Wicketkeeper Steve Rixon and non-striker Kirmani watch on.

Kim Hughes, who first became Australian captain against Pakistan in 1979, played 70 Tests for Australia.

Viv Richards in a full-strength West Indian side
helps demolish the Establishment players in 1978.

West Indian, Andy Roberts was known
for his effective use of bowling a slower
bouncer followed by a much faster one.

England warm up for their Australian tour with some table cricket.
From left to right: Bob Willis, Derek Randall, Mike Hendrick, David Gower and Ian Botham.

Rick Darling hooks against Victoria. The hook shot proved to be a stroke of mixed fortunes for the South Australian right-hand opening batsman.

Boycott missing out again, this time bowled Hogg for one run during the
Third Ashes Test at the MCG, 1978–79.

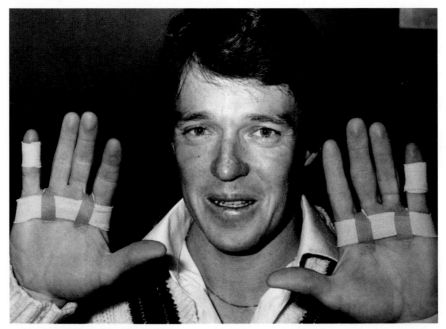

Australian wicketkeeper Kevin Wright took the full brunt of Rodney Hogg's
pace in the final two Tests of the Ashes summer.

Lambs to the Slaughter: the Australian side before the Second Ashes Test at Sydney, 1978–79.

Geoff Miller, English captain Mike Brearley, John Emburey and Mike Hendrick toast the 5–1 series win.

It's all over – a solemn looking Rod Hogg and Graham Yallop at the end of the Ashes series, 1978–79.

English player, Derek Randall gets a soaking after his second innings score of 150 in the decisive Fourth Test of the 1978–79 Ashes series.

The man destined for greatness, Allan Border.

A deft cut by Rick Darling
during his highest Test score of
91 at the SCG, January 1979.

Rodney Hogg on fire at the MCG.

Australian captain Graham
Yallop, successful as a batsman;
not so as a leader.

was better than par. England in response managed to put together 286. On debut, Hogg's 6–74 would be the best figures of his career.

A more buoyant Australian side started its second innings. The post-Hogg performance euphoria was short-lived. Cosier was bowled first ball by a half-pace Willis full toss.

> *I can still see it today, a big sloping in swinger that was a full toss. It was the first time I think that Willis's first ball had been on the stumps.*

Cosier can laugh about it now, but when he was bowled his head went back and his face turned grey, as if he couldn't believe what he had done. The string of low scores going back to the West Indies was starting to bother him.

Australia's 2 for 2 turned to 3 for 49 when Wood was caught shuffling across the crease on 19. When Kim Hughes joined his skipper Yallop on the third afternoon he must have realised this innings might be his last chance to perform. Maybe the encouraging words from Hughes' mentor Frank Parry were still ringing in his ears: 'There's only Bradman and you and then it's daylight to the rest.'

As a schoolboy Hughes had met the former club cricketer at the local nets, where he would watch and was eventually asked to join in. It was Parry who told Hughes he was good enough to play for and captain Australia. It was Parry who encouraged Hughes to be flamboyant in style, orthodox in technique. It was Parry who encouraged the high back-lift, lightning fast footwork and flashing blade.

On this third day of the First Test, baggy green capped and mitten-gloved Hughes looked calm, as if he for once had greater control of what he was doing, impetuosity put away for the day.

Hughes hooked Willis onto The Gabba's dog track but then when Brearley posted a second man deep, he showed restraint. He looked a player reborn. Another failure could well have meant returning to Shield cricket for an extended period.

Hughes batted like we hoped he would. Despite his lack of onfield success, Hughes was a favourite among school children around the country.

Perhaps it was his effervescent manner and willingness to play big strokes combined with the cheeky grin and that hair. In schoolgrounds around Australia, the question buzzing around was: '*Is Hughes still in?*'

And so with unprecedented patience, Hughes kept batting. It must have helped having Yallop at the other end, also batting with great discretion; a tuck around the corner here, a more extravagant drive there, countering the pace of Willis, Botham and Old and the canny spin of Miller and Edmonds (who surprisingly only bowled twelve overs). The right-handed Hughes and left-handed Yallop combined well, rotating the strike with nicely judged signals, egging each other on in mid-pitch chats.

As the partnership developed momentum, the response from the crowd grew louder, the events of the first day forgotten. The knives had been out for skipper Yallop before he even tossed the coin; now the gallant captain's knock helped the score to 4–219 before caught and bowled by Willis.

Yallop's century on debut as captain of Australia was the last until Steve Smith did the same at Brisbane against India in 2014–15. His innings was the perfect riposte for critics who said he lacked the ticker for the job, and for a batsman whose previous highest score at The Gabba was 35. He later wrote of his dismissal.

> *Willis sent down a half volley … I thought to myself, 'more honey for the bear' and stepped into it to drive. The ball went back like a rocket, low to his right, and he just threw out his hand and plucked in a most casual catch … I felt like I had made a duck instead of a century as I left the field.*

Hughes' combined aggression and patience took him into the nineties after an unusual half-pull off Old. A sweep off Miller took him to 99. Hughes faced Old. The first four balls were played carefully out on the off side, the next to mid-on, and the next to gully. Hughes then glanced a ball to leg to take him to 101 and end forty minutes spent in the nineties. A straight six off Miller followed, as if in celebration.

After Yallop's departure with Australia 49 runs ahead, Hughes kept on batting as partners came and went: Laughlin for five, Maclean fifteen, Yardley and Hogg sixteen, Hurst a duck. When Jim Higgs walked out to bat, Hughes finally went down swinging.

He was the last man out for 129 in 476 minutes in an intelligent innings where he allowed the circumstances to determine how he would bat. Hughes had batted for almost eight hours, collecting 52 singles off 411 balls. There was talk of a new maturity and ability to combine attack and defence, making not just impressions but runs.

Despite the positive signs of Australia's second innings, England knocked off the 176 runs needed for victory with seven wickets in hand.

Australia had lost and the ACB needed a scapegoat. Despite his second innings century, Yallop was soon the target of criticism of his leadership style and lack of tactical acumen.

For one so introverted as Yallop, it was never going to be an easy job. There were questions being asked, not just about the decision to bat on the first day, but also what appeared to be a lack of urgency in his leadership style. His own fielding was also disappointing so he moved from first slip.

The handling of leg-spinner Jim Higgs also raised some eyebrows. He didn't call on Higgs to bowl in England's first innings until the sixty-third over and had over-bowled medium-pacer Laughlin when most felt that spin would be more effective.

As Keith Miller put it, 'It took a dropped catch by Higgs to remind Yallop he was on the field.'

Second Test in Perth

Australia decided to bolster its batting for the Second Test in Perth by selecting opening batsman Rick Darling at the expense of all-rounder Trevor Laughlin. Gary Cosier was moved from opening bat and Peter Toohey moved down the order to number five. Kim Hughes was elevated to number three for his home-ground Test. Queensland medium-pacer Geoff Dymock came into the side in the place of leg-spinner, Jim Higgs. England brought in John Lever as the opening bowler replacing Chris Old.

The changes can be seen as a result of the domination of the bowlers the previous weekend in the first-class match between the MCC and Western Australia. Thirty wickets fell for only 300 runs in two days. The visitors had succumbed for 144 before bowling the home side out for 52 and 78, registering WA's first loss against any opposition in just under two years.

Although the Test strip prepared by curator Roy Abbott was not as green, Yallop took the centre square into consideration when he won the toss on a humid overcast day with rain forecast on the opening morning.

Australia's left arm medium pacer Geoff Dymock had wondered for over a year why he wasn't getting any calls from the national selectors. He had played Test cricket in the pre-Packer era. Although he was thirty-three, his form was good and he had taken wickets against England in the tour match. Dymock was at last brought into the side after being made Twelfth Man in the First Test at Brisbane. Cosier's one run in two innings in the unfamiliar opening spot had helped Darling's cause. Higgs was unlucky to miss out, especially at the WACA where fourth and fifth day's bounce had proved crucial in the past.

In the lead up to the second Test at Perth John Maclean was becoming frustrated at what he saw as an amateurish approach around the Australian side, not the playing group but rather the support staff – or lack of it. There was no set team manager (the State Association would fill the breach for the match), no medicos and an inexperienced captain. Having injured a hamstring in the days before the Test, Maclean had orders from a private physio to bind it in crepe tape. The message from the temporary manager was unsupportive: 'If you're not fit, you shouldn't be here.'

Before play, five RAAF men were sent into the murky skies with the idea of each carrying a coloured flare; green and gold for Australia, red, white and blue for England. One of the quintet carried the 150th anniversary medallion to be used for the toss. With a stiff easterly breeze hampering the skydivers' efforts, one of the parachutists landed half a mile away from the ground on the banks of the Swan River. Luckily the skydiver with the medallion landed within the WACA.

Yallop won the toss again and this time sent England in to bat. Hogg took the new ball and dismissed Gooch and Randall early. It was very slow entertainment for the crowd of 7,833, with only ten runs in the first hour. England was 3–41 when Dymock had the English captain caught behind for 17 (Brearley had taken 117 minutes). Enter 21-year-old David Gower.

Ducking into a Hogg bouncer caused some damage to the polystyrene protecting his ears, but didn't deter Gower from a well made Test hundred, leading his side to 3–190 at stumps.

Boycott finished the day on an undefeated 62. Dymock, in his last over of the first day, appealed for a caught behind off a Boycott inside edge. Not-out. This was the first in a number of mistakes made by umpire Tom Brooks, before creating some history of his own. Boycott was dismissed the next day for 77 runs that had consumed 454 minutes and 337 balls and contained no boundaries. It was the innings of a man struggling with personal issues (the death of his mother and loss of Yorkshire captaincy) a long way from home.

England made it to 309, helped by an increasing tardiness in the field. Peter McFarline described the Australians' efforts.

> *I have never seen an Australian side so slovenly in the field, so deaf or inconsiderate of its captain's instructions, so lacking in confidence.*

South Australian opener Rick Darling, who hadn't played a Test since his disappointing tour of the West Indies, was hoping to ride his luck. His promotion again brought him together with Australia's other jumpy and fleet-footed runner between the wickets, Graeme Wood. Their opening partnerships would soon resemble two anxious men rushing to the hospital for their medical results.

Darling was fiddly, a ball of energy who looked like he could explode at any minute. He was athletic in the field, pacing the cover region, ready for any opportunity that may present. At times Wood appeared ready to run for anything, like in a game of tip-and-run, like a fully-charged Eveready battery. *Drop and go* was often Wood's method; good when it worked, diabolical when it didn't. He was run out four times in his first 22 innings.

Wood was typically strutting around, tapping the bat steadily before receiving the ball, swaggering down the pitch like one of those cool kids at school. In Perth, he was dismissed early LBW, shuffling across the crease facing Lever. When he played the stroke, Wood almost fell over as if he'd trodden on his own toes.

In the first innings, Rick Darling was now faring better, with Toohey down the other end. But having avoided the threats presented by the new ball and capably making his way to 25, he charged down the wicket and ran himself out. Whenever Darling batted it seemed there was always impending doom just around the corner. The run-out happened in the last over before stumps to leave Australia at 4–60.

Meanwhile, Graham Yallop had a few problems of his own. He was already having trouble with Hogg, his main strike-bowler, and that lack of respect was seeping into the minds of other players.

On the first day the side's most senior Test player Cosier was asked to field at silly point to Boycott, with the instruction to sledge the England opener. Cosier refused, feeling uncomfortable bagging a player of Boycott's standing for no reason. Besides, as he explained to his captain, 'You don't sledge someone who is better than you.'

Cosier takes up the story.

> *Boycott gloved a few balls through leg gully and Hoggy came up to me at short point and yelled, 'I want another short leg.' I replied, 'Well tell him [Yallop] then' … 'I'm not telling that prick! You tell him I want another short leg!'*

Cosier was starting to worry that his poor form would see him out of the Australian side for good. Despite being vice-captain, his soft first-innings dismissal for four, caught in slips off Willis, was a very bad look.

I loved batting in Perth. It was just a crappy shot. I was hoping the selectors would take into consideration Woody's run-out in the first Test and let me get back to the MCG where I had made Test runs.

Before Cosier was given a chance to prove himself, there would be more controversy this time involving an umpire

An umpire's meltdown

The Second Test at Perth became known as the match in which umpire Tom Brooks lost the plot. He later admitted:

At one stage my mental and physical reactions weren't synchronising. I thought to myself, I'd rather be watching this match than standing in it. I felt it was time to retire.

By final day of the Test he had announced he was resigning. Brooks' struggles seemed even more unusual given that just a season before he was considered one of the world's best test cricket umpires.

Brooks made a good impression in 1977 as the first Australian invited to stand in England under an exchange scheme, He certainly knew how to handle a pressure situation. Brooks umpired the Sydney Test in 1971, when Ray Illingworth led England from the field after bottles and cans were thrown at fast bowler John Snow. Brooks and Lou Rowan told Illingworth that if he did not return, England would forfeit the Test. Illingworth led his men back and they won the Test and the Ashes.

Brooks also stood with Robin Bailhache throughout the six Tests of Ian Chappell's Ashes winning series in 1974–75 and officiated in the biggest match of all, the Centenary Test

Yet the frequency and obviousness of his errors during the 1978–79 Perth Test was hard to fathom. A sample of Brooks' errors reflects the performance of a man clearly out of his depth.

In the second innings, England's Boycott played and edged to Maclean and the Australians were certain they had their man. When Umpire Brooks called *'not out'*, Yallop threw his cap on the ground in disgust. Brooks had even apologised to Yallop after he gave Boycott not-out for the snicked catch. 'I'm afraid my error's cooked it for you,' he said.

A photo published in West Australian newspapers reveals the Australian's frustrations – a study of player emotions after the caught behind appeal against Boycott was turned down by Brooks. It looks almost staged: Boycott stands with hand on hip while the Australian fieldsmen are caught in various poses. Most noticeable is Cosier who is facing the camera, eyes skyward as if appealing to the gods. The bowler Bruce Yardley appears to have just completed a 360-degree pirouette. Like a policeman non-striker, Gooch stands at the other end, hands on hips and legs crossed. Brooks, realising his error, stands with his arms folded, looking as uncomfortable as a security guard who is no longer allowing patrons into a nightclub.

Half an hour later Gooch appeared to glove a ball to Maclean. Again *'not out'* was the call.

When Australia batted for the second time in the match, Peter Toohey found himself the victim of Brooks when he was given out caught behind off Hendrick for a duck.

> *It was frustrating as I didn't hit the ball … and after a really bad First Test. Although I didn't bat that well in the first innings, I made runs and was starting to feel more comfortable.*

Toohey felt doubly frustrated having some form in the first innings, scoring 81. Finally Gary Cosier looked like he was at last running in to some form when he rushed to 47 in the second innings before sweeping at England off-spinner Geoff Miller. Even though the ball hit Cosier in the chest, he was given out by Brooks LBW. When Wood was given out caught behind for 64 in the same innings, the fielding side looked as surprised as the batsman. These were not marginal errors – they were howling mistakes.

Years later the Australian players who felt the brunt of Brooks' decisions still feel a sense of frustration. 'Yeah, I was one of Brooks' victims,' laments Cosier in the manner of a man who realises that he had an opportunity taken away from him.

After the Test, Yallop as skipper, was ruing the misfortune his team was experiencing. The selectors however, had decided it was time to make some changes to the line up.

More changes to the Australian side

One bowing out of Test cricket, but not voluntarily, was Gary Cosier. The day after the Test match, Cosier fielded an early morning phone call from his mother in Melbourne: 'I'm sorry to tell you this but they've just announced the team for the next Test and you're not in it dear.' It could have been worse. A journalist, the usual communicator of such news, could have delivered it.

The axing marked the end of Cosier's Test career in which his batting average had dwindled to 28. When Cosier played his last Test he was just 25 years old.

Wicketkeeper Maclean may have felt frustrated before the Test but it was nothing compared to what followed afterwards, as all players sat at the Perth airport waiting to see if they had a flight out. The ongoing pilots' strike delayed the side's departure and Maclean loudly complained about venerated Alan McGilvray and ACB officials sitting in the first-class lounge while the players coped with the heat in the airport foyer.

> I carried on like a pork chop but the players were just in a herd not knowing what was happening and our allocated team manager did not help. It was a classic example as to why Packer happened: the Board just didn't look after its players. But when you play for Australia and get that sort of prominence in the public's eye you can get a bit ahead of yourself.

Maclean's anger was noted by the Board members who were present and had very long memories.

With two tests completed and Australia at 2–0 down, the Australian press was becoming more scathing by the day and the fans more disillusioned.

An Aussie win in Melbourne

The Australian selectors made two changes for the Third Test in Melbourne. Border came in for Cosier while Yardley made way for spinner Higgs to play at his home ground. England dropped left-arm quick bowler, Lever for off-spinner Emburey.

Brearley, while not disappointed by Border's inclusion, wrote that although Cosier was 'an ungainly batsman, his strength and unorthodoxy had earned our respect; we were not sorry when he was dropped.'

At least the Australians had a diligent fill-in manager. David Richards looked after them, providing a room at the hotel to gather as a team, engendering a more positive team spirit.

By the time the Australian side had checked into the Hilton in Melbourne, they weren't feeling as bad as a team 2–0 down suggested. Toohey felt they had let England off the hook in Perth. Maclean had similar views, blaming the umpiring more than anything.

> It could easily have been one-all as we headed to Melbourne and that would have put a whole different slant on the series.

The main frustration was with the some of the press who were starting to mock players' performances. The 'second rate' tag was becoming wearisome for players doing their best but outpointed by a stronger and more experienced line-up.

For Rick Darling, the Melbourne Test represented first hope and then another lost opportunity. Involvement in an increasing number of mix-ups running between the wickets was starting to have an effect. Peter McFarline described Wood and Darling's running between the wickets during the Third Test as so poor it resembled:

> ... an amalgamation of panic, despair and attempted suicide. Four times in the first hour either could have been run out by yards ... Darling seemed unable to control his legs, Wood unable to grasp the basics of running between the wickets.

It started well for Darling in his first Test at the MCG, a moment he'd longed for having watched a number of Tests and VFL grand finals on the family's small TV at their Riverland home. What would it be like to play in such a stadium on such a big occasion? Darling and Wood batted with poise but ran between the wickets in a way that made their teammates' hearts beat a lot faster.

With fleetness of foot to pace and spin, hooking and cutting with confidence, it had looked like this was going to be Darling's day. It was not to be. When the score reached 65, Wood drove firmly to Boycott at mid-on and started to run. Realising his mistake, Wood sent Darling back. Boycott's gentle lob to the bowler had Darling, at full charge, yards short of his ground, out for 33. It was for Darling, another in what was becoming a string of disasters. Darling recalls:

> *That was bloody disappointing to be run out in Melbourne. It was one of those days when I felt great and everything was going right. I just knew that I was going to get runs. Woody scored an even 100 that really kick-started his career.*

For Wood the Melbourne Test provided his first Test century at home and confirmation following his strong West Indian tour that he could excel at test level. Wood's century consumed 392 minutes and was the only half-century of the match. At the close of day one, the Australian innings sat at 4–234 with Wood undefeated on 100 and newcomer Border on 25. Border took thirty deliveries to score his first three runs. He finally gave a glimpse of what was to come when he pulled Miller over midwicket for a boundary.

Overall it had been a good day for Australia; out were the batting collapses and in was a sense of confidence that was previously lacking.

The Age newspaper exalted the effort with the headline 'Australia's tortured tyros tip the scales at last', a large action photo and a three-column commentary sharing the limelight with the Queen's New Year's Honours list.

Along with former motor racing champion John Brabham, opera star Joan Sutherland and singer and actress Olivia Newton-John, the *Weekend Australian* had a photographic sequence showing Darling avoiding a Willis bouncer across the top of its front page with the honours relegated to a less obvious position. A score of 400 was predicted. They collapsed to be all out for 258 and even though the total was less than expected, Australia's batting line up at last began to resemble players more at ease with the pressure of Ashes cricket. It was a different matter for one of England's batting greats who continued to struggle. Geoff Boycott was going through a time both personally and with the bat. He probably noticed the banner, *Watching Boycott bat is like going to a funeral* that was hung across the upper tier of one of the MCG stands. The owner would have been happy as Boycott again failed, out for one on the first innings as England stumbled to 143.

After a first ball duck on day one Kim Hughes top scored in Australia's second innings with 48 runs. Chasing 283 to win, Boycott lost his opening partner and captain Mike Brearley for a duck, before scoring 38 in just under three hours and 20 minutes.

England's crumbling innings ended on 179. Hogg took ten wickets and Australia won by 103 runs. It was England's first defeat in sixteen matches under Brearley's captaincy.

Even though Australia had won, the press questioned why Higgs bowled with just one slip to Botham and Miller, when it was clear that more pressure should have been applied with close-in fieldsmen. Yallop was still under fire. Ray Robinson noted:

> *The margin of Australia's probable win was shrinking while Yallop took 51 overs to bring the key bowlers to the ends where rough patches would aid them.*

Within seventeen balls of Higgs bowling from the north end, his leg-break and wrong 'un had Botham and Miller caught. With his 23rd ball from the southern end, Dymock ended the innings by trapping Gower LBW.

However, it seems that no matter what Yallop did, he appeared to have few friends in the press box. Yallop, more introverted than some of his predecessors, courted few favours with the press. More modern age man than part of Australia's hard drinking culture, some former players suspected him of being too self interested to make a good Australian captain.

Word had also spread as to how little Yallop's premier fast bowler Rodney Hogg respected him. While success in Melbourne brought a brief respite, the road ahead for Yallop was paved with obstacles.

Allan Border – cricket saviour

Allan Border had arrived on the scene almost without notice. He had failed to score fifty in six innings but then back-to-back first-class hundreds against West Australia and Victoria brought him to the notice of the selectors. The previous 24 months had been a time of great change for the gritty left-hander. Coming under the influence of former England player Barry Knight (then captain-coach of Mosman in Sydney), had made all the difference.

Border was fortunate to receive one of the club's scholarships to train at Knight's indoor cricket centre. There in the winter of 1975 for five weeks after work, Border caught the train across the Harbour Bridge and then a bus to the other end of Sydney where he was put through his paces and filmed. Knight worked on little things like a tendency to open the face when driving and keeping Border safer outside off-stump, but largely he was left to his natural style.

It was then that Border started to realise he could go a long way in this game. Border says he owes a lot to Knight.

> I was at that age of 16 to 19 when cricket was taking a back seat to my other interests. Barry reignited that interest. I was ebbing between A and B grade and Barry took me aside and talked me though some realities ... I went to his indoor centre and worked on a few technical things.

On his debut for New South Wales at 21, Border made 36. Captain David Colley predicted he would develop into one of the best batsman produced by the state. Border won the Australian Cricket Society award for

NSW's Young Player of the Year, enabling him to go to England. A note from Brian Taber to Frank Thistleton of Whitbread Breweries led to a season with the Gloucestershire seconds. The highest of his two centuries was 159 for Robins' Eleven against Cambridge University, which ranks as a first-class match. In height 174 centimetres, and weight 80 kilos, Border was compared with famous left-hand opening batsman Arthur Morris.

Then he was selected for the third Test in Melbourne – his Test debut. Border's first innings of 29 in 105 minutes was a resilient one, but was followed by a duck in the second, unluckily run out after some sharp work from Mike Hendrick at silly leg slip. It had been a pressure-packed experience, making Border feel he was probably propelled into Test cricket prematurely.

> I was very nervous; the good thing was that I had to field first before having to go out and bat so I was able to get a feel for the atmosphere of the Test match, the crowd and the expectations, as I'd never experienced anything quite like it.

However, for Border, that Melbourne Test was the beginning of a stellar career. Now considered one of the greats of the modern era, as a batsman and captain, he would go on to lead Australia through the turbulent 1980s building the foundation for Australia's return to the top of the Test cricket ladder.

The Melbourne win gave the Australians a window of hope. With three Tests down and three to come, and England ahead 2–1, the series was wide open for either team to win. If the Australians could just win in Sydney, the series would be on a knife-edge.

Trouble in Sydney

For the first time in three years, the Australian team was unchanged for the next Test. Despite the defeat, England went in unchanged too.

Australian wicket keeper John Maclean was having a strong series with the gloves having taken 15 catches by the end of the Melbourne Test. Like his teammates, he was keen to do well in Sydney to consolidate his place in the side and square the series. If they could win, then the critics might shut up. Maclean thought the press just loved twisting the knife when Australia lost. They didn't notice the things that went well, like when he snaffled edges off Brearley and then Edmonds in England's first innings at Brisbane. He was on cloud nine, the best catches he had ever taken. Not that the press noticed, they were too busy focusing in on Australia's seven-wicket loss.

Maclean was batting in the nets two days before the Fourth Test when things changed – for the worse. Batting in a helmet for the first time without a visor, he was struck in the eye by an Alan Hurst warm-up ball that sprung off a length, leaving him bloodied and bruised.

In Yallop's words:

> *All hell broke loose. I was watching the whole thing as I was bowling in the same net... Alan Hurst sent him down an ordinary half volley ... the ball exploded off the wicket and crashed into his left eye ... 'I'm gone, I'm gone!' he kept saying as Hurst helped him ... Macca had waited a long time to play for his country, and all he could think about was that this accident would keep him out of the Test.*

Maclean was hurt and needed help, not that there was much on hand. Bob Radford was the Sydney manager. He was an outstanding administrator who had a deep love of the game and its history, but player management wasn't necessarily his strong suit. Known for long lunches, Radford was once described by Sir Donald Bradman as the best cricket administrator in Australia – before lunch, he'd add jokingly.

Maclean had toured New Zealand with Radford in an Australian team in 1969 and observed the administrator pulling a bottle of vodka out of his suitcase as the flight departed at 10am.

'It's ok – it's 12 o'clock in Wellington,' was Radford's justification.

In Sydney for the Test, Maclean says Radford was nowhere to be found during the entire Test, nor was there a doctor present on the day he was injured.

Word of Maclean's injury soon reached Chairman of Selectors, Phil Ridings who called up the young Victorian wicketkeeper, Ian Maddocks as reserve in case Maclean failed a last-minute fitness test. Maclean was feeling the pressure and desperately wanted to play in the Test. To adopt Wally Grout's attitude of *'never give a sucker an even chance'*, he was determined to make the team ahead of Maddocks. He was passed fit, but was warned by Ridings only to play if he felt fully fit. He played, but it was a decision he later regretted.

Running around the Sydney Cricket Ground on the first morning of the match, Maclean felt woozy from the anti-inflammatories, diuretics and antibiotics he had taken. The 100°F temperature didn't help.

By the time England had slumped to 8–119 at tea, Maclean had caught Gower and kept well enough to keep England's collapsing top order on their toes. When Maclean returned to the dressing room, he couldn't undo his pads, and his whole body was cramping. He lost balance as he came out of the shower and was forced to lie down. Rick Darling felt spent, but thought that Australia's wicketkeeper was so affected by the extreme heat that he might die.

Even though Maclean soon returned to take back the gloves, the selectors, having seen Australian captain Yallop wicketkeeping (he had temporarily taken the place of a sick Maclean), were sharpening their knives. In the first innings, Australia had the better of the England side: Hurst's 5–28 had helped bowl them out for 152.

On the hill, a banner proclaiming the *Peter Toohey Stand* occupied prime position as the Doug Walters stand had done two years before. Only 20,824 people showed up, a disappointing total when compared with the 52,164 who had attended the corresponding day's play in 1974–75. The weather was hot but more importantly the competition from World Series Cricket was starting to take its toll.

Helped by Darling's 91 in 274 minutes with ten boundaries and Hughes' 48, Australia cobbled together 294. Kim Hughes, who charged at Willis and holed out to cover first ball after lunch, had again thrown his wicket away. After occupying more than three hours at the crease, this time Hughes was caught off a ball by England's off-spinner John Emburey. It was a reminder that despite Hughes' valiant century in the First Test, he was far from complete as a Test player. Frank Tyson diagnosed Hughes inappropriate stroke as some sort of mental seizure, calling him 'Impetuosity Hughes'.

When England began its second innings 142 runs in arrears, Hogg dismissed Boycott first ball. It was a loosener, catching Boycott on the back pad as he shuffled aimlessly across the crease; his only first-ball defeat in 136 Test innings. Randall on a pair made it to three before Dymock caught him plumb just before lunch. 'Not out' boomed umpire Bailhache. The Australians had gone from a mood of exhilaration and anything-is-possible attitude to disillusionment. Dymock takes up the story.

You could almost sense the air being sucked out of the Australian side.
I had Randall plumb LBW, padding the ball away. As we walked off
the field he came up to me and said, 'Sorry mate, that was plumb.'

England would have been virtually two for none. Dymock's next ball to Randall was driven for four and England went to lunch at 1–11. Dymock believes the English press coverage about the eight LBWs in the Melbourne Test off the bowling of Hogg and Hurst may have affected the umpire's decision.

Skipper Yallop was convinced Randall was out.

Honestly, I did not realise the umpire had made that extraordinary
decision until I was about twenty metres up the wicket ready to kiss
Dymock on the cheek, so convinced was I and the rest of the players
behind the stumps.

Maclean, well positioned behind the stumps, agrees, saying the not-out decision was crucial to the result of the series.

Randall went on to bat for ten hours in forty-degree heat. If we had
won that Test we were two-all. We could have won or at least drawn
the series and the team would have remained unchanged for the
Fifth Test.

Former New South Wales player, author and journalist Ray Robinson agreed but with a caveat.

Umpiring decisions are the shakiest ground for opinion, yet a reprieve, second ball, spared Derek Randall when he would have been willing to walk ... instead of going on to the largest and longest score of the rubber.

Randall scored 150 in 571 minutes, his hundred in 406 minutes remaining the slowest for either country in all Tests between Australia and England. Higgs added to his three first innings wickets with another five to give him match figures of 8 for 176.

Australia still had its chances and spilled them: six dropped catches in England's second innings, most off Jim Higgs. While commentary was critical of Yallop's ability as captain, especially when Higgs was bowling, the leg-spinner's main complaint was that Yallop wouldn't field at first slip often enough. Instead it was left to Kim Hughes, while Wood also missed chances at silly mid-off from Gooch.

Australia was rolled in the second innings for just 111 in the fiftieth over after losing its first wicket at 38 in 51 minutes.

Maclean ended his time at the crease in Australian colours, caught in close by Botham off Miller for a duck. Australia's overall batting performance didn't help Maclean's approach with the bat. Having batted aggressively in the first innings of the First Test, on the advice of his skipper, he forfeited his naturally aggressive style to play safe in this Test. It was an approach that had him stranded at the crease when it came to facing the spinners. Like all good keepers, Maclean generally played spinners well, but not in this series.

Uncertain as to whether he should be defending or attacking, he opted for the former – to his detriment. He was out to the gentle off-spin of Geoff Miller four times in eight innings. Maclean had taken eighteen catches in the first four matches, only two short of a record for an Australian in an Ashes series. Regardless, he was about to be dropped from the side.

Gary Cosier, who stood next to Maclean at first slip, thought his best years were behind him.

I noticed that season for Queensland that I was taking a number of catches on my left side from first slip, which you don't normally have to do when a keeper is at the top of his game.

The night after the Sydney Test, Maclean was out to tea at the Dolphin Hotel in Sydney with ABC broadcaster Jim Maxwell. 'Now do you think you should have played with your eye?' said Maxwell to Maclean rather too tartly. The words still sting, almost forty years later.

Maclean later discovered he had cracked his orbital bone, although no X-rays were taken. He also lost two teeth due to the pressure placed on the bone. It had been a cruel few days. He learned of his sacking during Queensland's next Shield match when some wag in the Outer yelled out, '*Hey, Maclean they've given you the arse!*'

In any event, Maclean's appointment as wicketkeeper seems to have been more a defensive move after the failure of Rixon. Maclean had been brought in to the side to add some experience in the leadership ranks. Now, he was out of the team.

While Victorian stumper Ian Maddocks, who was briefly called in as an emergency for Maclean in Sydney, may have thought he was the logical replacement, the man who was selected was 25-year-old Western Australian wicketkeeper, Kevin Wright.

By the summer of 1978–79, Wright's name was among those mentioned for possible selection for the First Ashes Test. He viewed himself a fifty-fifty chance but wouldn't have been too disappointed if the job had gone to a more senior keeper.

Red-haired, lean in build and agile behind the stumps, Wright looked more like a jockey than a cricketer. His father, also a wicketkeeper, introduced young Kevin to the gloves at a young age and the skill of taking the ball cleanly behind the stumps appeared as natural as walking.

The former Melville Senior High School student was soon recognised as a significant talent with the gloves, debuting in A-grade for Fremantle at fifteen under the guidance of former Shield and one Test player, Bob Meuleman.

Games with the WA state colts had Wright looking for higher honours. He'd left school to work in a Perth sports store, but after two years his father suggested that he work part-time on the family business accounts while he played, practised and watched as much cricket as he could. So began Wright's three years of life as a semi-professional cricketer, which proved crucial in Wright's progression toward the baggy green cap. Like most things Kevin Wright did, he immersed himself as much as he could in cricket and tried to learn as much as possible.

He first heard of his Test selection after a day keeping for WA against Victoria at the MCG in the middle of January. He'd just returned to the dressing room when Kim Hughes yelled out 'Hey Pops! You beaut, you've just been picked for Australia.'

Wright, who had become a father at the age of twenty, beamed with delight. His state captain John Inverarity was quick to ensure that Wright kept his feet on the ground, warding off press interviews to more senior figures. As Wright had a few beers at the team hotel with teammate Terry Alderman and ABC commentator Drew Morphett, he had high hopes for what Test cricket would be all about. Like many dreams, the reality proved different.

In some ways the Fourth Test at Sydney was both a blessing and a curse for Australian Test cricket. A curse, as Australia lost the sense of momentum it had built up in Melbourne and lost the match by 93 runs. England's win in Sydney gave them the Ashes. When Alan Hurst was bowled by Emburey on the fifth evening of the match, Brearley became only the second England captain after Sir Leonard Hutton to successfully defend the Ashes.

It was a blessing, as it marked the true arrival of Allan Border. On his home ground, Border had undefeated knocks of sixty and 45 as wickets tumbled around him.

There was also welcome news in the way Rick Darling applied himself in Australia's first innings in Sydney. He played like a man who had scored more than 33 and 5 from the Melbourne Test. Less jumpy from the start of his innings, he played with the confidence of a man who knew he had what it took to compete at Test level, scoring 91 before being caught by Ian Botham at leg slip. It would represent his peak moment in international cricket. Undefeated overnight on 35, Darling made his way to 91 the next day, but by the time he spooned Miller to Botham in close, Darling was spent. It was over 100 degrees Fahrenheit and players were taking drinks twice a session.

> *I thought this could be the chance for me to make a Test hundred but in the end I was buggered. We were all naturally fit but we didn't do much running. By then I thought I had proved I could make it at this level.*

One wonders whether the nerves Darling experienced had also drained him.

Australia's second innings collapse in which Darling managed only 15 echoed earlier batting performances and was as predictable as Geoff Boycott's derision of the crowds.

> *They are foul-mouthed and mindlessly repetitive; their brains were in their Eskys.*

By the time Australia had lost the Fourth Test, Peter Toohey was so out of form he believed that anyone from his hometown of Blayney could have dismissed him without difficulty.

In Sydney, Toohey had added to his meagre scores by another six runs in two innings. The success of the previous season against India seemed like a long time ago. He had lost confidence to the point where he would have happily have carried the drinks for the Fourth Test at Sydney even though it was his home ground:

> *I had no confidence in my technique. I'd been around in Test cricket for more than a year so maybe the bowlers were starting to work me out.*

When Toohey had played against India the previous season, he thought he would make runs every time he walked out to bat, but he struggled to get the same feeling against England. Toohey also believed the head injury he sustained from an Andy Roberts bouncer had an effect on his ability to counter pace bowling and probably contributed to his later failures against England. It gave him a sense of vulnerability he hadn't felt before and he struggled against fast bowlers after that.

By the end of the Fourth Test, any excitement about an Australian comeback had died. Again Yallop's handling of Higgs came under scrutiny. When England's batsmen began to rally in their second innings, Higgs again had no close-in fieldsman for support on turning and bouncing Sydney pitches where his wrong 'un could have enabled some bat-pad catches. As the series progressed, Yallop was seen as more a reactive than proactive captain.

The Fifth Test – fall from grace

Changes again were made to the Australian team. Dymock found himself replaced by Queensland teammate Philip Carlson. Yardley was brought back into the eleven to give Australia two spinners for the match. Mercifully, because of his woeful form, Toohey was dropped. England's side remained unchanged for the third Test in a row.

The first day's play in Adelaide's saw England batting first, dismissed for 169. Darling took the final catch of the innings, a skier off Willis who had swung his way to 24. Australia then went in to bat and by stumps, they had crumbled to 4–69.

Although the series had been decided, the first day was one of high drama. An enduring image that remains imprinted in the minds of Australian cricket fans is white-helmeted Rick Darling at the wicket clutching his chest as he collapses to the ground. He had been struck in the heart by a ball from Willis' long run, hair awry, arms flailing. Darling recalls it felt as though he'd been shot.

> When I was hit it took the wind out of me. It was as if everything was sucked in and collapsed. My chewing gum was sucked into the back of my throat so I couldn't breathe properly. It was quite scary at the time but didn't have any long-term effects.

He was saved by a precordial thump to his chest (a single blow of the fist to the middle of a person's sternum to interrupt a potentially life-threatening rhythm) by English cricketer, John Emburey, recently first-aid trained. Mick Mason, physiotherapist for the South Australia Cricket Association (ASAC) assisted by placing Darling on his side, pulling his tongue back and removing the chewing gum from his mouth. Darling was carried off the field on a stretcher, much to the concern of the Adelaide crowd. He resumed batting the next day only to be bounced and caught on the fence hooking.

The day's events were a far cry from twelve months earlier when Darling attracted great interest from the Adelaide Test crowd, opening his Test career with two half-centuries, playing on that occasion with childlike abandon and adult responsibility.

A lot had happened in the twelve months since. By the Fifth Test of the 1978–79 Ashes, although only 21, he'd experienced enough ups and downs to start thinking more about the game and what could go wrong.

> *I probably hooked too much, but I scored a lot of runs hooking and prided myself on the hook and the pull as they were my bread and butter.*

He was criticised heavily for falling to the hook when England had clearly set a trap for him. Although dropped for the next Test, Darling wasn't going to give hooking away.

It was at the Adelaide Test when long-requested help for the Australian skipper Graham Yallop finally arrive. Former Victorian and South Australian Shield cricketer Les Stillman was given the job as a liaison officer.

Yallop suddenly didn't have to organise practice sessions, book taxis to Government House for a reception, liaise with the press about whereabouts, oversee breakfast orders and ensure everybody was ready to leave for the ground on time. He could now focus solely on cricket. Even so, Test newcomer Kevin Wright was surprised at the lack of intensity at training when he first arrived in the Adelaide Oval nets.

*We were used to training much harder under Invers; the preparations
for a Test match I thought would be a notch above that of state level.
But that was just Yallop's way: he was more inclined to just sit back
and let things happen.*

When Australia, having won the toss decided to bowl, there was an audible groan from the Members' Stand. Adelaide's pitch was renowned for being a good one for batting. Yallop's decision again reflected a captain not confident in his own team's batting ability.

To say that Kevin Wright's first hour of Test cricket was a shock is an understatement. For years he dreamed of walking out onto a Test cricket ground with an Australian cap on and now all the sacrifices that he and his dad had made seemed worth it.

Wright couldn't believe his eyes. He'd just been getting used to his first moments in Test cricket and dealing with the pace of Rodney Hogg when it all exploded in front of him. England was 4–18 with Boycott, Brearley, Randall and Gooch in the pavilion. When Gower followed, it became 5–27 but then Botham with 74 and Miller 31 set about stabilising England. Seeing five wickets fall for just 27 runs was an amazing result for the struggling Australian team.

Phil Carlson gets his chance at last

Phil Carlson was one of those players who, given the right circumstances, could have been anything. An all round sportsman who found any games involving hand-eye coordination easy, Carlson had waited years for this chance to play Test cricket and he dearly hoped he would fulfill his potential at the elite level. Yet sitting in the dressing room after the first day's play in Adelaide, Test debutant Carlson was feeling pretty lousy, getting out from the fifth ball he faced. Ian Botham sat next to him, holding a long neck bottle of beer.

'You didn't get within a bull's roar of hitting that.'

'I know,' Carlson replied, 'but have a look in the paper tomorrow; it'll be in there.'

Carlson was given out caught behind by Max O'Connell after the ball had grazed his shoulder. It was not a good start for Carlson particularly as he had been twelfth man for the first two Tests at his home ground of Brisbane and then at Perth. 'Both places that had my type of wicket' he reminisced, After the Second Test carrying the drinks, he was dropped from the team for the third Test in Melbourne.

'What did I do, spill the drinks?' he asked selector Phil Ridings after a Shield game in Adelaide. Ridings was slightly taken aback, 'No, nothing at all,' he said.

Carlson thinks it probably wasn't one of his best moves to question the selectors. His attitude about the selectors didn't help to win him a place in the side.

> *Those blokes were high and mighty and didn't really have much to do with the players; they were too busy drinking wine in the VIP area.*

Carlson was yet another player who thought the Board was still not paying enough attention to the demands of the players, the ones who had to represent their country on the field and the ones who brought the crowds in to watch.

A tall and elegant batsman who could strike the ball hard, Carlson also bowled medium pace with an ability to break partnerships. That summer he'd scored a century and taken ten wickets against New South Wales, the first player to achieve this match double in Australia in the twentieth century.

The second innings of the Adelaide Test proved more productive for Carlson, who managed 21 and took two wickets.

A schoolboy prodigy, Carlson had been picked as a wicketkeeper for the Queensland state primary school side at eleven and captained the state to a national championship the next year. He was inspired by watching Garry Sobers hit Richie Benaud and his teammates around The Gabba on the first day of the tied Test in 1960–61 scoring a majestic 132, Having watched the first four days of the match, Carlson and his dad missed the final thrilling six hours when the match historically finished in a tie. He'd missed that last day because the family was travelling to their favourite family holiday destination on the Sunshine Coast.

Carlson went on to make his first-class debut at eighteen in 1969–70, where he had to face a rampant 'Froggy' Thomson on a Gabba green-top after he'd broken the arm of England's skipper and Test player, Tom Graveney. An undefeated 85 in his next match against New South Wales proved *the lad could play*. A maiden hundred against New South Wales the next season confirmed that he could indeed play.

Carlson became an all rounder partly by chance. Queensland captain Sam Trimble after facing Carlson in the nets with the new ball decided to elevate Carlson to all-rounder status. His status as all rounder saw him close to selection for Australia's tour of England in 1972 but Graeme Watson got the nod as the batting all-rounder. Even taking 6–32 against South Australia in January 1972, removing Causby, Rebbeck and the Chappell brothers in 21 deliveries, didn't convince the selectors. It was only after he had played 73 first-class matches over a decade that the call to Aussie colours finally came in the summer of 1978–79

Carlson would go on to Sydney for the Sixth Test with poor results. It was the last time he would play in a Test match. It was a disappointing end to career that had shown so much promise.

The Adelaide Test rolled on after Australia was dismissed for 164, with the home side coming back into the game during the first session of the holiday Monday. Carlson opened the bowling, beginning a spell that lasted more than ninety minute in severe Adelaide heat. Hogg was his bowling partner at the other end but not for long.

After only bowling four overs, without Yallop's approval, Hogg took himself off the ground because of 'stiffness of the inner thighs'. When Yallop saw him leaving and contested the matter, Hogg kept walking. When Yallop persisted that Hogg remain on the ground, Hogg told Yallop he thought it best for them to settle the matter out the back of the grandstand.

That Hogg should threaten the Australian captain is extraordinary. In more recent times, such defiance would have probably incurred at the very least a demotion from the Australian team. Hogg's attitude also reveals much about his arrogance and the prevailing attitudes at the time in disciplining recalcitrant players.

Drinks were taken with England 3–97 and a short time later Yallop left the field to see what was happening with Hogg. The argument continued in the dressing room, leaving Australia with nine players on the field and no captain.

While Kevin Wright found his first hour of Test cricket exhilarating, he couldn't believe the exchange between the skipper and premier fast bowler.

> I thought, this isn't the way Test cricket is supposed to be. Looking back though, this was all part of what was going on. The press were all over us, everyone was calling the side second rate, we were losing. There were a lot of external factors going on … the jump to Test cricket, keeping to blokes I hadn't kept to before, was hard enough without all of this going on.

The next day Bradman asked Hogg to apologise to Yallop.

> We can't condone this sort of behaviour and the way you've gone about what you've done. The captain of Australia is the most important person; he's the leader of his ship. You've got to show a lot more respect.

Hogg nonchalantly noted, 'So that's all I had to do, apologise to Graham.' Maybe this was the essence of the problem with Hogg that summer, that he wasn't really held responsible for his disruptive actions. Although Yallop says the selectors suggested sacking Hogg after he kept wanting to come off the field after short spells in the Second Test at Perth, he felt compelled to keep him in the side if they were to have a chance of winning the series. Hogg was after all, a great pace bowler. Yallop's simple response to the selectors' suggestion: 'If you sack Hogg who will you replace him with?'

And that was the bind that Yallop and the Australian selectors found themselves in. Teammates couldn't help but notice. Twelfth Man for the Adelaide Test Peter Toohey noted:

> *Graham was a good bloke but he couldn't handle Hoggy, who bowled when he wanted to. Graham just wasn't able to manage him.*

Despite his precision bowling, Hogg's antics must have affected team morale and the respect that players had for Yallop.

Later in his career, when Hogg tried to leave the field after bowling a four-over spell for Australia under Greg Chappell, he was told in no uncertain terms that if he did leave, he would never play for Australia again. Hogg stayed on the field. It was one thing for a player as respected as Greg Chappell to say this; it would have been another for the inexperienced Yallop.

After having England 6–132, England's wicketkeeper Bob Taylor led the recovery before being dismissed on 97. England's second innings total of 360 proved too much for the Australians, who were dismissed for 160.

The Test loss by 205 runs was another defeat for the Australians. The much hoped for on field success for the Establishment players was proving elusive. Hope for a victory in the Sixth and final Test in Sydney had all but faded.

Sydney again – the final humiliation

By now the one constant about the Australian selection policy was 'change'. By the end of the Fifth Test, Australia had played 17 Australians and more would be adding to the list for Sydney Test.

Given his atrocious form it was surprising that Toohey was brought back into the side for the Sixth and final Test and Allan Border relegated to Twelfth Man. New South Welshman Andrew Hilditch replaced Rick Darling who had fallen victim to the hook twice in Adelaide and was paying for it.

Hilditch's rise from club cricketer to Test player happened at warp speed. Having made his debut for NSW against Tasmania in 1976–77, he captained his state team the following season in only his third first-class game. At 21 years and 274 days, he was the youngest since Ian Craig to captain New South Wales.

Hilditch attended Sydney University and played cricket for Sutherland while studying law. A score of 93 for New South Wales against England in 1978–79 then brought him to the attention of the Australian cricket selectors. Orthodox and cautious in approach, Hilditch was more plodder than stroke player at this stage of his career. He was someone the selectors thought might take the shine off the new ball and blunt the effectiveness of England's new ball attack of Willis, Hendrick and Botham. However Hilditch failed twice, run out for three in the first innings and caught behind for one in the second.

When England scored 308 in response to Australia's meagre first innings of 198, any chance Australia might have had of securing a second victory in the series was gone. A second innings capitulation of 143 left the visitors with only 35 to chase, which they successfully did for the loss of only one wicket – Boycott for thirteen was a woeful end to his wretched series.

It was also wretched for the ACB. The attendance of 22,617 in this match remains Sydney's worst since 1888 (apart from one rain-ruined match in 1989) and it put paid to the idea of a six-Test series in Australia. Forty years earlier, 350,534 saw one Test match, nearly the attendance of the entire 1978–79 Ashes series.

Yallop's performance in Australia's first innings, scoring 121 out of the 198 runs scored, was by any standards extraordinary. It was the fifth highest individual contribution (61.11%) to a team total in Test history. To show how good this was, the next-best score was Kim Hughes' 16. Even the ever-critical Hogg had to concede the brilliance of Yallop, describing it as one of the best Test innings that he'd ever seen..

Despite his success and being named the Man of the Match award, Yallop couldn't help but feel bittersweet. He later wrote in *Lambs to the Slaughter*.

> *I couldn't raise a smile … because of all the work of the summer, wasn't all that bad from a personal point of view … against that so*

*much weighed heavily on my mind ... the Ashes are what the battle
is all about and we simply didn't show the grit and determination
in the Tests.*

The Ashes series: what was learned?

Yallop may have wondered how his team had been so comprehensively
defeated 5–1. Many had performed so well. Hogg took forty-one wickets,
Hurst twenty-five, Higgs nineteen; Yallop himself scored two centuries, Kim
Hughes one, Graeme Wood one and yet the side could not mount formidable
enough totals.

Of Hogg's forty-one wickets, twenty were either bowled or LBW, a much
higher percentage than Thomson in 1974–75 (ten out of 33) or Dennis Lillee
(five out of 25). Hogg also had thirteen batsmen caught behind the wicket.
By the summers end the man he had replaced in the South Australian team
the season before, Wayne Prior, had all but disappeared into the anonymity
of playing in the WSC country circuit with the Cavaliers, essentially a second
string side that played the major teams of Australia, West Indies and The World
in regional centres across the country.

Hogg had great support in the form of fellow paceman, Alan Hurst,
who took 25 wickets with pace and an ability to slide the ball off the pitch.
Hurst has fond memories of that summer.

> *Dismissing Boycott six times in the six Tests was a personal highlight
> of the series for me. Hoggy also took his wicket four times and Boycott
> really didn't have the great impact on the series it was expected he
> would. I guess 25 wickets would generally be considered pretty good
> in an Ashes series, but in this case my haul and Jimmy Higgs' nineteen
> paled into insignificance against Hogg's tally.*

Australia's batsmen against England were proven out of their depth in
their worst performance of the 20th century. Kim Hughes is a case in point.
After scoring a century in the second innings of the First Test, he failed to score

a half century for the remainder of the series and finished with a lowly average of 28. Allan Border headed the Australian averages but no one other than Graham Yallop (32) averaged more than 30. The series represented a period of lost opportunity for Australia's batsmen, although the selectors' scattergun approach to picking the team would hardly have inspired confidence or brought out the best in the players.

Allan Border, dropped for the final Test, was feeling uneasy. It had been a harsh introduction to Test cricket. Undefeated scores of 60 and 45 in a losing team in Sydney appeared to carry little weight with the selection panel. Border reflects on that time.

> *It was a tough time, the selectors were trying new players out and there was a little bit of looking over your shoulder to see who would cop the axe next, which was an unfortunate by-product of the battle between WSC and the Establishment. In the end I was fortunate; the selectors gave me a good run and there are lessons there for the current selection panel of the need to pick and stick.*

However, former English fast bowler Frank Tyson best summed up Australia's sixth Test humiliation.

> *Yallop's youngsters failed to anticipate, appreciate and combat the professional application of the England fieldsmen and bowlers. They also neglected to analyse and exploit the foibles of an England batting line-up, which by no stretch of the imagination could be described as outstanding. It was the old, old story of experience hammering home the final nail in the cricket coffin of callow youth.*

If the series were to be defined by the different abilities of the respective captains, Brearley for England, and Yallop for Australia, Test player Hurst makes some salient points.

> *Mike Brearley was certainly a major influence on the outcome, but not with the bat. As a captain and strategist, he was*

*exceptional. The Poms didn't panic or get flustered; they played
the game steadily and beat us hands-down in this department.
We didn't have respected leadership. Although Yallop did his best
and performed well with the bat, there were contentious decisions
in pressure situations and well-documented on-going conflict with
Rodney Hogg.*

To be fair, Yallop was like his most of his teammates, inexperienced in leadership and thrust into a role he was not really ready for or suited to. How much was his inability to effectively lead Australia related to the inexperience of his young and ever changing team?

Given Yallop's difficulty in dealing with chief complainant Rodney Hogg, it's worth noting that as general rule of thumb players who often complain the most about man-management are often those who are least prepared to follow.

Had Australia won more games, would Yallop's leadership style have been questioned to the extent it was? Losing has to be explained and it's much easier to blame one reason or cause. Leadership doesn't exist on its own; as we have since found in the modern game it is very much a collaborative process. Had Yallop a few more willing and experienced players behind him, the result may have been different. However, he must take some blame for lacking a proactive or experimental approach, but when it comes to trying to handle the likes of a Rodney Hogg, the question has to be asked, '*What exactly could he have done differently?*'

There was little doubt that Brearley's captaincy was first-class. John Meyer in *From the Outer* noted Brearley's acumen in the all-important Fourth Test:

*He conducted a long defensive campaign extending from the second
morning, right through to the earlier part of Australia's second innings.
At that point, when the home team was anxious to make a quick
start in their chase of the required runs, Brearley used Hendricks in
a containing spell of ten overs that yielded only seventeen runs and
also two valuable wickets. But as soon as the wickets began to fall,*

he immediately put extra pressure on the batsmen having the off-spinners Miller and Emburey together and crowding the bat with four or five close fieldsmen.

It's a testament to how a captain's call can influence the outcome. Mike Brearley believed that each of the Tests could have gone either way on the last day. Manager Doug Insole summed it up.

Fortune rather than lack of skill played an important part in Australia's defeat. We could easily have lost in Sydney and Adelaide and, had we done that, the Series would have been open until the last match. It was a great deal closer than the 5–1 result implied. Our feeling is that a much-maligned Australian side played against a very good English side.

In *The Great Escape*, David Frith's summary of the series in the *Australian Cricket Annual*, the author asks:

Was there that much between the two sides? The answer is more than likely yes, although an examination of the statistics provides some interesting reading. Australia's opening attack was at least as good as England's with Rodney Hogg and Alan Hurst taking 66 wickets as against 39 of Bob Willis and Mike Hendrick. But they lacked the strong support that the Englishmen had in Ian Botham, Geoff Miller, John Emburey and the barely-used Chris Old, John Lever and Phil Edmonds.

Would Australia have been better off with Inverarity as captain? Australia could have benefitted from John Inverarity's ability to read the game in 1978–79. Had he been captain, he would surely have been more proactive and willing to take risks. His mature temperament could also have provided assurance to younger players competing in the Ashes for the first time. Hogg might also not have had such a disruptive effect.

And so a summer of Ashes Test cricket was defined.

Australia had gone through four vice-captains during the previous two summers and was soon into its third Test captain, Kim Hughes, whose only previous captaincy experience was in ten games for North Perth.

The Australian Cricket Board had a lot to consider. Not only were Test match attendances down, they had received a report into the poor attendance rates of Sheffield Shield cricket as well. For the ACB, there was also the continuing situation with WSC. By the end of the series, the battleground of the bitter fight with WSC had extended as far as the High Court in London, with no end in sight.

Chapter Six

Pakistan, then the World, 1979

After the crushing defeat that was the Ashes tour in February, the Australian cricket team needed to regroup quickly for Pakistan's visit in March 1979.

The two-Test series was hastily arranged by the ACB in response to the deteriorating state of financial affairs and the growth of interest in Packer's brand of cricket. The first Test of the tour was held in Melbourne, and the second in Perth. Two first-class matches were included in the tour: one against New South Wales, the other against South Australia.

The Pakistan team for the tour was made up of – Majid Khan. Mohsin Khan, Zaheer Abbas, Javed Miandad, Mushtaq Mohammad (captain) Asif Iqbal (vice captain), Wasim Raja, Imran Khan, Sarfraz Narwaz, Wasim Bari, Sikander Bakht, Mudassar Nazar, Haroon Rasheed, Ashraf Ali, Talat Ali and Anwar Khan.

They arrived straight to Australia after a successful tour of New Zealand. It was perhaps a sign of the coming reconciliation between the ACB and WSC that all of Pakistan's World Series players were to play in the series, however Australian WSC players were not.

The World Cup, a 60 over championship involving eight countries to determine the best limited-overs side every four years, would follow later in June. The tournament had grown in stature due to the increasing success of one-day cricket around the world and the triumphant inaugural World Cup held in 1975. By the time of the 1979 World Cup, the cricket war was ending, and most countries – Australia excluded – chose to play their WSC players.

Australia's decision was as much about rewarding player loyalty and the Establishment demonstrating its control as it was about practical logistics (May 30 marked the official agreement between the ACB and Packer).

Although the broader cricket fan base was starting to view WSC players less as mercenaries and more as cricket professionals standing up for a fair deal, the prospect of an immediate return to Australian colours for the likes of the Chappells, Marsh and Lillee, would have grated on sections of the cricket loving public.

Battle for the cricket dollar

Before the May 30, 1979 peace agreement, the battle between the Establishment and WSC, despite some periods of cooperation, was still going strong.

After the hubris of the 1977–78 season, Australian cricket officials worried by the closing stages of the 1978-79 that they were now losing the cricket war. A meeting of Board delegates in Adelaide prior to the Fifth Test revealed the true extent of the problems Establishment cricket faced. Their marketing strategy for the season had collapsed and a report from Tom Worrell of Sportsplan Marketing added to the growing sense of pessimism. An assessment of the Sheffield Shield competition revealed that crowd figures for 1978–79 were the lowest they had ever been. The overall average gate was 1,458, far fewer than even Packer's country matches were attracting.

WSC cricket also encompassed a short spring tour of the New Zealand as well as a trip to the West Indies. The fifteen-day trip across the Tasman saw Australia play a World Eleven in one three-day and eight limited-overs matches. The WSC Australians later toured the West Indies, playing five Super Tests and ten one-dayers from February to April 1979.

But even before all of this Packer's shadow over cricket was growing. In the lead-up to the second season of WSC, Packer had signed more players and planned to field two more full teams from England and Pakistan. WSC's cost-cutting managing director Andrew Caro attracted increased support from sponsors and the public plus *that* song, 'C'mon Aussie C'mon', to this day a national anthem of sorts.

Day/night one-day cricket was growing in popularity. The agreement with the New South Wales Government to use the SCG with newly installed lights gave the Packer game greater credibility.

By the close of 1978–79 the writing was on the wall for the Establishment who were starting to look helpless to do much about the wave of support for World Series Cricket. Fans wanted to see the best players in action and were voting with their feet.

In Packer cricket 17 limited-overs matches around Australia ended with four finals taking place in Melbourne, where nearly 79,000 spectators watched as the West Indies won by three matches to one against the WSC Australians, collecting $35,000 in prize money.

The four Establishment one-day internationals attracted 43,448 fans as Australia defeated England 2–1.

Even in the traditional form of the game the test match, Packer was outstripping his opponent.

The final WSC Super Test between Australia and the World lured 40,000 over three days and the final official Test 22,000 over four days. WSC Super Tests and one-day fixtures attracted 585,240 people through the gates while the Establishment, with both England and Pakistan touring, pulled 551,007 for the same number of days of cricket. Nearly 700,000 had watched Packer cricket, a near trebling of those for the previous summer.

There was also on-field success as the Australian WSC side made the grand final against the Rest of the World, leaving Tony Greig to claim $61,000 first prize for the winning World side.

With the success of WSC, Packer was confident enough to announce, 'Unless there is reconciliation, WSC is here for years, and years and years.'

He then left the door open for compromise just a fraction with, 'but I don't want to appear anti-reconciliatory.'

He expressed his disappointment at the way the Ashes series had panned out, perhaps considered by the ACB to be the ultimate insult. As Packer is quoted as saying:

> *If they had performed better, it would have been better for us. There's a depression among cricket followers that has been very detrimental to us. I think it's been second-class cricket by comparison … but I'm disappointed as an Australian.*

The Pakistan Tour begins

The first match of the tour was a drawn (washed out) first-class match after just eight overs between Pakistan and New South Wales. Concerns that the SCG light towers, installed for the WSC matches, would cast a shadow over the pitch saw the match shifted to Canberra – the first time a NSW side had played an official match against a visiting touring side outside their own state.

Pakistan won a follow up one-day match against New South Wales by 12 runs. The match at least gave Andrew Hilditch (35) and Allan Border (53) a chance to have a look at Pakistan's bowling attack.

The Australian team selected for the First Test in Melbourne was Graham Yallop (captain) Kim Hughes (vice captain), Graeme Wood, Allan Border Davenell Whatmore, Peter Sleep, Kevin Wright, Wayne Clark, Rodney Hogg and Alan Hurst.

Despite the Ashes thrashing Yallop held his place as captain, although the selection of Hughes as his deputy was a hint that the selectors were considering a change to someone with a more proactive, although less experienced approach.

Five of the Australians selected for the First Test had played just seven Tests between them.

The effects of these changes on the confidence of the Australian players are worth considering. Given the calamitous result of the 1978–79 Ashes, summer players were given little chance to settle into the line up or given much support of they initially failed. The Australia side it seemed was in a state of constant flux. A player would be picked with the knowledge that he would be dropped after one or two failures making it very difficult for them to play with any sense of surety.

It's worth noting these constant changes made Yallop's job as the captain of an inexperienced Australian team even more difficult. The selection panel – consisting of Phil Ridings, Sam Loxton, and Neil Harvey – were undermining the players with their constant changes.

New to the side were South Australian leg-spinner Peter Sleep, Victorian middle-order batsman Davenell, Whatmore for debuts; medium-pacer Wayne Clark also returned from the wilderness after missing the entire Ashes series. Australia dropped Toohey, Carlson and Higgs from the side that lost the final Ashes Test at Sydney.

Newbies – Sleep and Whatmore

Nicknamed 'Sounda', (short for 'sound asleep') the Penola-born Peter Sleep was an aggressive middle-order batsman and wrist-spinner. Sleep was employed as a groundsman and would prepare the local club wicket. He rejoiced in the fact that he hadn't completed high school. A friendly man, Sleep would often chat with and help out youngsters who were struggling with their game.

Sleep first appeared for Kensington where he launched his debut for South Australia in 1976-77. He managed 3–73 in his debut for South Australia against Victoria at Adelaide Oval in February 1977. Sleep was able to bowl with a sense of calm amid an innings and 123 run defeat, with Victorian captain Richie Robinson's 185 marking his fourth century in successive Shield matches. Sleep followed up with a half-century and 2–71 in a tied match against Queensland. A disappointing wicketless drawn match against New South Wales rounded off Sleep's debut summer but it was his 8–133 against Victoria in Melbourne in 1978–89 set him up for Test selection.

Sleep had a windmill style of bowling, but was able to turn the ball sharply at times. He had a tendency to bowl too flat at times and would goad the batsman at every chance.

'I am gonna get you … I'm gonna get you,' he would state often with a toothy grin even if his previous delivery had been struck over the fence for six. His aggressive attitude at times more closely resembled a fast bowler's.

More than anyhting Sleep's lack of variation in flight and lack of a more deceptive wrong 'un probably went against his effectiveness. A hard worker in the nets, he was really just short of Test class as a top-order batsman or frontline bowler.

While 'Sounda' was an Aussie through-and-through in birthright and manner, Whatmore was an 'outsider', having come to the southern suburbs of Melbourne as an eight-year-old immigrant. Whatmore's English-speaking father moved his wife and three children from Sri Lanka in the mid–1960s when the government introduced Sinhalese as the first language at schools. Cricket was one of his few outlets in what was a difficult period of change.

Young Davenell found cricket a more than useful pathway to acceptance in Australian culture, not that it was always easy. His dark skin in 1960s' Victoria made him prey to racial abuse.

Victorian selector Sam Loxton first noticed his batting skills as a teenager when he first turned out for Prahran. Loxton's mentoring also led to Whatmore touring Apartheid-era South Africa with a Derek Robins side in 1976, as one of three promising young Australian players, along with Trevor Chappell and John Douglas. For someone of Whatmore's skin colour the experience was both shocking and exhilarating. What he saw made Whatmore appreciate his life in Australia, what he achieved made him realise he could play cricket at the highest level.

League cricket and County seconds in England added to Whatmore's game, leading to a first-class debut for Victoria against Western Australia in March 1976.

Whatmore was one of five players who made ducks when the home side declared at 7–44 against the green-top onslaught of Lillee and Malone.

His first match the next season was against a Queensland side containing Jeff Thomson; his 49 batting at number three gave him the assurance he was ready for first-class cricket.

At the end of the 1978-79 Shield season, Whatmore scored 108 in the first innings of Victoria's win against Western Australia, virtually a Shield final; his ambition of earning a baggy green cap was realised, making him Australia's first Sri Lankan-born Test player.

Before the First Test at Melbourne, Pakistan's WSC men Asif Iqbal, Majid Khan, Javed Miandad, Sarfraz Narwaz, Imran Khan and Haroon Rashid did little to hide their allegiance to Packer. In a warm-up match, a number of them practised in WSC shirts. Pakistan manager Ebu Ghazali was appalled and asked the players to at least cover their insignia, which they did.

Some positives were happening off-field for Australian cricket. Conciliatory moves were being made by ACB treasurer Ray Steele, who invited Packer for lunch at the VCA delegate's room. Steele may have made comment on his guest's Pakistan ties, but a polite lunch ensued.

Asif Iqbal ruffled a few Australian feathers by making derogatory remarks about the standard of the Australian cricket teams in that summer's Ashes series, providing a prelude – or perhaps a catalyst – for what was to come.

The First Test in Melbourne

On an uneven-looking MCG, Yallop won the toss and decided to bowl. Rodney Hogg continued his fine form taking 4–49 in Pakistan's first innings of 196. When Hogg bowled Miandad, the visitors were 5–83. A rescue by the skipper Mushtaq Mohammad (36), Imran Khan (33) and Sarfraz Narwaz (35) added respectability to the total.

With Australia now batting, Imran, fresh from rattling some Kiwi cages during a 1–0 series win, soon struck. Hilditch was dispatched from a lifter for three, Border bowled for twenty and Sleep caught behind for ten. Fellow newcomer Whatmore managed 43. Known for hitting the ball hard, Whatmore was unusually subdued, facing 147 balls in 206 minutes. Perhaps the pressure of playing for Australia for the first time took its toll on Whatmore. He was considered much better with the bat than he showed on this outing.

> *It wasn't me that innings, I went into my shell. I didn't play like I did when I batted for Victoria.*

By the end of the 1978-79 season, Whatmore had scored 750 first class runs at 39.47 with two centuries and a highest score of 113. Whatmore was clearly feeling comfortable at first class level but froze when it came to taking the next step, which players often say Is more to do with dealing with the extra pressure and publicity that comes with playing for Australia than any lack of ability.

Hogg discovered how hard the Pakistanis played when Javed ran him out as he wandered down the pitch doing some 'gardening'.

> *I blocked a shortish ball from Sarfraz. It was called a no-ball and I wandered down the wicket tapping at the turf doing my best Ian Chappell style ... Javed Miandad snuck around behind me and whipped the bails off and I was given out ... I started to walk and was about three paces away from stepping outside the ground when Mushtaq Mohammed approached me. 'We are sorry Rodney, we would like you to come back.' So I turned around and walked all the way back to the middle of the ground, but umpire Ray Harvey said, 'Look, we're sorry Rodney. They can't call you back. You're out.' So I lifted my bat, smashed all the stumps out of the ground and walked off.*

Hogg later acknowledged that he had acted like a schoolboy but also that he was never reprimanded by anyone about it. Graham Yallop responded that he was surprised Hogg had left one stump standing. Was this another case of where Hogg should have been pulled into line for his behaviour?

Majid showed his class with 108 from 157 balls. Then Border with a maiden Test century (105) and Hughes (84) appeared to be leading Australia to a challenging target of 382. The tide turned again when medium pacer Sarfraz took seven wickets for one run in a spell that included three runs through no balls, in 33 deliveries.

Grainy footage visible today on YouTube shows Sarfraz constantly shining the ball, ambling in to deliver medium-pace deliveries. It also shows Australia's exposed middle order and tail enders scrambling to lay bat on ball as the MCG wicket at times stayed so low some of the deliveries looked like they rolled into the stumps and pads of the batsmen.

Sarfraz finished with 9–86, the finest innings figures in any Test in Australia up to that time. Kevin Wright batted for forty minutes and remained not out on one, watching the final procession of Sleep, Clark, Hogg and Hurst all dismissed for ducks. Australia's 168 left them 28 runs shy of the visitor's first innings total – so near and yet so far – another loss to the Establishment players.

Border was the standout for Australia. His chanceless century consumed six and a quarter hours, contributing two out of every three runs scored while he was at the crease.

Peter Sleep left the MCG feeling he had much to learn at Test level, having made 10 and a duck and taken 1–62 off only eight overs. The match was Australia's eleventh defeat in fifteen Tests. Doing enough in a Test match to win was becoming a foreign concept.

A new skipper

The Second Test began nine days later on 24 March. Graeme Wood, out injured with wrist damage after colliding with opening partner Hilditch, made way for Darling to return. After taking one wicket in the match, Clark was dropped for Dymock, while Yardley replaced Sleep who had taken only two wickets in the First Test and struggled with the bat. The South Australian all rounder had failed to trouble extract enough spin from the MCG wicket to trouble Pakistan's top order batsman and done little with the bat in pressure situations.

Victorian middle-order batsman Jeff Moss was called in for injured skipper Yallop.

Yallop's season ended on crutches, his ankle injured in a grade match played between the two Test matches. It may seem odd now that the Australian captain would have the opportunity to play grade cricket, but this was a time before the one-day saturated summers that would see players appearing for their state less frequently, an absence that was even more pronounced at grade level.

Pictures of Yallop smiling while hobbling along on crutches showed a man at last freed from the shackles of leading a struggling and inexperienced Australian cricket side. The symbolism was hard to miss. Yallop had overseen six losses and one victory, giving him one of the poorest records of any international cricket captain.

After all he had been through that summer it must have been a relief to take a break. Kim Hughes took the reins for the Second Test in Perth. Yallop would never captain Australia again.

To say that at 25 years of age Hughes was an inexperienced leader would be an understatement. His leadership roles thus far included being head boy at primary school, student representative at Greylands Teachers College and captaining a handful of grade games. He later jokingly said, 'I got the job because I was someone with a heartbeat.'

Andrew Hilditch became Australia's fifth vice-captain of the past two summers in just his Third Test. A player of limited abilities, Hilditch was such a dedicated cricketer he was able to overcome his limitations to make it to Test level. Obsessive in his habits, he was not adverse to hard work and discipline. In many ways he was the perfect deputy, someone content to do the menial tasks without taking any of the glory.

Hughes brought in WA's state squad coordinator Daryl Foster to help, (similar to what Les Stillman had done to help Yallop in Adelaide). Foster immediately set to work, making practice more organised and purposeful.

The Australian team lacked senior players to lend assistance to newcomers and to players having a bit of a rough trot; and without that sort of guidance, a dressing room can be a lonely place when things aren't going well.

Foster admired the England model that had the experienced physiotherapist and physical trainer Bernard Thomas, as well as Ken Barrington, as Director of Cricket – although the job was more akin to a modern day coach. Barrington was the part coach, mentor, team manager and then some. Despite a stirring pep talk to his players, Hughes only lasted a few days in his new role before injuring himself stepping on a ball at practice. Hughes had been vice-captain since the Fifth Ashes Test at Adelaide so there is logic in his selection as Australian captain. But the decision looked like a reward for Hughes public displays of loyalty to the Establishment. Hughes' appointment as captain is an example of a lack of thought from the selectors. Australia was in need of wiser more mature heads in the side. John Inverarity who was coming off a strong domestic season could easily have been chosen, and was considered a more likely candidate to lead.

Jeff Moss – one Test wonder

For Jeff Moss, unlike Sleep and Whatmore, this would be his only Test. Tall with black curly hair, vaudeville moustache and upright stance, Moss played mainly off the back foot. His legacy of just one Test (an averaging 60) is to be one of those oddities in Test-cricket records.

Sent by his father to Lindsay Hassett's Elwood coaching school, Moss was invited by one of the coaches, former Bodyline-era batsman Leo O'Brien, to train with Melbourne at the age of eleven. At twelve, he was a record-breaker in the MCC's Dowling Shield team, impressing selectors in the Under-16s when just twelve.

The road to A-grade was paved with many obstacles, mainly the depth of talent at the prestigious club. Years in the fourths, thirds and seconds finally saw Moss make his senior grade debut at 21, and only then because Max Walker had a university exam. All these years playing against seniors toughened Moss' resolve and honed his technique. It took little time for him to consolidate his position.

Despite consistent performances at A-grade level, he was 29 years old when finally selected for Victoria in 1976–77, after 100 A-grade games. He made a duck, caught bat-pad off Thomson. His parents having made the trip to Brisbane especially arrived just in time to see their son walking from the ground.

Victoria was on a two-week tour having already played Kalgoorlie, Geraldton, Beaudesert and then Bundaberg, providing Moss a good break from his office-bound job with an insurance company. New South Wales was the second leg of his maiden trip, where he knew if he failed against an Andy Roberts-led attack, his state career would be brief.

All his life and cricket experience prepared him for this moment, in which he won the nickname of Stirling Moss by scoring 149 on the SCG, with powerful drives down the ground. Moss was Victoria's leading run-scorer in the Shield-winning seasons of 1978–79 and 1979–80.

Following a career-best 220 against South Australia in 1978–79, his Test cap arrived for the Second Test against Pakistan. He knew the press had been angling for his selection but didn't think it would ever come.

Journalist Rod Nicholson told Moss he was in the side six hours before he was officially told. After a laboured 22 in the first innings of the Second Test taking over two hours in the first innings, Moss relaxed and took more readily to Test cricket in his second chance at the crease.

Second Test at Perth: A new captain and a win

The Second Test couldn't have started more positively for Australia. Pakistan was soon one for nought, Majid Khan under a big white 'Greg Chappell-style' hat dismissed for the first of his two ducks in the match. Asif Iqbal was run out with the score at 5–90. Hurst and Dymock had troubled all but Javed (129) as Pakistan made it to 277.

When Australia batted, Hilditch achieved double figures, scoring 41 in an opening partnership of 96 with Darling, who relished his recall, hooking and cutting his way to 75. It was Darling at his vibrant best, full of confidence, calmer in approach, less prone to risky singles and more controlled in shot selection. Border fell fifteen runs short of consecutive centuries with a painstaking 85 in 347 minutes. Deep defensive fields and time wasting affected his progress to such an extent that the WACA members gave Border the slow handclap. Caught and bowled chances at 47 and 61 off Imran showed Border could hang in there, even when he was struggling to find the middle of the bat.

Australia had at last produced a first innings of over 300. By the time Hilditch led Australia onto the field for the third day, Australia was fifty runs ahead.

During Pakistan's second innings, in Iqbal's undefeated 134, he shepherded the strike so well that tail-ender Sikander faced only three balls in a last-wicket stand of 22 in 39 minutes. It was a reminder of his 152 not-out two summers earlier in Adelaide. Hurst disposed of Sikander by 'mankading' him following a tip-off from twelfth man, Trevor Laughlin.

Hurst had no regrets about the move. Each over, Sikander would lean on his bat for the first six deliveries with no intention of running, then on the seventh and eighth deliveries would head down the track looking for the quick single. He was moving well down the pitch before the ball was delivered. Hurst watched the non striker backing up on the seventh ball; Sikander was well down before the delivery. There was no run. Next ball Hurst stopped and took the bails off. Sikander was a good two metres down the pitch and just stood there, looking back at Hurst in disbelief.

Umpires Tony Crafter and Max O'Connell were also taken by surprise and consulted with Hilditch to check that the appeal stood. Hurst didn't see a need for a warning and saw Sikander's actions as blatant cheating. He cites the fact that a bowler will be penalised if he is no-balled by just a few centimetres, while in this case a batsman was gaining an advantage of more than a metre when running between the wickets.

Retaliation from Pakistan didn't take long during Australia's innings. Hilditch had made his way to 29 and in a gesture of goodwill picked up Darling's miss-hit drive and returned it to Sarfraz. Without touching the ball, Sarfraz began screaming. Pakistan successfully appealed for handling the ball. Darling, who was at the other end, recalls Umpire Crafter's bemused expression before realising he had to give the Australian opener out.

Hilditch waited for the Pakistani captain to intervene. He didn't. He was annoyed at missing out after making a start and wondered if his gesture had cost Australia the match. Iqbal thought the incident appalling.

I do not want to be associated with such incidents. There was no need for us to stoop so low as to appeal against Hilditch for handling the ball as a non-striker.

Darling made 79 before being run out in a mix-up with Border. In a search for quick runs, Yardley was elevated but only made one before caught short of the crease. Test debutant Jeff Moss, sensing it might be his only chance to play for Australia, handled the pressure of a final-day run chase like a veteran. Despite darkening skies, Moss lofted Imran over midwicket for six, helping ease the pressure. His 81-run partnership with Border was in a sense a glimpse at the future for Border. Three months after scoring his maiden first-class century on the same ground against Western Australia, Border was playing in his first winning Test.

Moss remembers the Test and what followed.

In the second innings we chased down a total with a storm on its way. I played my normal game for 38 not-out and hit the winning run.

New captain Kim Hughes was jubilant – one Test win as captain and a one hundred per cent result. When he took some beers and soft drinks into the Pakistan dressing rooms post-match in a bid to ease the tensions, he was met largely by cold stares and little conversation. Many members of the Pakistani team didn't drink alcohol for cultural reasons, and it's fair to say that not many would have appreciated Kim Hughes generally cocky demeanor from one so young and inexperienced. Even so, the behaviour appeared to be sending the Australians a clear message that the Pakistan players didn't have much time for their opposition.

Hurst noted the contrast of this tour with that of the English touring side. Against England, the players of both teams mixed after each day's play (with the exception of skipper Mike Brearley, who didn't socialise much with the opposition).

> Pakistan, apart from one or two players, was not at all interested in socialising and usually preferred to keep their own company. In fact, there was little spoken between the teams. They often left the ground quickly after play and as we stayed in different hotels we never saw them away from the ground.

Darling had provided Australia with some top-order stability, although run outs were still a problem. His latest run-out was his third in nine Tests.

Looking back, Darling is puzzled that senior players in the team did not support and help the younger, inexperienced players.

> No one sat me (or Woody) down to try and work out what was going on. It would have been good to have someone senior do this but we were just left to our own devices. I never said anything to my captains so I was never going to ask someone to help me sort it out.

Things were different in the 1970s. Were problems like Wood and Darling's running between the wickets sorted out, it would have made a huge improvement to the Australian top order and the careers of both players. Barely in their twenties and trying to cope with the challenges of a rapid advancement into Test ranks without much support, you can understand how problems such as theirs would arise and remain, without wise counsel.

By summer's end, the man Australia had picked as its number three the season before, David Ogilvie, retired from first-class cricket. His profile from the 1978–79 ABC book examined whether he should have been judged on his poor early form in Test cricket.

It would be unfair to form any judgments on his poor performances
in the West Indies, as disappointment at his original omission and
his rushed trip to join the team could have contributed to this failure.

Judged though he was. When Ogilvie was hit by a delivery from Bob Willis early in the 1978–79 season, critics believed that maybe his strength against pace wasn't quite as invincible as it appeared. Ogilvie, who called the blow 'a heavy one', believes the effect on his career was minimal, and remains baffled as to how he failed to duck.

I faced a thousand bouncers and was fairly comfortable against them
and then faced one from Willis and couldn't get out the way of it.
What was that all about?

Stranger still was that he wasn't wearing a helmet, despite selling them on behalf of C&D to the England players.

For Ogilvie the summer of 1978–79 represented a missed opportunity, making numerous starts but not converting. Ogilvie thought the selectors had stopped looking in his direction and lost some confidence and interest in the game. He no longer saw cricket as the path to making his way in the world.

The Pakistan Tour came to an end with a 1-all draw.

By now it was clear that cricket fans had swung in favour of Kerry Packer and the World Series Cricket competition. The Establishment side was struggling to win Test matches, and the Australian selectors had shown little faith in the players they selected – frequently dropping them after one or two failures. At the same time, WSC crowds and television ratings were out performing traditional cricket. The ACB's coffers were hemorrhaging, and while Packer was losing money, he continued to gain cheap television content for his Channel Nine stable.

The war is over

By the end of the summer, public and press attitudes to WSC had changed. Crowds at Super Tests now outstripped those of Test cricket. The ACB faced major challenges both on and off the field and a compromise seemed to be the only answer. WSC had an ageing player group, with almost half of its list over thirty. Players, although they may not have said so publicly, were hankering for some of the old tensions of Test cricket.

Ross Edwards puts it succinctly.

> *We would have had one great summer, the ACB would have had*
> *one disastrous summer and there would be nothing left for any of us.*

In May of 1979, ACB Chairman Bob Parish announced the formal agreement with Channel Nine. PBL Sports, a subsidiary of CPH's television holding company Publishing and Broadcasting Ltd (which held the WSC player contracts), was the ACB's new partner and would lease the Australian cricketers back to the Board. The war was over and Parish described the result.

> *I don't think either side has won. I think the game of cricket has won.*
> *It is peace with honour.*

In practice, PBL would receive exclusive promotional rights and WSC logos stayed as part of a tri-cornered World Series Cup - a new competition between two touring nations and Australia. The cricket Packer packaged was a version of his original concept, delivering at least 300 hours of cheap television involving Australia, England and the West Indies. It was a monumental win for the Australian businessman. Australian summers would never be the same. The one-day game, previously seen as a filler by Australian cricket officials, was to soon become a centre piece for the cricketing summer – as important, if not more so, than traditional cricket in terms of crowds and television ratings.

Meanwhile, there was of course a World Cup and a hastily arranged six-Test tour of India to play.

The World Cup

The World Cup was played in the immediate aftermath of the Packer revolution. Some saw it as a coming-together of the cricket brotherhood.

The Pakistan and West Indies Boards instantly welcomed back the Packer defectors – The English and Australian boards did not. Against weaker opposition, England had been coping well enough without the likes of Tony Greig, Dennis Amiss, Alan Knott, John Snow and Derek Underwood. The loss of the Chappells, Lillee and Marsh struck at the heart of Australian cricket. Even so, it would have seemed unfair not to select the Establishment players given the role they had played during the previous two summers; and there was the matter of selecting a team to tour India before domestic cricket in Australia resumed.

The Australian fourteen-man World Cup squad to England led by Kim Hughes and managed by David Richards was Border, Cosier, Dymock, Darling, Hilditch, Hogg, Hurst, Laughlin, Moss, Whatmore, Yallop, Wright and Graeme Porter.

Porter, who attended City Beach High School with Kim Hughes, was a tall, slim, steady medium pace bowler who could swing the ball either way. Known for his ability to bowl into the wind at the WACA and shoulder the bowling load, he had the wily ability to work batsmen out which was helped by serving as an apprentice under Dennis Lillee and Mick Malone.

Porter was quiet in demeanour yet a highly capable player who could also bat but would later inexplicably fade from favour.

All Cup matches were to be limited-overs contests, with an initial warm-up against Middlesex at Southgate rained off.

It would prove to be a disappointing tour of England for the Australians players and the twelve hundred supporters who had flown over for the tournament. Australia defeated New Zealand at Arundel, but lost to Kent by 73 runs before the fixture against Hampshire was rained off after an hour. Australia then lost its opening match at Lord's to England by six wickets in cold, drizzly weather, before a capacity World Cup crowd of 25,000.

With twelve of the English squad recent tourists to Australia, some in the dressing-room thought it was like the start of the Ashes tour again. The match had a similar feel.

Australia set a disappointing target of 9–159. Fourteen runs came in the first ten overs; all players were still learning the art of one-day cricket. Hilditch laboured over 136 minutes for 47 while Darling took 61 balls to score 25, amid several close calls risking the arm of David Gower. The cricketing world was beginning to appreciate the fielding abilities of Gower, who, with his blonde curly hair and angelic face was often underestimated as a fieldsman. He had a fleetness of foot, and an accurate throwing arm – running short singles to him at cover was like committing a cricketing form of suicide.

England lost early wickets then cruised to an easy victory as Gooch scored 53. Australian supporters at home had watched the match on the Ten Network because Kerry Packer said the BBC coverage was not up to standard. Australia's continuing failures were starting to wear thin with the Australian public, who were viewing the side as more second rate than ever with each performance.

Next stop Trent Bridge. As it had been in 1975, this match loomed as a crucial contest to see who would make it through to the semi-finals. The cold and damp weather was causing bronchial problems for Rodney Hogg, who missed the match.

Australia's 197 fell short of Pakistan's 286. Western Australian Graeme Porter opened the bowling in place of Hogg and captured 1–20 off 12 overs. Hilditch scored 72 and Moss completed his second and final appearance in international cricket by being run out for seven. It was better than Cosier's final batting appearance – he was caught and bowled by Majid Khan for a first-ball duck.

Australia defeated Canada at Edgbaston despite Hogg going for 26 off two overs, including four boundaries in a row by 39-year-old Glenroy Sealy in the first over of the match. Porter again did well (2–13 from 6 overs).

Australia's campaign had been a disaster, winning its only match against minnows Canada. Only Hilditch had scored a half-century and only Hurst had taken five wickets in an innings against Canada.

Hogg said that the Australians were the 'sacrificial lambs of the tournament, given virtually no hope from the outset' – a fair point given the tournament began in June, the three lead-up games were inadequate, as was preparation thanks to rain. Other teams were better prepared, with a number of the Pakistani, New Zealand and West Indians had already been in England, playing County cricket.

Jeff Moss has mixed memories of his World Cup campaign. Twelfth man at Lord's where he fielded most of his team's innings for an ailing Graham Yallop and run out for seven – that was the sum total of his contribution. He remembers his one World Cup match being played over two days because of rain; trying to sweep on one knee and the ball dribbling away; looking up and seeing Hilditch next to him. He could have stayed put, but ran to the other end, sacrificing his wicket. He never wore the green and gold colours again.

By the end of the championship, his teammate Dav Whatmore was wondering why he had been selected. He didn't play any matches for Australia, not even a warm-up game. He's not sure if his whites even needed a wash when he arrived home. The chance to play in England in front of his former league cricket mates evaporated without a trace. Whatmore thought his lack of opportunity eventually played in his favour.

> I thought, well at least I can't be dropped from the Australian team to tour India.

On that point he was correct.

By the end of July, Kim Hughes was seeking counsel from Ian Chappell about touring India. Border and Hilditch were at Barry Knight's nets promoting Dennis Lillee's new venture, the aluminum bat. Although he didn't say so to Lillee, Border thought, 'a tingling in the hands told me the willow people wouldn't be losing too much sleep.'

Border was about to make a name for himself with a wooden bat. Before the India tour at the start of 1979–80, Ray Robinson wrote under the headline *Allan Border: Shades of Genius:*

> As Allan enters he looks the sort of batsman bowlers find he is. He takes things as they come, without mannerisms that betray unsteady nerves.

Nothing had looked like getting him down. Border's dependability had added much needed consistency to Australia's batting.

Robinson didn't know the half of it.

Australia was soon to tour India. Cricketers from both the Establishment and WSC were now in a form of no man's land. No one knew where they stood within the context of the new cricketing format. Would Packer players be punished for their role in World Series Cricket? Would the Establishment players who had suffered such inconsistency at the hands of their own selectors be deemed good enough to play for Australia? Who would captain Australia given there were effectively two Australian captains – Kim Hughes and Greg Chappell? More to the point, now with all the players available who would be selected for their state teams and who would be able to lobby for selection?

The answers to all of these questions and more would soon arrive. The Establishment players selected for the tour of India knew that they would be out of the country playing for Australia when the 1979–80 Sheffield Shield season began. It was unknown as to how the selectors' would compare the form of the Establishment players to those playing domestic cricket in Australia. The Establishment players were feeling nervous, they would be out of view of the Australian selectors who would pick the side for the First Test at The Gabba against the West Indies on 1 December.

The Australian team was about to head off on gruelling tour of India where they would experience conditions, both on and off the field, that they had never seen before, against a full strength opposition. For some, it would be their making, for others, their last tour before they disappeared from the international scene forever.

Chapter Seven

Australia in India, 1979

This Test series was notable for a number of reasons, no less than it would be the last series by an Australian side that excluded players in the WSC. It was also the initial tour of India for 10 years and the first time the Indians beat Australia in a series.

Selectors Ray Lindwall, Sam Loxton and Phil Ridings picked a team of fifteen to tour India for the six Tests. The tour was quickly arranged; the ACB highly embarrassed that it had to call off India's planned visit to Australia in 1979–80 after the signing of the peace agreement between the Board and WSC. The schedule meant England the West Indies toured, thus beginning a revamped itinerary with a new key focus on the three national one-day competitions.

For the Indian tour, Kim Hughes was captain, and after only three Tests, Hilditch was his deputy. Eleven of the fourteen players who toured England for the World Cup held their places; all-rounders Gary Cosier and Laughlin, and batsman Moss were dropped. Spinners Higgs, Yardley and Sleep were all included, as was opener Wood.

Yallop, although relieved of any leadership duties, was one of the tour selectors and chosen as the backup keeper. Most responsibility for wicket keeping on this arduous visit would fall to Kevin Wright; neat and agile behind the stumps, he was also an orthodox middle-order batsman who could hold his own against pace and spin. Ten players had never toured before and not one of the team had been to India.

The ten-week trip was poorly timed. Never before had a Test series started so early – the second week of September, when the departing monsoon rains usually delivers a final sting. The timing of the tour also meant that the Australian players would miss the opening salvos of the Sheffield Shield season back home, where WSC players would have the chance to put their name front and centre in the eyes of selectors. The Australians in India were both physically and philosophically a world away from the gaze of the Australian selectors' and the public.

After the tour, the Australians would then face the challenge of readjusting to Australian conditions, two weeks into the domestic season, before home internationals started.

The first few days of the Indian tour were a learning curve; the Air India jumbo jet transporting the team lost power in an engine, resulting in an emergency landing and return to Singapore.

When the team arrived in Kashmir, the players were greeted by the unfamiliar sight of 14,000 troops deployed along the thirteen-kilometre route from the airport to the Broadway Hotel in central Srinagar. The troops were there by order of Prime Minister Indira Ghandi, as protection against the Jammu Kashmir Liberation Front (or Pakistan Liberation Organisation – PLO)

Higgs remembers being called with his teammates to Canberra before the tour.

It was explained to us that the PLO had threatened action if we played in Srinagar, saying it would be tantamount to agreeing to India's occupation of Kashmir. When we got to India it was pretty obvious to everyone that we'd be in more danger if we didn't go. We flew in on a 737 aircraft and later found out that the Australians were the sole occupants of the plane apart from journalists and security.

Senior security officers who had been assigned to protect Prime Minister Malcolm Fraser on his visit to India earlier in the year were attached to the touring party to Kashmir.

Concerns had been raised when the Australian High Commission in London received intelligence indicating the Australians would be in peril if they played in Kashmir. The information was passed to Canberra and for a while the tour hung in the balance. Minister for Foreign affairs Andrew Peacock advised the ACB against visiting Kashmir. The Board of Control for Cricket in India (BCCI), which had supported the ACB throughout the Packer period, felt betrayed and threatened to cancel the tour. Australia went back to the original schedule after tour manager Bob Merriman was briefed by the Australian High Commission to New Delhi.

Allan Border soon learned that the cool peaceful shadows of the Himalayas were a long way from home. One night he tried to enter his skipper's room via a narrow catwalk that ran between the balconies, rather than simply knocking on Hughes' door. He later wrote:

> I was halfway along the plank when … spotlight. Far from below the plank, Indian soldiers had fixed me with a searchlight and were bellowing commands like 'Halt' and 'Surrender' … I could see a marksman pointing something at me. It was probably an automatic rifle but it could have been a napalm thrower or a missile launcher … I managed to choke out 'Aussie cricketer, Aussie cricketer!'

The lead in to the First Test

An 8,000 strong police security blanket surrounded the North Zone Ground at Srinagar, the capital of Jammu and Kashmir State, where Australia was to play its first match. Despite the military presence, the Amar Singh ground was a beautiful sight, at the foot of a hill known as the Throne of Solomon, ringed by regal chinar trees planted by the Mughal Emperor early in the seventeenth century.

The match was played without incident. Victorians Hurst (5–33) and Yallop (83) supported captain Hughes, whose first outing on sub-continental soil yielded 70 runs.

Dymock enjoyed his first bowling outing in India marking a promising start for the wily thirty-three-year-old. The journeyman who was soon to come into his own as a Test player quickly gained a sense of the local umpiring customs.

> *I bowled a ball at this bloke who drove it to mid-off. The fielder was about to catch the ball when the umpire at my end called no-ball for over-stepping the mark. The batsman went on to score a hundred and was picked in the Test squad but didn't get a Test match. I thought that's interesting, maybe they wanted to give him a decent run before the series. But looking back, life might have been difficult for the umpire if he had given the batsman out. We later had heard that some umpires were reluctant to give some decisions through fear of reprisal, like having their house burned down.*

Dymock mentally prepared himself to be disappointed when he was bowling on the sub-continent. Not that he would experience many let downs. He began the tour well, taking 4–25 in the first innings of the drawn match against North Zone that saw the home side at 2–76 chasing 262 to win.

Darling, who had heard the tales of woe from former Australian players, was prepared.

> *I loved it. The culture of the place was an eye-opener, as third world as you could get and it was a hard place to play cricket, the heat and facilities were a nightmare. The wickets were hard as all hell, so were the balls and some of the umpiring was laughable. I liked all the grounds but Kanpur was a shit of a place.*

No wonder. A dead dog had lain stiff and untouched in the outfield for days, covered in flies and slowly eaten away by birds.

While the first-class match in Srinagar had been a draw, rain spoiled the second match against South Zone in Hyderabad. Border showed a glimpse of what was to come with a brilliant 113 with fourteen boundaries including a six. Hogg made his first appearance taking 3–27 as Higgs and Sleep grabbed three wickets each. Darling proved injury-prone again with a fielding mishap on the first day. Six stitches above the left eye hindered his vision, ruling him out of the First Test. Hogg was also fortunate not to be hurt after being pelted with stones on the final day's play of the drawn match.

The Australians would discover that things had not changed much since earlier tours. Stories of surviving a tour of India were passed on by Australian players from the 1950s and 1960s, when conditions were primitive. Horror tales of Gavin Stevens almost dying of hepatitis and others picking up exotic diseases filled the players with a sense of dread.

In some parts of the country the current players thought they had returned to the Middle Ages. Bathrooms in the hotel at Nagpur consisting of a concrete slab on the floor for a toilet and open showers. The rooms had no blankets and one ceiling fan in each. *'The Board has spared no expense again!'* was an ironic comment often heard as the Australians left their hotel.

Local water and salads were to be avoided; tinned fruit sent was at times the only reliable solid. Imported Swan Lager (detained for a period by customs, much to the players' dismay) was the best drinkable liquid.

Hughes followed former keeper Barry Jarman's view of tackling India: 'Eat and drink everything you see, including the local beer.' Hughes, like Jarman, was the only player in his squad who, by the end, remained healthy throughout.

Despite some highlights on the tour, it was an administrative debacle as well as an playing disappointment in terms of match results.

There were several cricket-related problems. Graham Yallop managed to break five bats from the all-cork-no-wool style of balls. LBW decisions ran against the Australians at a ratio of 23–8. Their catching didn't help, with 22 missed chances in six Tests (with the odd one possibly related to to mirrors flashing in eyes) and the stinking heat was so bad at some grounds, there was a need to wear cologne-laced necklaces.

Forty-year-old Team Manager Bob Merriman also had to be patient with the BCCI as it initially failed to provide a letter of remittance. Jim Higgs' photograph of a slogan seen on a piece of graffiti, *To lose patience is to lose the battle,* became the team's rallying cry.

An added frustration was that after four weeks, Australian journalists were telling players that it was all over for them; thanks to the reconciliation back home their Test careers were over. They implied the tour was really just a smokescreen to get them out of the country to help the returning WSC players settle into their Shield sides.

While struggling to complete an arduous Test series, the players inevitably had one eye on the first-class cricket season at home and how to retain their positions in their respective state teams. There was legitimate concern that their performances in India might not count for much. There was a feeling in the squad that no one back in Australia really noticed what they were doing. It was after all the peak period for Australian Rules football and Rugby league finals. Any mention of cricket was likely to be about a new summer of international cricket with everyone available. It was also an era when Australian tours to India attracted minimal media attention. There was no *Fox Sports* to beam cricket from the sub-continent into the living rooms of cricket fans.

Andrew Hilditch said he would have enjoyed the tour had he not felt locked away from what was happening in Australia. Trying to impress selectors rather than team unity was uppermost in the minds of the players. As *Pelham Cricket Year* put it:

> *The Australians played like young men under the sentence of death.*
> *This in cricket terms is exactly what they were.*

The circumstances in which the Australian side toured India were unique. For the first time, players were uncertain as to how much their performances would be noticed by the Australian selectors. Also, never before had such an inexperienced Australian side toured the sub-continent, led by a captain and senior players with such limited experience. The tour schedule was hectic, containing six Tests and numerous provincial matches all to be played within the ten weeks. It was a tour that would have tested the most resilient and experienced Test cricketers – let alone the younger, newer players.

It was under these circumstances that the players went into the six-Test series.

The Test Series: a test too far

The Australian side for the First Test at Madras was made up of Hilditch, Wood, Border, Hughes, Yallop, Whatmore, Wright, Dymock, Hogg, Hurst and Higgs. Left-arm orthodox spinner Dillip Doshi debuted for India replacing Bishan Bedi who had played his final Test at the Oval. Thirty-one-year-old Doshi had been waiting in the wings for three years for Bedi to retire. The Indian side included Gavaskar, Chauhan, Kirmani, Viswanath, Vengsakar, Yashpal Sharma, Yajurvindra Singh, Kapil Dev, and Venkataraghavan.

Australia began the Test series confident that it could take on India at home, mounting an impressive total of 390. Border dropped on nought, turning Kapil Dev to short leg Yajurvindra Singh – went on to create a stand of 222 with Hughes. The partnership fell just short of Bradman and Barnes' record stand against India at Adelaide in 1947. Border spent twenty minutes on 99 before bringing up a maiden Test century abroad on his first attempt. His 162 ended when a Yallop straight drive ricocheted onto the stumps off bowler Doshi's hand.

Their innings were important stepping-stones for Hughes and Border who were now establishing their credentials as Test players. It also showed a growing maturity; Hughes, as he had done in Brisbane, partnered defence with aggression. To have done so as skipper was another indication that maybe he had what it took to lead his country. Border and Hughes put pressure on the fielding side by rotating the strike. The left-hand, right-hand combination made it hard for the bowlers to bowl a consistent line.

India responded with 425. Bad light and heavy rain ended the drawn match two hours early, with Australia 177 runs ahead.

Higgs, who with 7–143 returned the best figures of his 22–Test career, remembers:

> *I took seven wickets without turning a ball; it was so hot that*
> *the quicks bowled in two-over spells where the main aim was to*

not let the sweat drip down onto the ball. It was hard going. We
often lost the toss and had to bowl first on very flat pitches and I
didn't get much of a chance to bowl on the wickets when they were
breaking up.

The Bangalore Test was also drawn, the southwest monsoon wiping out more than seven hours of play.

Darling came in to open the batting with Hilditch, and all-rounder Yardley brought in to replace Whatmore and Dymock. For India, Yadav came in for Singh.

Australia's 333 was more than matched by India thanks to a 159-run stand by Vengsakar and Viswanath who both scored centuries.

Hogg was bowling too many no-balls; four in one over and promptly kicking middle stump out of the ground. It raises the question as to what was wrong with Hogg; whether he was consistently no-balling on purpose in protest at the wickets being so lifeless.

The Third Test was held at Green Park in Kanpur, where heat, humidity and basic facilities made the venue an even bigger challenge for the Australians. Dymock was back for the injured Hurst and Whatmore took the place of an ailing Wood. India's team remained unchanged.

The Test was a career high for Geoff Dymock, who made the most of the grassy, unexpectedly fast pitch, transformed from its normally flat and lifeless surface. His twelve wickets made him the first Australian and third bowler ever to dismiss all eleven batsmen in a Test match (along with Jim Laker, Srinivas Venkataraghvan, Abdul Qadir, Waqar Younis and Muttiah Muralithran).

India at tea on the first day was sitting comfortably at one for 204. Dymock, playing in his 87th first-class match, had taken one for 87. Given this is cricket's unlucky number, he thought the omens weren't good. He had toiled in hot humid conditions in Brisbane, but he felt spent. He recalls:

Kevin Wright saw the state I was in and how much the heat was
affecting me and he ran up to me and said, 'Your bowling today has
been the gutsiest I've seen on a cricket field.' I've never forgotten the

words and they inspired me to just keep doing my best. The secret to doing well in India was working hard and not giving up.

Just after lunch the next day, India was all out for 271; Dymock had taken 5–99 from 35 overs. Seven more followed in the second innings, including Sharma caught behind for a pair. Australia needed 279 in 312 minutes but fell short, collapsing against the pace of Kapil Dev and off-spin of Yadav – Australia lost by 153 runs.

Hughes continued his fine form with 126 against West Zone in Ahmedabad for another drawn match. Everything Hughes touched seemed to turn to gold, taking the new role in his stride, dealing with the challenges of an arduous tour with a smile always on his face while publically saying all the right things. Team manager Bob Merriman had rarely seen a more impressive captain.

Peter Sleep for Yardley was the only Australian change for the Fourth Test at Feroz Kolta in Delhi. India dropped Venkat for leg-spinner Narasimha Rao.

Dymock (4–135) again led Australia's bowling in another drawn Test. Higgs (3–150) was the only other bowler to have much of an effect on India's 510, marking the second time in the series that they had compiled their highest total against Australia. It wasn't without controversy. Dymock says he saw Sunil Gavaskar (115) clearly run out by several metres at the bowler's end when still in single figures.

The first chink in captain Hughes' armour was starting to show. Australia lost to East Zone after veteran Ramesh Saxena steered his side to a four-wicket victory in Cuttack. Hughes displeased locals when he bowled his batsmen rather than bowlers, to end the match early.

India was unchanged for the Fifth Test at the famous Eden Gardens ground at Calcutta. The visitors, facing enormous parochial crowds of up to 80,000, experienced their finest hour mounting an impressive 442 in the first innings. Hughes (92) took part in his second double-century partnership of the series, this time with Yallop (167 off 392 balls over fifteen fours) who opened for the first time. It was to be Australia's highest individual score in India until 1986–87.

The Australians had dismissed the home side for 347 and by close of play on the fourth day, India had reduced Australia to five for 81. Hughes scored a quick-fire 64 including a dramatic straight six off Shivlal Yadav, and then declared, setting India 247 to win in 65 overs.

Once Gavaskar, Vengsakar and Viswanath had fallen to reduce India from a comfortable none for 52 to 3–70, any thoughts of chasing the total disappeared. Yashpal Sharma guided India to safety with an aggressive 85.

Had the series finished there on five Tests, the Australians would have gone home with honours even. They would have lost 0–1, saved a Test where they had followed on, and gallantly forced the issue in another.

The final Test proved one too many for the Australians.

Kevin Wright remembers everyone in the side being out on their feet, exhausted by the constant illness, travel, and playing in the humid conditions. Yardley, who had been so sick with a stomach bug he needed a nurse to administer a drip to him overnight, was replaced by Sleep.

For India, after just two wickets in two Tests, Rao made way for Mohinder Armanath.

Australia lost the Sixth Test at Mumbai's Wankhede Stadium by an innings and one hundred runs after capitulating for 160 and 198 in response to India's first-innings score of 458. A second-innings 80 by Hughes and 61 from Border in a defiant partnership of 132 mirrored their achievement in the First Test.

Gavaskar scored his 22nd Test hundred, putting on 192 in 147 minutes with his opening partner Chetan Chauhan for the first wicket, a record for India–Australia Tests. Wicketkeeper Kirmani with an undefeated 101 became the third nightwatchman to score a century at Test level.

So hard up was Australia for wickets it used seven bowlers including Yallop and Whatmore. Doshi took eight wickets for the match, giving him 27 wickets at 23.33 for the series.

The final outcome, Australia had lost the six-Test series 2–0.

Rick Darling ended his Test career retired hurt in the second innings, carried off the field on a stretcher. He'd been struck a blow on the right temple by a Kapil Dev bouncer and been lucky not to have been more seriously injured. Had he been struck a few centimetres lower, he could have died. Darling spent several days in the care of doctors and nurses tending to yet another head wound. It was a hell of a way to end a tour.

This was a tough tour by any standards, let alone one undertaken by a young and inexperienced side. Kevin Wright, who later lived in India for three years and worked closely with its people for the past fifteen years, has tried to put the tour out of his mind.

Wright was the only keeper in the squad, playing all six Tests and five four-day games. He remembers a diet of boiled eggs and being wary of the food at the grounds for fear of getting ill. When the players had break for drinks, they would be served from a bucket that was as hot as the temperature inside the ground. Step outside the hotel and you'd have to be accompanied by security. Such was the political situation. Most players chose to stay within the confines of four walls.

Wright believes that the team was never really appreciated by the Australian Cricket Board for its efforts, and that the players, because of the circumstances, performed under unprecedented pressure.

> When your livelihood depends on you playing to the best of your ability, the Australian team environment wasn't the best place to be. Kim Hughes was a terrific captain but the whole time I played Test cricket it felt like there was an axe hanging over my head … we were all learning our trade and if we made a mistake it was amplified. It was a massive learning curve for all of us.

When Wright arrived home, he found he had gone from being the Australian Test wicketkeeper to an unemployed district cricketer in 24 hours. There was no communication from cricket officials about his future. As a father of two young children, he secured the only job he could – as a car salesman.

Graeme Wood, after a miserable tour with just 138 runs at 13.80, was also about to experience the dramatic fall, as he went from playing in front of massive crowds as an Australian cricketer to playing local district cricket. Once one of the more prominent Establishment players, he was starting to feel like an outsider. He had been dropped from the side for the 1979 World Cup, with speculation that his delay in signing his ACB contract before the Ashes series may have had something to do with it.

Geoff Dymock, who finished the series with 24 wickets, was the surprise find for Australia. It was as though he was tailor-made for the challenges of the sub-continent. Hailing from the Queensland country town of Maryborough, Dymock revelled in any chances cricket provided. He was also no stranger to the disappointment of being overlooked as a junior cricketer. It was only when State squad member and left-arm bowler member Rob Pascoe visited Maryborough State High School to run a special coaching clinic that 15-year-old Dymock considered becoming a bowler.

Asked by Sandgate Redcliff keeper Ian Emerson to have a run at the club, Dymock got to meet former Australian opening batsmen and captain Bill Brown. He began the next season in A-grade and stayed for two years. After graduating from Teacher's College in Brisbane, he found himself first based in his hometown, and then later in the Aboriginal community of Cherbourg. Dymock played in the country leagues representing Queensland Country against the MCC before joining his mate, rugby player Col Reynolds for a trip to England.

A chance conversation with a fellow passenger made him aware that the fitness trainer on board the boat was a relative of former Victorian batsman John Grant, then a pro at a club in Lancashire. Calls were made and by the afternoon of Dymock and Reynold's arrival, they had a club line up to play for.

At Central Lancashire club of Milnrow, Dymock first met former NSW player and club pro Ken Grieves, who was to become a great influence on Dymock's life. Grieves provided gems of advice that Dymock has himself passed on numerous times throughout his career. *Bowl at the stumps, they miss we hit,* was an example

Dymock's return home was timely. Two years later while playing at Pascoe's North's club in Brisbane he was selected to play for Queensland against the Rest of the World. His three wickets for the match included Indian opener Farook

Engineer and Pakistan's Zaheer Abbas. When Bill Albury withdrew because of a fear of flying, Dymock was on the plane to Sydney for the next match.

Five wickets against New South Wales cemented his place in the Queensland side. He was a winner on all fronts, getting married after the match. More cricketing commitments meant a three-day honeymoon had to suffice. Two years on the Australian selectors called. But he faced a worrying question just before he found out about his Australian selection.

On the second last day of the Shield game against South Australia, Dymock was interviewed by Eric Beecher from *Cricketer* magazine and asked about the rumours that he 'threw' rather than bowled. 'Lou Rowan, former Queensland and Test umpire, reckons you chuck,' Beecher told Dymock.

That afternoon, the Test side for the Adelaide match was announced. Dymock was in. Fretting that the allegations that he threw the ball would reach a wider audience, Dymock rang South Australian Test umpire Col Egar who confirmed that Rowan was the source and that Egar had received numerous letters from Queenslanders about Dymock throwing. Egar provided the reassurance Dymock needed, telling him that he had checked his action from all angles and there was nothing wrong with it.

Dymock believes that it was the flick he gave the ball with his wrist and finger when he bowled leg-cutters that gave some the impression he threw. The magazine article never appeared and nothing more came of it. A relieved Dymock made his Test debut a few days later and toured New Zealand at the end of the Australian summer, although he believes that Ian Chappell didn't rate him – hence no WSC offer.

By the end of the tour Davenell Whatmore was feeling frustrated. He'd failed to convert starts early in the series. He scored 76 in the Fourth Test at Delhi and followed it up with 54 in the second innings. The good form didn't last long He scored ten runs in his next four innings revealing the doubts that sometimes consumed and brought a disappointing closure to his Test career.

Looking back, I had more ability than many Australian batsmen around then, but I never had the mental strength. I had self-doubt and I needed a coach to sit down with me to tell me I was good enough. Sadly we didn't have them in those days.

This notion of a lack of support throughout the Packer period was voiced by a number of players. But the ACB was merely doing what it always had done – that is not giving much thought to the welfare of the players There was little consideration of the effects that such a crowded schedule would have on the young Australian side, who were forced to criss-cross around India playing matches in an illogical geographical sequence.

The lack of senior players was problematic on this tour. There was no Bobby Simpson with years of experience to pass on and the touring side was a long way from traditional home supports. This really should have been recognised by the Board.

Yet their predecessors had similar experiences. By the time a player reaches Test level he is close to complete *as a cricketer*. The Australians of 1977–79 would have been exposed to the usual club and state coaches and mentors, in other words the traditional support services. Those who reached Test level had adjusted to the standard of first-class cricket well enough to be selected to play for Australia. But Test cricket is never easy; it must have been worse when most of your senior players are competing in an alternative competition.

Would a coach have made a difference? This was not an era of coaches at national level; all players had to do the best they could without them.

Some players maintain that a coach isn't needed. While Ian Chappell is the most staunch critic, even Allan Border says the amount of coaching staff around the side now is excessive, a situation which as captain he would have found intrusive.

Border believes the tour to India provided a perfect learning environment and launching pad for his career.

It was a hard tour in so many ways. It was a great learning experience and we learnt how to play on turning wickets. It was just a good education all round as it was a totally different lifestyle to what you would experience in Australia. We all had difficulties with getting crook and not having supplies of bottled water (no such thing in those days). We had to boil our own urns each morning to kill off the bugs in the water, not that many of us drank the water; we were too busy consuming this Indian lemon drink called Lemco which wasn't very helpful for us when it came to rehydrating.

Despite scoring a big century and three half-centuries, Border had his own issues on tour, as Bob Merriman noted.

By the time we got to Kanpur he'd gotten a couple of failures and complained about where he was. And it was difficult to get him out of bed. I even talked to Kim about sending him home … we had him in for a talk and he pulled his socks up right away and became an excellent tourist.

A captain shows promise

After all the false starts as a batsman, Kim Hughes appeared to have matured into the type of player that Australian cricket so badly needed. His captaincy was also well respected. He received high praise from the Australian team manager Bob Merriman.

At all times Kim showed proper diplomacy with officials and in my view, with the press … neither the Indian manager nor Gavaskar would talk with any member of the media.

Fellow teammate, Higgs liked Hughes' innovations.

He was very different from Graham Yallop, he'd try new things like put Yardley in as a night watchman, so he didn't hang around too long on the next day slowing play up. No amount of captaincy would have made any difference to our fortunes on that tour. We had good individual batting efforts led by Hughes but we hardly ever put it all together.

Hughes by nature was a risk-taker and tried to make things happen on the field. Also perhaps because he was leading a side away from the pressure of home with limited news coverage, he was able to take better charge of the side and grow into a style of leadership without too much scrutiny.

One of the Ashes bowling heroes had at last been put in his place by the captain, the other already home due to injury a month early.

Rod Hogg's 41 Test wickets against the touring England side may have given him the impression he was untouchable, but by the time he had kicked down a stump, squabbled with umpires and been no-balled 42 times in two Tests, his sense of invincibility was starting to evaporate.

I left India with only a handful of wickets, but still quite proud of what I achieved. I bowled well in extremely hot conditions but my body wasn't ready for it and my back collapsed. Along the way we stayed at a string of three-star dumps, especially in Bangalore and Jaipur. It wasn't like one of today's tours where an Australian team only goes for a short time, only visits major cities and stays at five-star international hotels.

Hughes said the tour was a disappointment for Hogg who had suffered the second-year blues. Hogg bowled better in the final three Tests, where he only took four wickets but toiled hard. Hogg's persistence was a sign that he respected Hughes more as a captain than he had Yallop.

Hogg was grateful for Hughes' hands-on approach. 'It was a nightmare tour. Kim had faith and I'm thankful for that. Kim led from the front. Most captains would have been hopeless under those conditions.'

Homeward bound to uncertainty

After just two Tests, Alan Hurst's back gave way and he was later sent home. Hurst finally took the advice of his orthopaedic surgeon who since 1974 had advised him for the sake of his back to give the game away or risk permanent disability. Hurst had managed the injury throughout his career until he broke down in India where he was hospitalised and placed in traction for two weeks.

A young tearaway from New South Wales, Geoff Lawson, was called up.

The Sydney Morning Herald carried the headline '*Is it RSVP or RIP?*' The story began:

> When is the invitation you have waited for all your life, not the invitation you need? When it's an invite to be a fast bowler in India.

After a series of vaccinations (including for yellow fever), Lawson found he couldn't lift either arm or sit down and had a temperature of 102 degrees. It was a similar reaction to Ian Callen's, although Lawson didn't have to play his debut Test the next day. In India, Lawson played no Test cricket but was made to feel a part of the touring party. He was only there for a few weeks but the sight of a countless number of people living in houses constructed from soggy cardboard and plastic bags stayed with him.

It was a strange time indeed when Australian players wearing the baggy green were wondering when their next Shield game might be. Or that the captain of the side who had had his best series ever might not even make the team. This is where the Board should have been more communicative to let players know they were aware of their efforts in India, although the Board had a few of its own problems in dealing with the demands of PBL executives in the lead up to the new summer of cricket.

When eleven experts writing in the magazine, *Cricketer* named their preferred 1979–80 sides, not one included Kim Hughes as a batsman. Interestingly, nine chose Graham Yallop, eight picked Rick Darling as a preferred opener and two picked Kevin Wright over Rod Marsh.

Hughes, on whether he believed that Greg Chappell was better credentialed for the job, answered, 'Yeah, I think basically for this particular season, he's the only player above being dropped.'

Did Hughes expect that he would become Australia's next captain? 'Oh yes, naturally, I'm the vice-captain. But it all gets back to form.'

This comment reveals that Hughes had confidence in himself, not only as a batsman but also as a captain. The logical choice as vice captain of the Australian side, Rod Marsh, was Western Australia's captain and a far more experienced players, however for a variety of reasons, including his documented outspoken nature, he missed out.

Those dropped catches

To have dropped 22 catches in India, roughly three or four per Test, was really to surrender the fight.

Dropped catches don't make the record books but they represent significant moments in a match. If a player is dropped early in an innings and goes onto a big score, the tenor of the game can change dramatically. A batsman who might otherwise have been walking back to the rooms with a duck or low score next to his name instead returns with a score that turns around his series.

Likewise, for a bowler to have catches dropped off his bowling can drastically affect the figures he records and ultimately his confidence.

Baggy Green and the second eleven accusations

So what is the value of the Australian cap to these men who represented their country when many senior players were absent? Do they consider themselves to have been a second eleven? The overwhelming consensus is 'no'.

Rick Darling takes great pride in his caps. He has a hat-rack of all caps from his playing days. At the top is his prized possession, the baggy green.

But he gets the impression there are some cricket fans that don't value the Establishment players.

> Some blokes say that because we played for Australia during WSC,
> it wasn't really like playing for Australia. We didn't play with the
> big boys.

It's a sentiment that's given him angst over the years, and it is easy to understand why Darling feels this way. In defense, he is quick to point out how many of the Establishment players went on to play significant roles in cricket either as players, coaches or administrators. Allan Border, Bruce Yardley , Rodney Hogg, Kim Hughes and Graeme Wood all went on to have substantial careers. Davenell Whatmore went on to coach several International sides, Yardley coached Sri Lanka, Wayne Clark coached Western Australia and Yorskshire, Wood was also the CEO of the Western Australian Cricket Assocation for four years.

Graham Yallop sees the baggy green as iconic and always has. His remaining cap is framed and displayed on one of the walls of his home. It's a symbol of pride despite the turbulent period in which he wore it.

David Ogilvie thinks very little about the Australian caps he earned. His caps are all on loan to schools he has attended or taught at. The culture and history of cricket was something he never really appreciated. He admits now it was probably to his detriment – but Ogilvie is always one to live in the here and now. While players have always taken pride in earning and wearing an Australian cap, the talismanic association attached to it has evolved in the last twenty years. Mark Taylor, when he was Australian captain in 1994, decided that each member of the Australian team should wear the cap in the first fielding session of a Test match. There is now a ceremony on the morning of a Test in which debutantes are presented with their baggy green by a former Test player. Gone is the tradition of being given the baggy green on every tour; now the players are just given one to last their career.

Gary Cosier was one who had plenty of caps to share around, which he did. He first received his baggy green at the Melbourne Hilton from VCA secretary David Richards.

> It was a matter of 'here's your package, now buzz off'. There was no ceremony associated with it at all.

Cosier wasn't one to wear caps, although he did when he scored his century on debut against the West Indies. He's given away most of his baggy greens; the few he has left are kept in a drawer with some old Australian jumpers that he checks occasionally to make sure they aren't moth-eaten.

I gave one to a bloke who I stayed with in Rockhampton. I ran into
him a few months later and he told me that his house burned down
a few months later and with it the cap. It saved me from asking for
it back.

Kevin Wright still has his two baggy green caps that will be passed on to his daughters. He will forever be grateful for the chance to play for Australia, but the association can bring out mixed emotions.

I'd be with a group of people and someone would say, 'Do you know
Kevin was an Australian Test wicketkeeper?' They'll then ask your
surname, they'll say 'Aaaah' not really recognising it. Then they'll ask
what era you played in and you'll get the response: 'You played for the
other Australian team.'

Wright has grown to value his baggy green more as time has passed.

Some of the Establishment players valued the cap more than others. At the 1979 World Cup (where baggy greens were awarded even for one-day championships), Rodney Hogg remembers swapping his for a police officer's lapel identification number, baton and handcuffs.

No such flippancy from Tony Mann, who had a great sense of what the cap meant. He was thirty-two by the time he played for Australia. His baggy green means the world to him, a reminder that the years of toil practising helped him earn the highest honour for an Australian cricketer.

Oddly enough, one could argue that Kerry Packer was responsible for making his players more aware of the importance of the Australian cap. When it was mentioned that WSC players should have their own baggy green caps, he was quick to point out '*No, you have to earn those son.*' Packer's 'Australian' Super Test and one-day teams always wore the wattle yellow and not the traditional green and gold of Australia. Packer believed that the baggy green was for Test cricket only.

For a number of Australian players in the 1960s and seventies, the cap was seen more for its practical purpose. On tour in England in 1968 and

1972 John Inverarity felt out of place wearing his cap, such was the anti-establishment sentiment at the time.

Australian cricketers had worn the baggy green playing one-day cricket before the reconciliation. They never again did in the new format. There was always a one-day outfit of canary yellow for cap and uniform, very different to the whites and the Australian cap of the Test arena.

Chapter Eight

Reconciliation

The war ended at noon on 30 May 1979 when Bob Parish made a public statement on behalf of the Australian Cricket Board. It began:

> *I am pleased to announce that the agreement between the Australian Cricket Board and PBL Sports (Public and Broadcasting Limited, henceforth known as PBL Marketing) has been signed and will be lodged with the Trade Practices Commissioner.*

The Board had granted PBL Sports the exclusive rights for ten years to promote cricket organised by the Board and to arrange television coverage and associated merchandising. World Series Cricket would cease promoting cricket matches in Australia and elsewhere but its logo would continue to be worn by Australian players in One-Day International matches. For the first three years, PBL Sports were allowed to arrange a contract with the Channel Nine Network.

The new era of Test series combined with an ODI program had begun.

It was a new cricketing world in all manner of ways. After twenty years, the ABC-TV had lost its Test broadcasting rights to Channel Nine. In December 1979, the ABC won a Federal Court case gaining television rights for areas of Australia not covered by Channel Nine; but at the cost of paying Channel Nine $600,000 per year, indexed annually.

Chris Harte in *A History of Australian Cricket* wrote that while a total of $265,000 prize money was to be provided for that first season, the overall deal gave the Board $1,150,000 annually for ten years, non-indexed, but by 1986 inflation had diminished this figure to such a small percentage of cricket income that the Board's plea for a revised figure was accepted by PBL.

In the early days of 'the peace', Parish flew around the world explaining the deal, especially to other countries' cricket boards. As he did so, PBL executives started their takeover and players were suddenly handed new contracts that told them for whom they could and could not do promotional work.

When it came to arranging the touring sides for the first season, PBL executives were adamant that the Board must confirm that the visit by India had been put on hold, so that England and the West Indies could play three Tests each plus an ODI series.

PBL wanted the Frank Worrell Trophy to be part of the West Indies deal, but Lord's refused to do the same with the Ashes.

The relationship between Australia and England fundamentally changed.

When England and the West Indies toured Australia in 1979–80, the TCCB (Test and County Cricket Board) wanted $600,000 for England, a daily rate 49 percent higher than in 1978–79, on grounds of demands for more money from players. PBL replied in their letter of instruction to Parish writing that $500,000 was sufficient. The less well-off West Indies Board accepted a small improvement in the guarantee, being offered $485,000.

The TCCB was fuming at the high-handed approach from a group they had worked with just two years earlier in the High Court. The Board were told that coloured clothing was to be worn for one-dayers; gross gate receipts and the supply of auditors was PBL's responsibility; the rules for ODIs would be rewritten; white balls would be used in these matches and the individual awards would be under the titles of *Classic Catches, Strike Rates, Player of the Match, Player of the Series* and *International Cricketer of the Year*. England rejected the use of coloured clothes.

Concessions for the elderly, unemployed and social security cardholders were to be introduced; the Board had resisted the idea for years. There were also to be black sightscreens for white ball matches, revised hours of televising all types of cricket and on-ground entertainment. PBL would produce the official programmes and tour brochures and have the final say on boundary advertising; the public address system would announce the new batsmen and bowlers; an electronic drinks buggy would be used at intervals.

The only thing more surprising than the PBL's dictatorial attitude toward the Board was the way Australian Cricket administrators showed little real resistance to the demands, illustrating how weak the Board's bargaining hand was by the time of the reconciliation.

The schism had cost the Australian Cricket Board $810,000 in lost income. In relative terms to its money flows of the past, it had been financially hemorrhaging. The extent of Packer's wealth on the other hand was demonstrated when the man was presented with a bat signed by all WSC players to thank him for turning the game professional. Packer would often stroke the bat, calling it 'my six-million dollar bat' – although the financial returns would have more than compensated.

The players were better off financially but were strongly bound to their employer. From then on, any Australian cricketer had to sign a contract with the Board plus a commercial agreement with PBL Marketing. In the early 1980s it was not an uncommon sight to see professional cricketers involved in numerous and varied in-store promotions. In trying to exert its authority over the game, PBL Marketing crammed a busy schedule into 1979–80. As well as the six Test matches involving the West Indies and England, there were fourteen ODIs, a revamped domestic McDonald's Cup limited-overs challenge, and the traditional Sheffield Shield.

The Establishment Men and some of the WSC-signed players faced an uncertain future.

Twelve of the sixteen Australian tourists to India did not feature in the Tests that summer, and five never did again. The Board faced a new reality of players demanding more. A nascent Australian Cricket Players' Association was born, but only briefly. Players were much more aware of their rights and the tension between players and the Board would only grow.

The 1979–80 season was also a difficult time for the selectors. For the First Test they were Australian captain Kim Hughes, Phil Ridings, Sam Loxton, Ray Lindwall and Alan Davidson. Whatever side they selected, there would be accusations of favouritism toward the WSC or the Establishment.

At the start of the season, New South Wales coach Peter Philpott posed the rhetorical question in the *ABC Cricket Book*:

> *Could anything go wrong in such a year? Unfortunately a great deal.*
> *For it is also a delicate season, a season when players, officials and*
> *supporters of the once World Series Cricket and the still Establishment*
> *group must learn to come back together and live and prosper.*

He went on to explain the ongoing tensions between some in the Establishment who believed the Packer period was an assault on all that cricket stood for, while there was still a distrust from the ex-WSC players suspicious of administrators who, they believed, had exploited players for many years.

It could be the most meaningful season of cricket Australia, or indeed the world had experienced. Alternatively, if the wounds did not heal there could be a permanent division within the game, as clear-cut as that which divided rugby league and rugby union early in the century.

One potential point of division was the money that the WSC players would continue to receive was substantially more than the Establishment players. For example, Clive Lloyd, Viv Richards and nine of their WSC mates were paid twice for their efforts in Australia; contract fees as well as the split-up of bonus monies. Ian and Greg Chappell, Dennis Lillee and Rod Marsh were all to reap at least $35,000. Englishman Derek Underwood was the highest-paid member of the team, collecting a $25,000 WSC fee while settling for a reduced tour payment. Nonetheless, he finished around $8,000 ahead of his teammates. Underwood was the only WSC player in the touring party and the low numbers of Establishment players who would represent Australia and the West Indies made player payment less of an issue than it could have been.

As if noting this critical junction in the game, the ABC released a sound cassette special of what they called *4 Great Tests*. Advertised on the back of the

ABC Cricket Book as a cricket flashback, the tapes featured stories about the Tied Test and 1960–61 tour by the West Indies; the final Test at Leeds in 1948 and the 1977 Centenary Test. It was as if they were promoting the dual series concept while simultaneously reassuring the public that everything was back to normal again.

Australia needed a strong side to take on the West Indies at The Gabba but there was also pressure to include some Establishment players, for their loyalty over the previous two seasons. Greg Chappell was named captain of the side that included only four Establishment players, Hughes, Border, Thomson and Hogg, in a team, which drew with the West Indies in Brisbane.

There could be no argument about the inclusion of Greg Chappell, Marsh, Lillee and Thomson. McCosker and Laird were undoubtedly fine players but their figures from the Super Tests were no guarantee of selection. Yallop, a former Test captain and proven Test batsman missed out for Hookes, who really was still coming to grips with his game at international level. Bright came in for Higgs, which was strange given their early-season form; in the Shield games before the first Test Bright had taken just 2 wickets in two games and Higgs 12–99 in his only game against WA at the MCG. Laird justified his selection, batting for more than ten hours for scores of 92 and 75, while Hookes proved he was up to the challenge with 43 and 37 in the drawn encounter. Bright bowled 25 overs, capturing one wicket for 36.

Then in Perth, Australia, with five former Establishment players (Hughes, Border, Toohey, Dymock and Thomson) achieved a 138-run win against England (and Lillee displayed an aluminum bat, delaying play and creating a memorable fuss).

A subsequent loss to the West Indies by ten wickets at the MCG involved six Establishment players, Hughes, Border, Dymock, Toohey, Hogg and Higgs. A six-wicket win over England followed at Sydney, with Hughes, Border, Dymock and Higgs on board. Then in Adelaide the home side lost by 408 runs in the final West Indies Test with only three Establishment players (Hughes, Border, Dymock) in the team. The topsy-turvy season ended with Australia defeating England by eight wickets at the MCG with the same trio.

For Australia, it had been a Test summer of mixed success. The win over England was encouraging but the results against the West Indies merely a sign of what was to come. It was the West Indies' first success in six tours to Australia and a welcome change for nine of the party who had been part of the 5–1 loss in 1975–76.

Dymock remembers the season of 1979–80 as one of tension around the Shield and first-class cricket fraternity. Players from both camps were worried that they would be ignored by state selectors – some friendships were lost.

Dymock found the team harmony was fine within the actual Test side. Allan Border said the same, that camaraderie was better because there wasn't this mad rush to impress selectors.

Ian Davis, post-Packer, also felt ostracised from official cricket. He'd even started to get the feeling he was on the outer of WSC when he told Ian Chappell that the Commonwealth Bank was reluctant to grant him leave on the tour for the West Indies a week before departure.

In hindsight, and even though Davis managed to buy a house with the money he earned from Packer ($22,500 each year for three years), he may have been better off staying with Establishment cricket. His career was finished by the age of 28, and he never felt fully accepted on his return to Shield cricket.

Ian Chappell dismissed the claims, saying that whenever it comes to selection, some players will always have a beef about it. It is true that selectors eventually have to pick a side, and there will be disagreement from some quarters with whichever players are chosen. Selectors for whatever reason also do have personal preferences, as does any employer seeking employees.

By the end of 1970–80, there had been a tremendous shift in the age and socio-economic fabric of those who attended games. The vast majority who passed through the turnstiles were under forty, with women attending in much greater numbers than before.

Australian fans would now be fed a diet of day/night ODIs and a large number of tours by the West Indies. The players were now benefitting from greater remuneration but there were soon signs that the pressure of increased matches across the season cricketers would play to earn their reward would bring their own issues – such as Greg Chappell ordering his brother Trevor to bowl an underarm to close off the match versus New Zealand in 1981 – but that was all in the future.

Former England captain Tony Lewis in *Cricketer* of February 1980, described the summer as 'a multi coloured road show.' He objected to the lunchtime entertainment of pop bands playing at high volume. *Age* journalist Peter McFarline lamented the loss of rest days, meaning an end to his visits to Yalumba vineyards in the Barossa Valley, where Wyndham Hill-Smith had hosted Test cricketers for more than a quarter of a century – the highlight of the summer for many players and press. The up-country matches, where players could sample local hospitality and the regions experience international cricket, were gone.

Questions were being raised about the marriage between the Australian Cricket Board and PBL Marketing. Cricket was being turned into big business with a commercial bottom line.

This new world also meant Australian players were rarely available to play for their states. In 1979–80, Kim Hughes did not play one game for Western Australia. This also meant fewer if any appearances in grade cricket.

A number of first-class and Test players interviewed described the value of playing alongside or against Test cricketers when they first played grade cricket. It helped youngsters learn some of the finer points of the game by simply watching top players close-up on the field. There was also the value of spending time with them after the match to discuss what had happened in the game and what could be done to improve next time. This sharing of information and stories was becoming a lost treasure.

After the gold rush

So what became of the Establishment Men after the cricket war?

Four of Hughes' touring side to India never played Test cricket again. Rick Darling (despite his prolific first-class scoring in 1981–82 when he made 1,011 runs and topped the Australian averages with 72), Alan Hurst, Dav Whatmore and Kevin Wright.

Border went on to play until 1993–94; Hogg played thirty-eight Tests and took 123 wickets at 28; Hilditch eighteen Tests to 1985; Wood 59 to 1988; Higgs played until 1980 with 66 wickets; Sleep fourteen Tests to 1989; Hughes seventy Tests averaging 37; Yallop thirty-nine Tests at 41; Dymock twenty-one Tests, bowling average 27; Hurst ended on twelve appearances; Jeff Thomson, twenty-two Tests before playing ten times for the Establishment side and then several WSC Super Tests before playing another nineteen official Tests for Australia, retiring in 1985.

Dyson added twenty-seven Tests to his three Super Tests for WSC; Rixon thirteen appearances between 1977 and 1984; Toohey played just a few more Tests and finished on fifteen, averaging 31; Cosier finished with eighteen and Serjeant twelve.

Cameo Test appearances during the Packer period were made by Callen (1), Carlson (2), Clark (10), Gannon (3), Hibbert (1), Laughlin (3), Maclean (4), Mann (4), Moss (1) and Ogilvie (5).

Geoff Lawson, who played one provincial game on the 1979 Indian tour, would play forty-six Tests between 1980 and 1989, taking 180 wickets at 30. Graeme Porter toured England for the 1979 World Cup and India, but despite strong performances never played a Test.

The question needs to be asked: *Why didn't more Establishment players kick on?*

Toohey and Darling were tipped to become prominent players but hardly featured at all post-Packer. Ian Chappell thought they were both good cricketers but just below Test standard. Bob Simpson clearly believed they were up to it, but didn't develop at the rate they should have.

Why not? Of course in any dressing room some young players will benefit from advice and help from older senior players, others won't. You only have to look at the way Bill Lawry encouraged John Gleeson as a leg-spinner but didn't have much time for Ashley Mallet. The same could be said of the way Bob Simpson favoured Rixon over Maclean, or later Steve Waugh over Matthew Hayden. Ian Chappell had his favourites too. He didn't much like Yallop or Hughes but appreciated Allan Border's talents.

Despite the Chappells' success as Test captains, there's an alternative point of view that they did little to guide younger players in their sides. The players who succeeded, such as Border, Marsh and Lillee, were enormous talents who could largely be left to their own devices. But what of players like Davis, Hookes, Cosier, Yallop, Turner, Hughes, Toohey, and Wood? How much help did they receive?

The Chappells inspired more by what they did than what they said.

So profound was Ian Chappell's effect on the 1975–76 series that Michael Holding thought he won the series single-handedly for Australia by his deeds with the bat.

> *He always got on top of the bowlers and others like Greg got the benefit: the same role Viv later fulfilled for us. Other batsman could get on top of you but Ian would embarrass you.*

Chappell was also one to occasionally lend a hand. Haigh in *The Cricket War* related a conversation that WSC and three-time Test player Martin Kent had with Ian Chappell in the 1979 Packer tour of the West Indies.

> *'What do you think of yourself as a cricketer, Super? Where do you think you've got to?' Chappell asked. 'Oh, I'm not bad but I've got a lot to learn,' replied Kent.*

Chappell replied:

> *It's OK to say that, but the sooner you believe in yourself, the better you're going to be. Back yourself. You're in this company, so you can play. Believe it. Don't always think you're always just starting.*

For Kent, the conversation proved a significant turning. He realised he deserved to be batting between the Chappells. But then Kent was one of those chosen to play WSC from Shield ranks. He was someone Ian Chappell backed.

Clearly Ian Chappell couldn't back everyone he played with, but the Australian cricket team was so clubby that they 'picked and sticked' with little regard for other players' development. One example was the way Graham Yallop was treated when he first earned the baggy green.

Success hides many faults. Perhaps Australia's decline in the post-Chappell era had some of its roots in the lack of any real succession plan for a post-Packer world. For Kent, the conversation proved a significant turning point. Had there been more support for the likes of Kim Hughes and Allan Border, the move to the era minus the big three of Chappell, Lillee and Marsh could only have been smoother.

Chapter Nine

Where are they now?

Twenty-three Establishment players made their Australian debuts in the twenty-four official Tests played during the two years of the schism. Many would not have had the chance to play for Australia were it not for one powerful man's lust for broadcasting rights and a tradition bound national cricket board's rejection of his approaches.

With the significant exception of Allan Border and to a lesser extent Kim Hughes and Rodney Hogg, most of those Establishment Men are largely forgotten.

Occasionally names like Carlson, Callen, Maclean and Moss crop up in an article recalling back-in-the-day or as answers at a trivia quiz night, but not much more than that.

Bob Simpson's name endures. Retired from Test cricket for more than a decade, in 1977–78 for two Test series. When Simpson looks back on those times he admits his players were all on a hiding to nothing. He was a brave man to put his record and reputation on the line, having been out of senior cricket for so long.

Simpson averaged 48 in 52 Tests to January 1968, then added 783 runs at the age of (just under) 39 in the five months from December 1977 during his second coming with the Establishment boys. On a wall in his study is a sketch by cartoonist Frank Benier. The central figure is surrounded by tots half his size; one is wearing a nappy, the other sucks a dummy, the third holds an Icy Pole. One of them, with trousers hitched up to his armpits, raises a hand and asks, Please Mr Simpson, if we're playing the Indians, can we be the cowboys?

He received a congratulatory telegram from Kerry Packer after captaining a 3–2 series win and scoring two hundreds against India. It got harder in the West Indies, a tour Simpson describes as 'daunting, and very, very awkward against a backdrop of so much going on, against an opponent that wanted to kill us'.

It was a sad finish to a Test career that ended more than twenty years after it began, with Simpson escorted off the ground by riot police after a crowd disturbance in the final Test at Jamaica. But he would stay in the game. His influence over the game continued for much longer, as a coach and selector.

With Australian cricket again struggling in the mid-1980s and the captain Allan Border finding the demands of leadership straining, the ACB once again turned to Bob Simpson, this time as coach. He held the position for over a decade, taking Australia to the top of the cricketing world by winning the World Cup and regaining the Ashes and the Frank Worrell Trophy. His 'pick and stick' policy helped the careers of Steve and Mark Waugh. Some promising players such as Greg Ritchie and later Dean Jones fell by the wayside, arguably before their time was up, because they didn't completely fit the Simpson mould. His zeal for honing the fielding and batting techniques of his charges became legendary, pleasing most, but not all. Simpson later went to England and coached Leicestershire and Lancashire.

At the time of writing, nearing eighty, Simpson is found more often these days on cruise ships with his wife Meg, travelling together in a way that was impossible during his cricketing days. They live close to Sydney's Olympic Park, in an apartment that housed Korean athletes during the 2000 Olympics. He is still involved with the Parramatta Grade club and has many requests for his coaching services – but has been happy to take a backward step.

Ian Callen's memories of Test cricket involve an aching back and an

Australian Cricket Board that didn't really look after its players. The injury from his one and only Test still causes such acute pain that he had to lie down for days on end. Callen had to deal with the back injury – which he believes destroyed his international career – alone, with no support. It took two years to identify that he had a stress fracture, and he now has a degenerative spine condition with problems in the nerves and lower disc.

The injury initially took Callen out of the game for two years. He knows he was never the same bowler again. He never really gained the same pace or momentum, having to change his action to compensate for bending his front leg, losing height and bounce.

> *I learnt to bowl within myself, was more like a stock bowler drying things up. But I could still let the odd one go.*

He toured Pakistan in 1982 (when Lillee, Greg Chappell and Pascoe opted out) but was struck down by dysentery and spent eight days in bed, losing two stone (13 kilograms). A knee injury followed and he lost two more seasons.

Most disappointingly, Callen believes that some people still think he was just a 'Mad Dog' who didn't prepare himself properly.

> *I worked as hard as anyone on my fitness and I could outrun anyone and bowl on line for overs on end. I had a lot of stamina. Looking back, I may have been too light and not physically strong enough for the workload I put in that Adelaide Test.*

Taught the art of bat making by the Warsop family during one of his early English summers in Lancashire League, Callen has spent the last twenty years making cricket bats from his own trees on his property at Tarrawarra near Healesville.

Archie MacLaren, the famous cricketer who captained England between 1898 and 1909, believed that the Yarra River flats near Healesville racecourse replicated the conditions where English willow had for centuries been grown. In the 1990s, Callen acted on MacLaren's theory. In wasn't all smooth sailing.

His business was forced into bankruptcy in 2005 when he says he was the victim of misinformation and listened to people he shouldn't have. For a while he stopped making bats, but was able to keep his trees and has carried on. Each morning he goes to work turning willow clefts into bats. He plans to teach the craft.

A young Phillip Hughes used one of Callen's bats to make his first hundred as a 12-year-old. The poignancy given Hughes' early death is not lost on Callen. He and his wife Susan have travelled widely, including to Pakistan where he sent a consignment of bats to refugee camps.

He was a coach, both online, and in the Dandenong Cricket Association where he says he is experiencing probably the most challenging job he has ever had, trying to inspire the players and open their minds to the game's history. Callen now provides bats to the Vatican cricket team and is hoping to meet the Pope later in the year.

Callen believes Kerry Packer was the best thing that happened to the game, and has recently benefited from the generosity of the Packer Foundation via the Australian Cricketers Association. Financial help enabled Callen to pay for surgery for a shoulder injury that was so severe he could not lift his arm above 45 degrees.

Gary Cosier still wonders why he wasn't asked to join World Series Cricket. Perhaps he nearly found out when a number of former Australian Test players gathered at the funeral of allrounder Gary Gilmour, who was farewelled by more than 1,000 mourners at Newcastle's Christ Church Cathedral. The list of former teammates and former top players attending would have made for a strong Australian side – the Chappells, Marsh, McCosker, Bright, Davidson, Matthews, Holland and Cosier.

At the reception in the local RSL, Ian Chappell turned to Cosier who was chatting with Ray Bright and said 'Cose, I hear I'm being blamed for you not being picked for World Series.'

Cosier replied, 'I've never said that, Bertie [Ian Chappell's nickname].'

'No, I know it hasn't come from you', responded Chappell.

Nothing more was said but it is widely assumed that Ian Chappell didn't want Cosier in WSC.

After a stint as Queensland vice-captain, Cosier returned to Victoria, playing grade cricket well enough to win the Ryder Medal. Although picked in the state squad, he rarely played; Victoria was looking to its youth.

For a while, Cosier owned some indoor cricket centres and worked for a rent-a-car company. He was also a selector, but the disappointment lingered.

> *I found it hard in Australia to watch Test cricket. I was always trying not to be a cricketer and find other paths.*

In the early 1980s, Cosier was offered a position with International Management Group (IMG) in Jakarta that started an international career. He spent seventeen years overseas working from the early 1990s in places like Tangier and Morocco in northern Africa where he ran golf properties. He was later CEO of Queensland's largest private golf club, Indooroopilly.

Tony Mann often jokes with his mate Sam Gannon about the time they played for Australia. They think themselves fortunate to have had the honour.

> *I thought I'd run my race and was very happy to have had the chance to have the success I did. By the time it was obvious I wouldn't be playing any more Test cricket, I was just happy to be playing full seasons for WA.*

By the end of the Indian tour in 1979, he had bowled 552 balls in four Tests – more than fellow leggie and captain Simpson, who got 524 in five. As the specialist leg-spinner, Mann would have liked to bowl more. By the time he retired from cricket in 1987, he'd played 28 years with Midland-Guildford, University and Mount Lawley. A maths teacher throughout his playing career, Mann's last full-time appointment was as Head of Maths as Guildford Grammar School (GGS), where he served until 1989.

He was Cricket Manager at the WACA for the next seven years before setting up a vineyard, returning to GGS for a part-time teaching and coaching role. These days Tony Mann takes pleasure in watching cricket, tending to his vines and admiring his view of the Darling Ranges. His attitude to life is similar to what it was for cricket: appreciate every moment.

Jeff Moss only played one Test for Australia and could be considered a little hard done by. He doesn't complain, and puts the success he had at top-level cricket down to a decision not to play the hook shot. Fast bowlers got the message and rarely bounced him.

In 1981–82, playing for Victoria, Moss hit an undefeated 200 against Western Australia, adding 390 for the third wicket with Julian Weiner but lost his place after two more matches and was never selected again.

The Australian selectors opted for Weiner to open the batting for Australia against England and the West Indies post reconciliation; it could just as easily have been Moss. He was Victoria's leading run-scorer in their Shield winning seasons of 1978–79 and 1979–80 and in the following year he scored 85 in the final, topping the batting list with 711 runs at 50.

As Victoria failed to continue its winning run, the selectors opted for a youth policy. Richie Robinson, Max Walker and Moss all finished up at the same time.

> *I was disappointed but I never had ambitions to play first-class cricket, so the six seasons I had were a bonus. I am sure if I had been selected in the State team at an earlier age I would have played more Tests.*

Moss enjoyed a lengthy period post-state cricket working in the insurance industry, spending twenty years with the Government Workers Compensation Authority. There was also a coaching stint at the behest of Ian Callen with Carlton, where he captained the B-grade into his fifties before taking up triathlons. He lives with his wife, Victorian state MP Lucinda McLeish, on their farm in Eildon, having recently fallen for the charms of horse racing, after his wife took on the role of Racing Minister in the Napthine Government. It took some time before Andrew Hilditch next played a Test match. Hilditch went from Australian vice-captain to district cricket within a week of returning to Australia. Only in 1981, after spending a Scottish summer leading Forfarshire to a county league title, did he regain his vigour for the game and moved to South Australia. The cricketing wheel eventually started to turn. There he made runs with a Spartan approach to batting, perfecting the leave-outside-off-stump, honed by hours in front of the bowling machine at Pembroke College where one John Inverarity was middle school headmaster.

Hilditch went on to play Test cricket with some success against the West Indies and England, but eventually fell prey to the hook shot on the Australian tour of England in 1985 and then against New Zealand at home. He is remembered to this day for that handled-the-ball dismissal against Pakistan in Perth in 1978–79. Later, Hilditch became a somewhat controversial Australian Chairman of Selectors. He still works as a lawyer.

Rick Darling's enduring legacy of his time in cricket are the head injuries he accumulated on top of the traumas he experienced as a typical country boy water skiing and shooting.

Now semi-retired, he works as a gardener at a retirement home. After twenty years of experiencing mini-blackouts been diagnosed with post-traumatic epilepsy. He still has problems with light entering his bad left eye and takes medication daily for his epilepsy. He has identified stress as one of the triggers for the seizures, which can sometimes last as little as five seconds.

> *I experience an overwhelming feeling of doom … it feels like the blood is being sucked out of my body. It's taken a lot of my confidence away, but I've got to the stage with medication where I know if I am having a turn and can snap myself out of it. I tend to avoid stressful situations like meetings in confined spaces, where if I have a mini-seizure I might be judged for it.*

Test cricket for Darling represented a chance for him to play the game at the top level and challenge some of the best bowlers in the world. Sadly at times the bowler didn't need to, Darling's jumpy demeanour making him prone to erratic running between the wickets, exacerbated by his sometime opening partner Graeme Wood's occasional scatter gun approach.

Darling was only twenty years old when he was first picked for Australia; his Test career was over before he turned twenty-three. He says he was 'immature and naïve and didn't know who to turn to when the runs dried up' and that 'there wasn't the guidance there is today.' Some guidance may also have helped his compulsive hooking habit.

> *I would always have a go at it. I could never duck. I might sway out of the way of it or get inside if it was too high or too quick, but I used to score a lot of runs hooking.*

After the reconciliation, Darling played a season of one-dayers for Australia in the early 1980s and topped the Australian Shield aggregate in 1981–82 but missed out on the Australian tour to Pakistan. A few seasons later he was hit by Queensland speedster John Maguire.

> *The one that finished my career was when I got hit in my eye by John Maguire from Queensland. He got one to really rear up, and I got back to hook and it went between the visor and the top part of the helmet and smashed in my eye. That finished me. After that, I didn't want to be there. I thought of other things I wanted to do in life. Even though I continued playing on in Shield for two or three years, I just didn't want to be there.*

He had a famous run in with David Hookes in the mid–1980s when he wanted to drop down the order for South Australia. He'd been hit too many times in the head opening the batting and wanted a change. Hookes saw him as an opener and refused to budge. Darling retired a few season later. Darling must wonder at times what his Test record would have looked like if he had been given as many chances as Hookes to consolidate a place in the Australian side.

Darling is disappointed that when he first played Shield cricket, off-field discipline was not more enforced. He wished he hadn't smoked and drunk quite so much and partied the way he did.

> *As a young kid I had to keep up with the Chappells and Malletts in the drinking stakes and I'm sure most of us would have been better players if we'd learned to toe the line a lot more.*

While playing cricket, Darling worked for the Electricity and Water Supply department as a surveyor, in public relations for the Hindmarsh Building Society with Rodney Hogg, and at Adelaide City Council as a machine operator. Post-cricket he continued his twenty-one-year service with South Australian Research, followed by three years as General Manager of the Adelaide Turf Cricket Association.

John Maclean, known as 'the Ghost who Walks' from *The Phantom* comic strip, for his habit of plastering his face with zinc cream, gave the game away for good the season after he was dropped by the Australian selectors. He wanted to make a proper living.

Maclean was once jokingly referred to by Greg Ritchie as 'the godfather of Queensland cricket'. He remembers how easy it was as a Test cricketer to 'get your head up your arse', to get carried away with your status. When Queensland won its first Sheffield Shield in 1994–95 Maclean with tears in his eyes was one of the first to congratulate opener Trevor Barsby whose first innings 151 had helped set up the win. Maclean knew the value of success but also more importantly what was learned along the way.

He still works as an engineer and for a period was President of the Queensland Cricketer's Club. If you cast your eye around the Brisbane skyline you will see many of Maclean's projects, including the Storey Bridge, Victoria Bridge, Somerset Ivanhoe and North Pine damns, as well as the Riverside Expressway.

Despite Jim Higgs' 66 Test wickets at 31, he was not picked again after the Third Test of the 1980–81 home series against India. He was dropped for the Adelaide Test and he asked skipper Greg Chappell what was going on.

'They [the selectors] don't want you in the touring side for England. They don't think leg-spin will work over there', the captain responded leaving Higgs speechless.

Higgs is generally considered Australia's best leg-spinner of the years between Richie Benaud and Shane Warne. Looking back, he sees things he might have done differently, such as concentrating more on cricket for ten years rather than combining a career in engineering with playing at the top level. He's still involved in the game as Vice President of the Richmond Cricket Club in Victoria and still plays the odd game at the age of 64.

> *I was proud of what I did and the fact that I taught myself to do*
> *something that not a lot of people could do. It would have been better*
> *if I had been more of an athlete.*

Higgs at various times has been a state and Test selector; taught a young Shane Warne how to bowl a flipper; and is currently a member of Cricket Victoria's Board of Management. An engineer by training, Higgs is principal shareholder and director of a traffic-engineering company with offices in Melbourne, Sydney, Brisbane and the Gold Coast.

Geoff Dymock, the left-handed batsman, for such a long time the man most likely to fade into the background because the selectors continually overlooked him, went from strength to strength. One enduring memory of his playing days is of when he was at the other end when Lillee famously came out with his aluminum bat. Struggling to hit the ball off-square, the bat was more noise than substance in a farcical scene ending with Lillee hurling it in the direction of Twelfth Man, Rodney Hogg.

Still playing Tests at thirty-five, the years may have finally caught up against him. But even in his second last Test, he took five for 104 against the West Indies in a match Australia lost by 408 runs.

Test cricket has brought Dymock many good memories, but interestingly, he says that some of his recollections of playing cricket as a child at Maryborough rival them.

Like many of his teammates, he saw the advent of WSC as a long overdue win for the players.

At the time of his interview for this book, Dymock was 69 and still obliged to work. As a school teacher, he found the dual life of cricketer and teacher a major financial burden. He now runs coaching clinics in country New South Wales and Western Australia with Doug Walters and does some relief teaching. He is disappointed in the little money he sees going to grassroots cricket and the number of Queensland bush competitions that are no longer running.

Dymock's state teammate David Ogilvie's Test experience amounts to a depressing underachievement. Despite his Bradmanesque first-class scores in the summer of 1977–78, in terms of Test success he failed to deliver. Not that it concerns him much now. Ogilvie, a school counsellor, says he lives very much in the present and his days of running around a cricket field are long gone.

Dismissively admitting it was nice to play Test cricket but that it didn't bring the personal success he had hoped for, Ogilvie gets the occasional request from autograph hunters. Once in a while someone will stop him and ask if he is the David Ogilvie who once scored all those runs for Queensland.

Nowadays Ogilvie goes to the occasional cricket reunion but that is as far as his connection with the game takes him. He's moved on. He is studying a PhD in education on 'The influence of the internal conversations on development in adolescent vocational identity', or as he translates for me:

> *I'm looking at the way the internal conversations young people have with themselves has any influence on the decisions they make about their career. Overall I don't think we spend enough time thinking about thinking.*

Asked if he was the victim of his own over-thinking on the cricket field, Ogilvie dismisses it as quickly as he dispatched balls through the leg side when on song with the bat. He regrets not being more involved with the *culture of cricket*, saying that this omission had been to his detriment at all levels of the game.

Craig Serjeant, Australia's vice-captain for the India series, dropped by the Fifth Test, feels that being made vice-captain did nothing to advance his cricketing career.

> *The vice-captaincy was the worst thing that happened to my career in many respects because I hadn't established myself at international*

cricket level. I'd played three Tests on a tour of England then there was this sort of heir-apparency that was bestowed upon me that I wore very reluctantly. That had a significant impact on my form over that series. It was like a big weight had been removed when I lost it.

A poor start to the domestic season in 1978–79 saw him dropped, never to return, having committed the sin of only passing 50 once in seventeen Test innings after his debut 81 at Lord's.

Serjeant thinks his file was closed after the West Indies tour. He's not sure why; perhaps the selectors saw the choice for the middle-order spot between him and Hughes; maybe they thought his improvement wasn't as good as it should have been.

Having never thought that he would play for Australia, Serjeant is glad he did, and acknowledges that he should have made more of the opportunities he was given. Like others, he believes one of the disadvantages of playing for Australia during that period was that players were given little time to develop their Test legs. He cites Steve Waugh, who took four years to score his first Test hundred and find his feet at international level.

Serjeant, who changed career paths in his mid-thirties to become a financial planner, says he lives by the creed of '*never die wondering*'. But he will. As he puts it, 'I didn't have the courage to try and become a professional cricketer.'

It's worth considering whether his lot would have been any better had he joined WSC. But by the time of the reconciliation he was no longer a part of the Australian side. The decision had effectively been made for him.

Wayne Clark, who took 44 wickets at 28 in his ten Test matches, has every reason to feel bitter about aligning himself with the Establishment. He still harbours annoyance at the way he was treated by Australian cricket authorities but is ultimately glad of the path he took.

If I'd gone with WSC I don't know what would have happened. As it was, I was able to play Test cricket and have stayed in cricket since. But the fact that no one from the ACB explained to me why

I was wasn't selected to play for Australia during the Ashes series of 1978–79 is a great disappointment.

If Clark had gone to WSC, there is every chance he could have been seen in higher regard during the post-Packer period.

Clark went on to become a successful coach of Western Australia for ten years, leading them to three Shield wins as well as two one-day titles. He was also coach of Yorkshire when it won its first championship title for thirty-three years in 2001.

Alan Hurst's Test career was a case of what might have been, his career effectively ending after breaking down with a back injury following the 1979 tour of India. He believes he would have played many more Tests for Australia if it hadn't been for his injuries.

He cites the names Border, Yallop, Hughes, Yardley, Wood, Higgs and Hogg, who totalled just four Tests against their names before Packer, but went on to play 417 Tests.

Hurst felt he had been cheated of achieving what he was capable of in cricket by the frailties of his own body. He did little related to cricket for several years – never even went back to his much-loved MCG to watch a game.

Hurst describes his time playing Test cricket during WSC as difficult. The Australian side was hastily put together and allegedly second-rate cricketers, but determined to do well despite lacking support, experience and leadership in an environment where the hierarchy was busy trying to mend fences and bring the cricket world back together.

There was always the thought that the Packer players would be back and that we had to do well as a group and individually to cement futures at that level. There was never a doubt that the public, the media and the administration saw us as a stopgap, and there is no doubt there were players who in normal times may not have played at that level, but we did the best we could in the circumstances.

A primary school teacher, Hurst was appointed as a physical education adviser, supervising about 35 PE programs, and later worked as a commentator for ABC radio and TV. Hurst became an International Match Referee for the ICC for seven years from 2004.

Maybe it's the former phys. ed. teacher in him, but Hurst finds it interesting that today's pace bowlers are injured as often as they ever were, despite all the technology, range of support personnel and supposed cutting edge training methods. And that's despite teams often being away for shorter periods. He notes that on a four-month tour of England in 1975, with a squad of sixteen players and with just a manager, a masseur and a baggage man and scorer, not one player was sufficiently injured to miss a game.

Davenall Whatmore looks back on playing for Australia with great pride if not a little disappointment. That he could represent his country and be paid for it was enough. He wishes he had made more of his talents; he averaged 22 from his seven Test matches. As a player he says that he never learned to read the game properly, a skill he better applied as a coach. Whatmore also applied what he learned from his own doubts as a player to coaching, ensuring the players knew that they had his support.

> *I wanted players to know that I cared, because that wasn't directed at me when I played. I would have just loved to have Bob Simpson or someone like him as coach when I played. I also wished I learned how to read the game better. I learned, but it was too late for me as a player. After finishing his first-class career in 1989 Whatmore went on to coach Sri Lanka, Bangladesh and Pakistan, the latter of which he found the biggest challenge because of what he described as an 'undermining' media. He coached Sri Lanka to its World Cup win in 1996.*

For Australia's reinvented off-spinner Bruce Yardley, the advent of WSC was a Godsend. He started as a relatively innocuous medium-pacer for Western Australia. Appearances for his state in 1966 and then again in 1970–71 did little for his future prospects. On the advice of a teammate having seen his quality slower ball, he became an off-spinner and was back in the WA team in 1973–74.

A call to play for Australia in 1978 at the age of thirty marked one of the great comebacks in Australian cricket. He went on to play thirty-three Tests and seven ODIs to take a total of 126 wickets. He missed out on the 1981 tour of England, having taken 33 wickets at 37, including 7 wickets for 31 in the final two Tests of the 1980–81 summer.

Yardley's 'card had been marked' as far back as the 1977–78 season; once you have been reported for a suspect action, the taint is hard to wash off, or at least it was in the 1970s and 1980s.

The following summer (1981–82), he took 51 wickets in nine Tests against Pakistan, the West Indies and New Zealand and won the International cricketer of the year. He also performed strongly against England in 1982–83 when the Ashes were regained, taking 22 wickets for the series. He missed out on selection for the 1983 World Cup and retired after playing just one more Test, taking seven wickets against Sri Lanka.

Yardley went on to coach Sri Lanka and the Western Australian Aboriginal side that plays in the annual Imparja Cup in Alice Springs. He later became an advocate for melanoma research after losing an eye to cancer.

Kevin Wright never heard from the selectors again after returning from the six-Test tour of India. There had been some debate in the press as to whether Wright should retain his Australian place ahead of Marsh, given what he had shown on the Indian tour. But he went from Australian wicketkeeper to unemployed cricketer in 24 hours, and so took a job selling cars.

Curiously, Wright says he never really enjoyed playing Test cricket. He liked being known as a Test player, but the experience of playing in an inexperienced side with so much pressure of players to retain their place made it hard to enjoy.

He believes the timing of the end of the cricket war did few favours for those who played in Tests during the WSC years and that if there had been another twelve months, a number of players could have had an extended run and established themselves at Test level.

For a time post-reconciliation, Wright and Marsh played together at the same club but never had much to do with each other. They had different styles of keeping. Marsh was more reliant on his reflexes and more likely to take the spectacular catch; Wright was more orthodox. No surprise really that the keepers had little to do with one another given they were both after the same places in the state and Australian teams.

In 1979–80, Wright played six more games for Western Australia then after some encouragement from South Australian selector Barry Jarman continued his Shield career. Wright again found himself playing alongside John Inverarity for the South Australian side and club side, Kensington.

After three seasons in South Australia, his cricket career took a turn for the worse. David Hookes, who was touring the West Indies with the Australian side, rang him one Sunday afternoon to inform him that Kim Hughes wanted Wayne Phillips to wicket keep for South Australia and would hold vacant the Western Australian spot for Wright.

Wright, who had just captained South Australia to a McDonald's Cup final win against a Western Australian side which had Lillee and Marsh, was unimpressed that the selectors had gone with Phillips. The state selectors originally sided with Wright but when Phillips threatened to move to Western Australia, the parochial local press supported him. The selectors backtracked.

Wright retired from first-class cricket at the age of thirty, a move he says was one the best he made. Working for Australian Eagles Insurance, he was promoted to State Manager in New South Wales and played for the Manly club ... but the passion for cricket was gone.

He worked his way up the corporate ladder to become a senior executive of Prudential Australia in the mid–1990s. From there he went on to start up the Indian operation of Prudential, becoming Managing Director for Asia. It's an amazing journey for someone who left school at fifteen. Wright admits that his status as a former Test cricketer opened doors for him, but also found he had to work twice as hard to convince people he had corporate value.

His professional life took him away from Australia for years to India, Hong Kong, Korea and Singapore and many cricket connections were lost. A reunion in 2002 of all Australian Test players made him feel more welcome.

The Packer players never made any reference that we weren't deserving members of the Australian Test cricket club. After that night, I walked away thinking that playing for Australia during that period was no different to someone who played Test cricket when two or three players were injured. I felt that night and still do that I am a member of a very special club.

Queensland's Phil Carlson must be one of the few Australians to play Test cricket while living in the bush, at Childers, 325 kilometres north of Brisbane.

A teacher by training, Carlson's time in front of the blackboard (while he also plied his cricketing trade in the Lancashire league and Leicestershire seconds) was limited: 'The kids drove me nuts.'

In Childers, he worked in a fuel, fertiliser and agricultural chemical business, playing in the local competition, driving down to Brisbane for Shield matches. Encouragement from state selectors to move back to the capital fell on deaf ears, "Why? I'm playing the best cricket of my life."

Carlson was an early starter and bloomer on the first-class stage. When he finally got the chance to play Test cricket, he failed in his two matches and was never called upon again. By the time he'd taken his last two Test wickets, Mike Brearley and Graham Gooch, Carlson knew his chances had come and gone.

By the end of the 1980–81 season, the Queensland selectors were no longer prepared to select him because he couldn't train with the squad, and delivered an ultimatum. Carlson refused to commute for training from Childers and gave the game away at the age of 29.

His life turned around thanks to the request of a Childers' customer, to help struggling farmers sell their farms. He sold nine in nine months and moved back to Brisbane to work in property development.

He's been on the Queensland Cricketer's Club Board for the last fifteen years; his background in property development has helped with the redevelopment of The Gabba as a modern stadium and shifting the cricketers' club from behind the bowler's arm to a glass-encased room above midwicket.

Now in his sixties, Carlson has had health issues and recently short-term memory problems because of early-stage damage to his frontal lobe, possibly caused by a late diagnosis of diabetes when he was 47.

Carlson injects insulin twice a day for his type one diabetes. It's a condition he monitors closely and requires a regular diet of exercise. He is currently involved in a study at Sydney's St Vincent's Hospital to see if there is a link between his brain injury and diabetes.

Graham Yallop in many ways has been the scapegoat for Australia's performance during the schism. He is remembered as the man who led Australia to a 5–1 Ashes loss, but his batting feats rarely rate a mention. During the period, he scored four centuries and four half-centuries in Tests against India, England and the West Indies. Once given the opportunity, he was one of Australia's most consistent performers with the bat.

Yallop is a man very much defined by the era in which he played, a forgotten captain of Australia, not that it bothers him. Yallop says he had the chances to go into a media role when he retired but chose not to. Instead, he has spent the last thirty years coaching.

> It's only after you give the game away and people refer to you as a former Australian captain and that's when it hits you that, OK, I was at the pinnacle of the sport ... I had no idea when I was a teenage that I was even going to be playing for Australia, let alone be captain.

Yallop was also one who continued to play Test cricket post-Packer, but not as much as he should have, initially missing out post-reconciliation. Not that he's one to dwell on it.

*There were a lot of good players returning, plus back then we didn't
question the selectors — we just went back to Shield cricket with the
aim of scoring runs.*

He regained his place for the 1980 tour of Pakistan, scoring 172 at
Faisalabad but found himself dropped two Tests later. He was one of a number
of Australian batsmen who found the 1981 England tour tough going. Again,
despite scoring a century at Old Trafford, he was dropped two games later.
He scored 268 against Pakistan at the MCG in 1983, an innings that consumed
twelve hours and 517 balls. During this innings, Yallop passed a Bradman
record set in 1929 — most runs scored by an Australian during a calendar year.
The aggravation of an existing knee injury put an end to Yallop's fine season.

Remarkably, he played only three more Tests. Just before the final
Test, Yallop's predecessor as captain, Bob Simpson, praised the play of the
Victorian and characterized his treatment as 'the most maligned and poorly-
treated Australian player of his considerable experience'. Yallop later joined the
Australian rebel tour of apartheid-era South Africa.

Like Kim Hughes, he went from Establishment captain to rebel. Yallop
explained that a number of players were told that their Test careers were over,
which made the offer to be part of the rebel tour more appealing. It was,
though, a time of mixed emotions.

*On one side were people who believed we shouldn't be touring because
of the apartheid regime, and on the other side, people were arguing
you should never mix sport and politics. We were torn between the
two. It wasn't a decision I took lightly.*

Yallop was perceived as lacking what was needed in the Ian Chappell
led dressing room of the period, even thought by some to be faint-hearted.
His performances on the difficult tour of the West Indies where he scored
three half-centuries against blistering pace was evidence to the contrary.
Maybe the perception arose because Yallop was the first batsman to appear in
Test cricket wearing a helmet.

How does he reflect upon his role in such a tumultuous time in the game?

I was thankful for any opportunity to play for Australia … to represent your country is a huge honour. I was grateful for the career I had and have no regrets.

What about his time as Australian captain?

It was a huge challenge against close to full strength international sides with an incredibly inexperienced team. We were competitive in all the Tests; it was just a lack of experience in knowing how to win.

What is Yallop's relationship with his nemesis Rodney Hogg now? They play golf together.

Yallop has spent much of his professional life running sporting centres and coaching cricket. He says helping youngsters has been a lifelong passion. Having coached at district level, he is now in charge of suburban club Elwood in Victoria. The club has 21 teams, fourteen of which are juniors. Yallop also has a connection with Indonesian cricket development, providing funds and objects like his baggy green cap to sell off in order to help the game there. The main cricket oval in Jakarta is named after him. Graeme Wood was dropped and recalled for Australia fourteen times over a career that spanned a decade. Yet unlike his former opening partner Rick Darling or state teammate Craig Serjeant, Wood found himself frequently given another chance. The experience of consistently playing Test cricket (fifteen out of a possible twenty Tests since first being picked) against strong international sides during the WSC era taught him to graft to earn back his place in the West Australian side.

Wood marked the occasion of the 1980 Lord's Centenary Test with a hard-earned 112. He became a regular fixture opening the batting for Australia, often against the might of the West Indies with their four-pronged pace attack. Another Test recall in at the age of thirty-three saw him score a final century, but he was dropped after the next match.

Inconsistency was Woods' worst companion. He was probably fortunate to play as many Tests as he did. Only twice in fifty-nine Tests did he score a half-century in each innings.

He passed John Inverarity's Sheffield Shield record for WA in 1991–92. After averaging 31 with a highest score of 172, the following season he was sacked as a WA player and captain, the reasons for which have never been made clear.

Wood, who is seen as a one of the success stories of the Establishment players, would later work for Fosters and go on to become CEO of the WACA. He now works in the wine industry and doesn't look much different to how he looked in the 1970s and 1980s.

Peter Toohey still has a scar to show for the blow he took from fast bowler Andy Roberts in the Caribbean in 1978. The fact that Steve Rixon had to scratch out his guard in a pool of blood makes the whole scene even more chilling.

Toohey recently spoke of his close call in the context of Phil Hughes' death.

My wife got quite emotional about it because it brought back all these memories. I went back out to bat at the fall of the eighth wicket. Looking back, it seems pretty bloody stupid.

The next summer he was hit again, this time by Carl Rackemann in a Shield match, something Toohey at the time saw as a blessing of sorts. 'It allowed the doctors to clean up both head scars.' He is understandably less inclined to view it that way now.

Toohey is not one to regret much. He still voices surprise at why he was called up for two Tests after the reconciliation, yet wasn't selected for the tour of India where his batting style was suited, in a weakened Australian side just months before.

He never really felt part of the Australian dressing room post-reconciliation, sensing that perhaps Greg Chappell didn't really rate him. Toohey is a man happy to talk of his limitations as a cricketer. 'I don't think

I was ready to play Test cricket again at that stage. After that my name was scratched out.'

He worked for Toohey's brewery (no relation) using his degree in food technology to rise to the head of manufacturing with the Baxter Group, making IV and renal solutions for Australian and New Zealand hospitals. He spent three years as a NSW selector, helping usher Mark Taylor and the Waughs into the team.

The man who was most affected by WSC was Kim Hughes. He was the one who became the Establishment's symbol of hope, the golden-haired boy who went on to captain Australia – the one who, when news of WSC broke, announced publicly that he was always going to play for Australia. Hughes did himself few favours in telling journalists about an approach from World Series that he'd turned down because he wanted to captain Australia. Sadly for Hughes, his inheritance of the captaincy and the timing of his record-scoring tour to India were both helpful and destructive. After the reconciliation when the West Indies and England toured in a dual series, it helped give Hughes a place in the full Australian side.

When Rod Marsh was awarded with the captaincy of Western Australia, Hughes felt it should have gone to him, asking 'How can I be vice-captain of Australia and not captain of my state?'

In fact, WA teammate of both Marsh and Hughes, Ian Brayshaw thinks Marsh should have been made Australian captain after the reconciliation. Impressed by Marsh's leadership in 1976–77 when he led his team to the double success of Sheffield Shield and Gillette Cup, Brayshaw wrote in *Miracle Match*:

> *Not only would the team have embraced his 'do as I do' brand of leadership but this would also have left Kim Hughes free, for the time being, to express himself solely with his flashing blade ... having seen at close hand the dimensions of Marsh's leadership qualities – his man-management skills and grasp of the strategic side of the game – I felt sure there would be life after cricket for him... in cricket.*

However, when Hughes was later appointed captain of Western Australia, when wiser and more more senior players could have taken the role, it smacked of a move to appease the Establishment. Kim Hughes was establishment, Rod Marsh was WSC. Hughes was cocky and convinced of his own talent. He also had a habit of not listening to the advice of senior players. Some saw him as simply a big head, only interested in his own welfare and fulfilling his own dreams. Others viewed him as the obvious successor to Greg Chappell, as captain of Australia, when Chappell retired.

In the four-year period post reconciliation, the captaincy fell to Hughes when Greg Chappell was not available for overseas tours. This arrangement was put in place for the first time for the disastrous 1981 Australian tour of England, where Australia, having led the series, was defeated 3–1 by a famous Botham-led recovery. It was the series of the 500–1 bet that Marsh and Lillee had on Australia losing the Leeds Test, a move they surely would not have made under the leadership of Greg Chappell and one that reflected the disrespect the two senior players held for Hughes. Marsh in their eyes, and with some justification, was the obvious replacement for Chappell.

Not everyone agreed, a number of players interviewed for this book spoke of their disappointment as to the way Lillee and Marsh in particular had treated Hughes. Lillee would bounce Hughes in the nets on the morning of a Test and other senior players displayed obvious disrespect on the field. Hughes, not wanting to appear soft, never spoke out about the anger and hurt he felt.

When he eventually inherited the full-time captaincy in 1984, he faced back-to-back series against the West Indies without Greg Chappell, Marsh and Lillee. Hughes' dreams of the captaincy of Australia all ended at The Gabba in 1984 after an eight-wicket defeat.

The fall was a long time coming. For months, Hughes' state teammate Wayne Clark saw what Hughes was going through.

I told him just to let the captaincy go, to start enjoying himself as a cricketer, but he wouldn't have a bar of it. He was so paranoid about it all that he became ill. He didn't listen to anyone, and he went into a shell. He just wasn't going to relinquish the captaincy. It got to the point where he didn't trust anyone, not even me. It certainly affected him health-wise. It wasn't a nice situation.

Clark, who thought Hughes was experiencing a breakdown, doesn't blame Lillee and Marsh for what they did to Hughes saying, 'That's just the way they were.' Others took a dim view of the treatment handed out to Hughes. John Maclean has little doubt.

Kim Hughes could have been anything. Lillee and Marsh treated him appallingly. You may not always agree with someone but you should treat them as a fellow human being.

Hughes later spoke about what had happened to him.

At the time the Aussie attitude – especially if you were a male – was that it was unAustralian to show signs of weakness. You didn't squeal but it wasn't much fun being a leader when every mistake is highlighted and the only way to survive is to put a shell around you but then you don't develop as a person. Nastiness creeps into your personality and it affected my relationship with my wife and kids.

Hughes will forever be remembered as the Australian Test captain who shed tears when he resigned. He played three of the best innings in Test cricket history, an undefeated hundred against the West Indies on the minefield of the pitch that was the MCG in the early 1980s. It was a mixture of courage, bravado and luck.

His other masterpieces, a dual 117 and undefeated 84 at Lord's in the 1980 Centenary Test, were combinations of finesse, textbook, perfect drives and power.

By 1985, Hughes was leading an Australian rebel tour to South Africa. Hughes initially declined the offer but when he discovered that Murray

Bennett, Wayne Phillips, Graeme Wood and Dirk Wellham had signed and been financially lured back to the touring side to England in 1985, he lost faith in the Establishment.

When Hughes returned from the rebel tours, the Western Australian Cricket Association attempted to ban him from club cricket. In response, Hughes took action against the WACA for restraint of trade; he won the case in the Federal Court of Australia, the WACA losing several hundred thousand dollars in court costs.

He played first-class cricket for Western Australia for two more seasons then captained Natal in the Currie Cup before retiring in 1991. He was seemingly *persona non grata* in Australian cricketing circles for a number of years before resurfacing as one of the coaches of younger players at the WACA.

Hughes, often heard these days on ABC radio, has partnered with former AFL player and coach Ken Judge to give inspirational talks to corporates, including a lot of work with the mining industry. He is now the Director of Coaching at Hale School in Perth.

When Hughes finally resigned, the captaincy went to Allan Border who wasn't happy with the circumstances that led to his teammate's demise.

> *When I saw what happened to Kim and the desperation he felt where he wasn't enjoying his cricket and took the desperate step of resigning the Australian captaincy I thought to myself, why would I want this job? I was very reluctant to accept the job and it took quite a few years to come to grips to grabbing the job with both hands and running with it. It's something I regret and if I had my time again I'd like to have another crack and be more positive about doing the job straight away.*

The lesson about the support needed for the captain was beginning but it took some time and was consolidated in 1985 when Bob Simpson was again called back to the Australian side, this time as a coach.

Allan Border was the great winner of all the Establishment players. Eventually, he was so well known he would be referred to only by his initials,

AB. He learned to adapt his game and to properly play spin bowling on a tour of India in 1979 and had time to develop as a batsman without the pressure initially of having one of the WSC players come in to take his place. He also managed to adapt to the extreme pace of the West Indian bowling line up and prospered in the post-Packer environment.

Border went on to represent Australia's stability in the middle order. When Hughes abdicated the captaincy, Border was his replacement and after a few rocky years went on to assert Australia's dominance over England and build the foundation for Australia's success against the West Indies.

Border was long known as the great saviour of Australian cricket. The author of a number of great Australian escapes. There was comfort in knowing he was at the crease. One Test match in particularly epitomises this rear-guard action: in March 1984 against the West Indies at Port-of-Spain, he batted in two innings for 630 minutes and 198 runs, defying Garner, Marshall and Daniel for 535 hostile deliveries on a damp pitch without losing his wicket. It was Border at his strongest, the man who could block everything out of his mind except the next delivery.

Border had resilience that brought longevity in the game. By the end of his career, he had seen and done everything possible on a cricket field. Throughout the 1980s he *was* Australia's middle order. Forever it seemed he held up while his teammates collapsed around him. At press conferences, he was always guarded and edgy, bristling at any suggestion of controversy but with a self-deprecating smile. He finished as the man who played 156 Test matches for Australia, scoring 11,174 runs.

By his Testimonial season of 1993–94, Border was a pop star for cricket fans indeed, U2's legendary singer Bono rang him from a concert at Brisbane's ANZ stadium, to the delirium of the crowd. Bono told the big crowd to sing to him; the words to the song *I just called to say I love you* filled the air. Border had been confirmed by a rock god as a legend. Border later went on to become an Australian Test selector and now works in the media for Fox Sports and is sometimes heard on the ABC.

And in the end ...

There is little doubt that World Series Cricket provided the foundation for a number of players to establish significant Test careers for players such as Border, Hughes, Dymock, Wood, Yallop, Higgs, Hogg and Yardley. Although there were some disappointing results for Australia during the Packer Period, there was also some excellent cricket played.

Test cricket was kept alive by the Establishment players in an era when the game was veering dramatically toward the commercial one-day style. The Establishment players performed against full-strength opposition as they kept Australian colours flying. They deserve acknowledgement of their role in Australian cricket by the Australian team.

Some questions about this period remained unanswered. Sometimes the truth is hidden for fear of embarrassment or upsetting a former teammate. There is, however, truth in what Tony Greig noticed about the ways that senior Australian cricketers of the 1970s and 1980s portray their history.

Winners write the history, and in this case, the winners were those playing for Packer. The period during the schism in cricket is now largely perceived by the public to be about Packer's WSC (although it took some time for Packer's cricket to be properly recognised). Ian Chappell has been given an enormous opportunity through his broadcasting on Packer's Channel Nine as well as newspaper and magazine articles to give his perspective on cricket in his time. Former front man for Word Series Cricket, Richie Benaud, for decades was the voice of cricket in Australia and has written extensively about the game. Bill Lawry returns to the microphone every Boxing Day Test. They are all Packer men through and through.

The voices are the same, the stories are the same, talking about the Test matches they were a part of. There are many anecdotes of the past but not so much analysis.

Graham Yallop thinks that one of the reasons Test cricket's role in the Packer period was largely forgotten was that the television coverage moved from the ABC to Channel Nine.

They didn't want to give credence to what the Test side achieved during WSC. They were pushing their own barrow and wanting to market the new form of cricket that was big business. I understand where they were coming from.

As author LP Hartley wrote in his book, *The Go-Between*, which featured a cricket match:

The past is a foreign country; they do things differently there.

For the Establishment cricketers, it seems at times as if the period between 1977 and 1979 does not exist. There has been little or no room for Establishment cricketing tales or footage in the mainstream media. Like the first-class cricket played during the major wars, Test cricket played during the schism is largely forgotten.

Past and present Australian teams are often remembered with reverence, or given special mention at celebratory occasions. It appears there is no place for those who played in losing sides considered as stop gap measures. The time has come for this period of Australian cricket history and its players to be recognised by the ACB and beyond.

Yallop thinks Cricket Australia doesn't have a great eye to its history and certainly not the Australian team during the schism, although since the formation and consolidation of the Australian Cricketers Association, things have improved.

There should be greater recognition of the Australian players and what was achieved during the Packer time. The Australian Test side put in an admirable performance under the conditions.

Perhaps the amnesia from Cricket Australia about Test cricket played in the era relates to how the Board conducted itself during the cricket war, which could hardly be seen as admirable or as having the players' best interests at heart. We need look no further than former ACB Chairman Bob Parish's reluctant admission twenty years after the first bullet in the cricket war had been fired.

I'm not certain World Series Cricket was a bad thing. It brought the Australian Cricket Board ahead in two years what may have taken thirty years, or never happened.

World Series Cricket had a special Twenty Year anniversary broadcast and gala event in 1997 to celebrate its significance. The TV minis series *Howzat* (2013) has promoted the legend of Kerry Packer and World Series Cricket even more. I'm not suggesting these events shouldn't be given some prominence; Packer did after all take on the Board and win. In doing so, changing the way cricket was played and marketed forever. He gave the game broader appeal through the promotion of innovations WSC introduced to one-day cricket. It meant the growth of the ODIs, which helped bring revenue for the State Associations to develop the game.

Former New South Wales captain and cricket broadcaster Alan McGilvray, famous for his pioneering of the 'synthetic broadcast' during the 1938 tour of England, once titled one of his books *The Game is Not the Same*, featuring a lament of what the game lost as it moved into the professional era. But perhaps the game of cricket itself has changed little. The battle between bat and ball is essentially the same as it was when the cricket war broke out.

Bowlers deliver balls to batsmen and fielders try to catch them out and stop them scoring runs. The game is capable of delivering the highest of highs and most devastating of lows. Despite the increase in limited-over matches, the players, when testing their skills, still value Test cricket above all else.

The accoutrements surrounding the game have certainly changed. The marketing and scheduling of cricket are now tailored to appeal to a mass audience – a valuable contribution that Kerry Packer began. Heavier bats, shorter boundaries and US baseball style entertainment in the T–20 matches are major features of modern cricket.

English journalist Alan Lee, who wrote about England Ashes series in 1978–79 in *The Times* in 2014, titled an article 'A Test of Traditions:

Eight reasons to be cheerless about the insidious trends ruining international cricket'. It's worth a read.

> *The hordes of hangers on who mill around the square before play begins, citing an England team huddle that had 27 people, that scarcely stood out among the crowd flocking around them; Twelfth men in day-glo jackets running on the field with drinks at every opportunity; television cameramen walking backwards just a few feet in front of dismissed batsmen, corporate clap-trap; everything sponsored these days; modern players being sheltered celebrities; decision review system; jingoistic crowds citing that this is not a cricketing issue but a cultural one.*

This says a lot about the commercialisation, not just of cricket but sports in general.

The cultural effects of Kerry Packer's foray into international cricket have been long-lasting. Important lessons have been learned. The main one is not about the commercialisation of the game but that it is the players and what they achieve on the field that keeps the game going. The Board must look after those on the playing field.

Player power has grown enormously since the 1970s and with it players' incomes (aided by a strong Australian Cricketers Association). Bob Simpson believes that the players are now attracting just reward.

> *I think it's marvellous that the players are able to earn big money as long as the means that they are doing this – that is T-20 cricket – is kept in perspective within the broader context of the importance of Test cricket.*

How this balance will be achieved is yet to be determined.

Back in 1977–78, because of the exodus of senior players from the Australian cricketing scene, those dubbed the Establishment Boys were given a unique opportunity to find a place in the Australian Test side. It was never going to be easy. Some seized the opportunity with open arms to help cement a place. Others let it slide. Some held their own, but effectively they had their files in Australian cricket closed for different reasons.

They all wore the baggy green cap with pride. They all did their best. These men who played Test cricket during the turbulent years of 1977–79 deserve some acknowledgement and credit for keeping Test cricket alive, when it could easily have died.

It's time to bring the Establishment Boys home.

Bibliography

Interviews conducted with:

Rob Bath, Allan Border, Ian Brayshaw, Ian Callen, Wayne Clark, Phil Carlson, Bob Cowper, Rick Darling, Ian Chappell, Gary Cosier, Mike Coward, Geoff Dymock, Gideon Haigh, Chris Hamilton, Jim Higgs, Kim Hughes, Alan Hurst, Barry Jarman, Dan Lonergan, Tony Mann, Norman May, Ashley Mallett, Jeff Moss, John Maclean, David Ogilvie , Roland Perry, Ken Piesse, Craig Serjeant, Mike Sexton, Bob Simpson, Peter Toohey, Paul Twiss, Dav Whatmore, Bernard Whimpress, Kevin Wright, Graham Yallop.

Annuals

Allan's Australian Cricket Annual; *Baggy Green*, Whimpress, Bailey, Trevor (ed); *World of Cricket*, MacDonald and Jane's, London, 1977-80, Piesse Ken (ed.) *Cricket Digest*, Newspress, Melbourne, 1979, Lemmon, David (ed); *Pelham Cricket Year*, Pelham Books, London 1979-81; *Wisden Cricketers' Almanack*; *Wisden Cricketers' Almanack Australia*; *Who's Who in Australia*.

Newspapers and Magazines

ABC Cricket Book 1975-1985; The Advertiser; The Age, Australian Cricket; World of Cricket; Australian Cricket tour guide; Courier Mail; Cricketer (Australia); Cricketer (UK), Inside Edge; Inside Sport; The News (Adelaide); Sunday Times (Perth); Sun-Herald; Sydney Morning Herald; The West Australian.

Websites

www.cricinfo.com

www.theguardian.com.au

www.theconversation.com.au

www.cricketweb.net

DVDs

The Australian Cricket Collection, ABC, 2006, Sydney.

Cricket 1977–78 Australia v India – First Test Day 1 Highlights, ABC Commercial, 2014.

Cricket 1978–79 Australia v England – First Test Day 1 Highlights, ABC Commercial, 2014.

C'mon Aussie C'mon, 20th Anniversary of World Series Cricket, Wide World of Sports, 1998, Sydney.

Books

Barry, Paul. *The Rise and Rise of Kerry Packer Uncut*, Bantam, Sydney, 2007.

Barker, Anthony. *The WACA: An Australian Cricket Success Story*, Allen and Unwin, Sydney, 1998.

Beecher, Eric. *The Cricket Revolution*, Newspress, Melbourne, 1978.

Benaud, John. *Matters of Choice: A Test Selector's Story*, Swan Publishing, Dalkeith, WA 1997.

Benaud, Richie, and others. *Ten Turbulent Years*, Swan Publishing, Sydney, 2009.

Blofeld, Henry. *The Packer Affair*, William Collins, London, 1978.

Bowerman, Martin. *One Test: One Dream, One Baggy Green*, Bowerman, Hobart, 2006.

Border, Allan. *Allan Border: The Autobiography*, Methuen, Sydney, 1985.

Border, Allan. *Beyond Ten Thousand: My Life Story*, Swan Publishing, Nedlands, 1993.

Bose, Mohir. *A History of Indian Cricket*, Andre Deutsch, London, 1990.

Boycott, Geoffrey. *Put to the Test*, Arthur Barker, London, 1979.

Brayshaw, Ian, *Caught Marsh bowled Lillee, The legends lives on* ABC Books, 2001.

Brayshaw, Ian. *The Miracle Match: Chappell, Lillee, Richards and the most electric moment in Australian cricket history*, Hardie Grant, Melbourne, 2014.

Bromby, Robin (ed). *A Century of Ashes, an Anthology*, Resolution Press, Sydney, 1982.

Brearley, Mike and Doust, Dudley. *The Ashes retained*, Hodder and Stoughton, London 1979.

Brearley, Mike and Doust, Dudley. *The Return of the Ashes*, Pelham Books, London, 1977.

Brearley, Mike. *The Art of Captaincy*, Hodder and Stoughton, London 1985.

Butler, Keith. *Howzat*, William Collins, Sydney, 1979.

Caro, Andrew. *With a Straight Bat*, Sales Machine, Hong Kong, 1979.

Cashman, Richard; Franks, Warwick; Maxwell, Jim; Stoddart, Brian; Weaver, Amanda; Webster, Ray (ed). *The Oxford Companion to Australian Cricket*, Oxford University Press, Sydney 1996.

Chappell, Greg and Frith, David. *The Ashes '77*, Angus and Robertson, London, 1977.

Chappell, Greg. *The 100th Summer*, Garry Sparke and Associates, Melbourne, 1977.

Chappell, Greg. *Fierce Focus*, Hardie Grant, Melbourne, 2011.

Chappell, Ian. *Chappelli*, Hutchinson, Sydney, 1976.

Chappell, Ian. *The Cutting Edge*, Swan Publishing, Sydney, 1992.

Coward, Mike. *Beyond the Bazaar*, Allen and Unwin, Sydney, 1990.

Coward, Mike. *Caribbean Odyssey, Australia and Cricket in the West Indies*, Simon and Schuster, Sydney 1991.

Coward, Mike. *The Chappell Years, Cricket in the '70s* ABC Books, Sydney 2002.

Coward, Mike. *Rookies, Rebels and Renaissance, Cricket in the '80s*, ABC Books, 2004.

Coward, Mike. *Champions: The world's greaTest cricketers speak*, Allen and Unwin, Sydney 2013.

Davis, Charles (compiler). *Test Cricket in Australia, 1877-2002: The Test Match Archive*, Charles Davis, Melbourne, 2002.

Davis, Ian. *More than Cricket: His Remarkable Story*, Brian Wood, 2004.

Dunstan, Keith. *Sports*, Sun Books, Melbourne, 1981.

Fahey, Michael and Coward, Michael. *The Baggy Green: The pride, passion and history of Australia's sporting icon.* The Cricket Publishing Company, Pennant Hills, 2008.

Fraser-Simpson, Guy. *Cricket at the Crossroads: Class, colour and controversy from 1967 to 1977*, Elliot and Thomson, London, 2011.

Frindall, Bill (ed). *The Wisden Book of Test Cricket 1976-77 to 1977-78*, MacDonald and Jane's London, 1979.

Frindall, Bill (ed), *The Wisden Book of Test Cricket Volume Two, 1977 to 1994*, Headline Publishing, London, 1995.

Frindall, Bill. *Frindall's Scorebook, Jubilee Edition*, Lonsdale Press, London, 1977.

Frith, David. *The Ashes '79*, Angus and Robertson, London, 1979.

Gower, David and Taylor, Bob. *Anyone for Cricket*, Pelham Books, London, 1979.

Greenidge, Gordon. *Man in the Middle*, David and Charles, London, 1980.

Greig, Tony. *My Story*, Stanley Paul, London, 1980.

Haigh, Gideon. *The Border Years,* The Text Publishing Company, Melbourne, 1994.

Haigh, Gideon. *The Cricket War: The Inside Story of Kerry Packer's World Series Cricket*, Melbourne University Press, Melbourne, 2007.

Haigh, Gideon and Frith, David. *Inside Story: Unlocking Australian Cricket Archives*, News Custom Publishing, Melbourne, 2007.

Harte, Chris. *A History of Australian Cricket*, Andrew Deutsch Limited, London, 1993.

Hogg, Rodney and Anderson, Jon. *The Whole Hogg: Inside the mind of a lunatic fast bowler*, Wilkinson Publishing Pty Ltd, Melbourne, 2007.

Hookes, David with Shiell Alan. *Hookesy*, ABC Books, Sydney, 1993.

Hutchinson, Garrie. *Test Team of the Century: The anthology of the greaTest Australian Test players of the Twentieth Century*, Harper Collins, Sydney, 2000.

Juddery, Mark. *1975 Australia's GreaTest Year*, John Wiley and Sons, Sydney 2005.

Knox, Malcolm. *The Captains: The Story behind Australia's second most important job*, Hardie Grant, Melbourne, 2010.

Lawson, Geoff. *Henry: The Geoff Lawson Story*, Ironbark Press, Sydney, 1993.

Lee, Alan. *A Pitch in Both Camps,* Pelham Books, London, 1979.

Lillee, Dennis. *My Life in Cricket*, Methuen, Sydney, 1982. Lillee, Dennis. *Over and Out,* Methuen, Sydney, 1984.

Lynch, Stephen (ed). *Wisden on the Ashes: The Authoritative Story of Australia's GreaTest Rivalry*, John Wisden and Co, 2011, London.

Mallett, Ashley. *Spin Out*, Garry Sparke and Associates, Melbourne, 1977.

Mallett, Ashley. *Thommo Speaks Out: The Authorised biography of Jeff Thomson*, Allen and Unwin, Sydney, 2009.

Mallett, Ashley with Chappell, Ian. *Chappelli Speaks Out*, Allen and Unwin, Sydney 2005.

Marsh, Rod. *Gloves, Sweat and Tears: The Final Shout*, Penguin, Sydney, 1984.

Martin-Jenkins, Christopher. *The Jubilee Tests*, MacDonald and Jane's, London, 1977.

Martin-Jenkins, Christopher. *In Defence of The Ashes, England's Victory, Packer's Progress*, MacDonald and Jane's, London, 1979.

MacFarline, Peter. *A Game Divided*, Marlin Books, Melbourne, 1978.

MacFarline, Peter. *A Testing Time*, Hutchinson, Melbourne, 1979.

McGilvray, Alan. *The Game is Not the Same*, ABC Books, Sydney, 1985.

McGregor, Adrian. *Greg Chappell*, William Collins, Sydney,1985.

Meher-Homji, Kersi. *Cricket Conflicts and Controversies*, New Holland Publishers, Sydney 2012.

Meyer, John. *From the Outer: Australia versus England 1978-79*, John Meyer, Wembley, 1979.

Moss, Stephen (ed). *Wisden Anthology 1978-2006, Cricket's Age of Revolution*, John Wisden and Co Ltd. Hampshire, 2006.

Nicholls, Barry. *You Only Get One Innings: Family, Mates and the Wisdom of Cricket*, Harper Collins Publishers, Sydney, 2013.

Nicholson, Rod with Williams, Ken. *100 Not-out: A Centenary of Premier Cricket*, Wilkinson Publishing, Melbourne, 2006.

O'Keeffe, Kerry. *Turn, Turn, Turn… Please. Musings on Cricket and life by Kerry O'Keeffe*, ABC Books Sydney, 2007.

Smith, Rick. *Australian Test Cricketers, An A-Z profiling every cricketer who's donned the Baggy Green.* ABC Books Sydney, 2006.

Robinson, Ray. *On Top Down Under*, Cassell Australia, Sydney, 1981.

Ryan, Christian. *Golden Boy: Kim Hughes and the bad old days of Australian Cricket*, Allen and Unwin, Sydney, 2009.

Ryan, Christian. *Australia; Story of a Cricket Country*, Hardie Grant, Melbourne, 2011.

Simpson, Bob. *Simmo – Cricket then and now*, Allen and Unwin, Sydney 2006.

Simpson, Bob. *Bob Simpson's Young Australians*, Lavardin, Melbourne, 1978.

Steen, Rob. *Desmond Haynes: Lion of Barbados*, H.F. and G.Witherby, London 1993.

Steen, Rob and McLellan, Alistair. *500-1: The Miracle of Headingley '81.* BBC Books, London 2001.

Wards, Kirwan. *Put Lock On,* Rigby, Sydney, 1972.

Webster, Ray (ed). *First-class Cricket in Australia Vol 2 1945-46 to 1976-77*, Ray Webster, Glen Waverley, 1997.

Whimpress, Bernard and Hart, Nigel. *Australian Eleven: Test Cricket Snapshots 1945-1995,* Bernard Whimpress, Adelaide, 1997.

Whimpress, Bernard. *On Our Selection: An alternative history of Australian Cricket*, Bernard Whimpress, Adelaide, 2011.

Whimpress, Bernard. *Chuckers: A history of throwing in Australian cricket*, Elvis Press, Adelaide, 2004.

Woodward, Ian. *Aussies versus Windies: A History of Australia-West Indies Cricket*, Walla Wall Press, Petersham, NSW, 1998.

Yallop, Graham. *Lambs to the Slaughter*, Outback Press, Melbourne, 1979.

Yardley, Bruce. *Roo's Book*, Bruce Yardley, Perth, 2007, Gary Allen, Smithfield, 2004.

Acknowledgments

As always when putting together a book of this nature there are many people to thank. Writing a book is no more a solo enterprise than putting a three-hour radio program to air each day. Bernard Whimpress and Mike Sexton encouraged me to write the book when I first mentioned the idea to them and they kept on encouraging. Bernard was also instrumental in helping with the structure of the book. Rob Bath – thanks again for your editing skills and ensuring I always look on the bright side of projects such as this. Dan Lonergan, Tony Hargreaves and Ian Brayshaw were invaluable when it came to passing on contacts that otherwise may had been hard to find. Dan also kindly read through the manuscript and was a terrific sounding board throughout the completion of this story and provided continual encouragement. Michael Steel provided some useful ideas, while Terry Alderman, Brian Wood and Ashley Mallett were also generous in sharing contacts. Dr Tony Best, a wonderful doctor and an even finer man, was a great help. Chris Hamilton as always was a terrific support. Thanks to my father Les Nicholls for reading the manuscript more than once, and Nick Moschetta who was always there to check details. Phillip Carlson, Wayne Clark, Gary Cosier, Rick Darling, Geoff Dymock, Alan Hurst, Tony Mann and Craig Serjeant kindly supplied some of their photos. Thanks to Pip Doyle at Fairfax for helping give my article about this story a run. If not for that I doubt this book would have seen the light of day!

I could not have been written this book without the benefit of the talents of the men who in 1970s covered both Packer Test and WSC Cricket, including Alan Sheill, Peter McFarline, Phil Wilkins, Mike Coward, Ken Piesse, John Benaud and Alan Lee. Peter Hanlon's more recent profiles 'In Packer's Shadow Series' for Fairfax was also a valuable resource. I also owe a special debt to the fine work of writers and historians especially Gideon Haigh, Christian Ryan, Chris Harte, Bernard Whimpress and Nigel Hart who have all written about various aspects of the era featured in this book.

This edition wouldn't be in your hands if it weren't for Alan Whiticker and Patsy Rowe, who saw value in the telling of the story, and their colleagues at New Holland Publishing for their fine editing and presentation of the end product. Huge thanks to all the past players, administrators and members of the media who so gladly gave so much of their time to me. Mum and Dad thanks for the on-going love and support and to Sue and Arthur Mercer for all you have done. Finally, words cannot describe my appreciation to my partner Ann and our four children, Jacy, Ambrose, Harry and Ellie, for their support, patience, love and understanding, affording me the time and energy to write this book. It was tough going at times but I got there!

Other Books By Barry Nicholls

On cricket
Cricket Dreaming – the Rites of Summer, 2009.
For Those who Wait – the Barry Jarman Story, 2011.
You Only Get One Innings, 2013.

On Australian Rules football
Triple Blue: Jack Oatey, John Wynne and the Whole Damn Thing, 2002.
The Story of 78: How Norwood gave Sturt the Blues – 30th anniversary edition, 2008.

India tour of Australia, 1977–78

1st Test: Australia v India at Brisbane, Dec 2-6, 1977

Australia won by 16 runs

Australia 1st innings		R	M	B
PA Hibbert	c †Kirmani b Amarnath	13	89	77
GJ Cosier	c Madan Lal b Amarnath	19	51	32
AD Ogilvie	c Viswanath b Bedi	5	15	8
CS Serjeant	c Gavaskar b Bedi	0	2	4
RB Simpson*	c Gavaskar b Bedi	7	5	6
PM Toohey	st †Kirmani b Bedi	82	142	142
AL Mann	lbw b Madan Lal	19	43	54
SJ Rixon†	c Amarnath b Bedi	9	21	14
WM Clark	c Gavaskar b Chandrasekhar	4	13	11
JR Thomson	b Chandrasekhar	3	19	18
AG Hurst	not-out	0	24	9
Extras	(b 3, lb 1, w 1)	5		
Total	(all out; 46.7 overs)	166		

Fall of wickets 1-24 (Cosier), 2-33 (Ogilvie), 3-33 (Serjeant), 4-43 (Simpson), 5-49 (Hibbert), 6-90 (Mann), 7-107 (Rixon), 8-112 (Clark), 9-132 (Thomson), 10-166 (Toohey)

Bowling	O	M	R	W	Econ
S Madan Lal	10	3	27	1	2.02
M Amarnath	13	4	43	2	2.48
BS Bedi	13.7	3	55	5	2.97
EAS Prasanna	4	2	2	0	0.37
BS Chandrasekhar	6	1	34	2	4.25

India 1st innings		R	M	B
SM Gavaskar	c Cosier b Clark	3	18	14
DB Vengsarkar	hit wicket b Thomson	48	165	115
M Amarnath	lbw b Clark	0	20	17
GR Viswanath	c Hurst b Mann	45	111	90
BP Patel	c Serjeant b Clark	13	31	27
AV Mankad	c †Rixon b Thomson	0	14	9
S Madan Lal	b Clark	4	14	5
SMH Kirmani†	c Ogilvie b Thomson	11	72	53
EAS Prasanna	c Thomson b Mann	23	62	61
BS Bedi*	not-out	2	11	6
BS Chandrasekhar	lbw b Mann	0	7	8
Extras	(nb 4)	4		
Total	(all out; 50 overs)	153		

Fall of wickets 1-11 (Gavaskar), 2-15 (Amarnath), 3-90 (Viswanath), 4-108 (Vengsarkar), 5-110 (Patel), 6-112 (Mankad), 7-119 (Madan Lal), 8-149 (Prasanna), 9-151 (Kirmani), 10-153 (Chandrasekhar)

Bowling	O	M	R	W	Econ
JR Thomson	16	1	54	3	2.53
WM Clark	18	5	46	4	1.91
AG Hurst	7	0	31	0	3.32
GJ Cosier	3	1	6	0	1.50
AL Mann	6	0	12	3	1.50

Australia 2nd innings		R	M	B
PA Hibbert	lbw b Madan Lal	2	12	12
GJ Cosier	c Prasanna b Madan Lal	0	2	2
AD Ogilvie	b Chandrasekhar	46	170	158
CS Serjeant	b Amarnath	0	2	2
RB Simpson*	c Viswanath b Amarnath	89	311	269
PM Toohey	c Bedi b Chandrasekhar	57	94	105
AL Mann	c Amarnath b Madan Lal	29	66	56
SJ Rixon†	c †Kirmani b Madan Lal	6	29	19
WM Clark	b Madan Lal	12	45	36
JR Thomson	not-out	41	61	53
AG Hurst	run out	26	30	23
Extras	(b 6, lb 11, nb 2)	19		
Total	(all out; 91.5 overs)	327		

Fall of wickets 1-0 (Cosier), 2-6 (Hibbert), 3-7 (Serjeant), 4-100 (Ogilvie), 5-184 (Toohey), 6-233 (Simpson), 7-237 (Mann), 8-246 (Rixon), 9-277 (Clark), 10-327 (Hurst)

Bowling	O	M	R	W	Econ
S Madan Lal	19	2	72	5	2.84
M Amarnath	8	1	24	2	2.25
BS Bedi	18.5	2	71	0	2.85
EAS Prasanna	20	4	59	0	2.21
BS Chandrasekhar	26	6	82	2	2.36

India 2nd innings (target: 341 runs)		R	M	B
SM Gavaskar	c †Rixon b Clark	113	320	264
DB Vengsarkar	b Clark	1	10	2
M Amarnath	c †Rixon b Thomson	47	100	79
GR Viswanath	c Ogilvie b Thomson	35	84	85
BP Patel	lbw b Thomson	3	8	6
AV Mankad	b Hurst	21	56	60
SMH Kirmani†	c Serjeant b Hurst	55	137	133
S Madan Lal	c †Rixon b Clark	2	12	9
EAS Prasanna	c Hibbert b Clark	8	29	11
BS Bedi*	not-out	26	50	30
BS Chandrasekhar	c †Rixon b Thomson	0	10	7
Extras	(lb 6, nb 7)	13		
Total	(all out; 84.7 overs)	324		

Fall of wickets 1-7 (Vengsarkar), 2-88 (Amarnath), 3-147 (Viswanath), 4-151 (Patel), 5-196 (Mankad), 6-243 (Gavaskar), 7-251 (Madan Lal), 8-275 (Prasanna), 9-318 (Kirmani), 10-324 (Chandrasekhar)

Bowling	O	M	R	W	Econ
JR Thomson	19.7	1	76	4	2.86
WM Clark	26	1	101	4	2.91
AG Hurst	15	3	50	2	2.50
GJ Cosier	5	1	10	0	1.50
AL Mann	15	3	52	0	2.60
RB Simpson	4	0	22	0	4.12

Match details
Balls per over: 8; **Toss** – Australia, who chose to bat; **Series** – Australia led the 5-match series 1-0; **Test debuts** – WM Clark, PA Hibbert, AL Mann, AD Ogilvie, SJ Rixon and PM Toohey (Australia); **Umpires** – TF Brooks and MG O'Connell

2nd Test: Australia v India at Perth, Dec 16-21, 1977

Australia won by 2 wickets

India 1st innings		R	M	B
SM Gavaskar	c †Rixon b Clark	4	28	33
CPS Chauhan	c Gannon b Simpson	88	195	151
M Amarnath	c Gannon b Thomson	90	228	156
GR Viswanath	b Thomson	38	50	55
DB Vengsarkar	c †Rixon b Clark	49	105	76
BP Patel	c †Rixon b Thomson	3	9	8
SMH Kirmani†	c †Rixon b Thomson	38	76	64
S Venkataraghavan	c Simpson b Gannon	37	83	60
S Madan Lal	b Gannon	43	44	35
BS Bedi*	b Gannon	3	0	4
BS Chandrasekhar	not-out	0	27	10
Extras	(b 1, nb 8)	9		
Total	(all out; 79.6 overs)	402		

Fall of wickets 1-14 (Gavaskar), 2-163 (Chauhan), 3-224 (Viswanath), 4-229 (Amarnath), 5-235 (Patel), 6-311 (Kirmani), 7-319 (Vengsarkar), 8-383 (Madan Lal), 9-391 (Bedi), 10-402 (Venkataraghavan)

Bowling	O	M	R	W	Econ
JR Thomson	24	1	101	4	3.15
WM Clark	17	0	95	2	4.19
JB Gannon	16.6	1	84	3	3.76
AL Mann	11	0	63	0	4.29
RB Simpson	11	0	50	1	3.40

Australia 1st innings		R	M	B
J Dyson	c Patel b Bedi	53	257	220
CS Serjeant	c †Kirmani b Madan Lal	13	40	32
AD Ogilvie	b Bedi	27	87	65
PM Toohey	st †Kirmani b Bedi	0	13	13
RB Simpson*	c Vengsarkar b Venkataraghavan	176	388	355
SJ Rixon†	c †Kirmani b Amarnath	50	120	115
KJ Hughes	c Patel b Bedi	28	80	75
AL Mann	c Vengsarkar b Bedi	7	20	24
WM Clark	c Patel b Chandrasekhar	15	58	44
JR Thomson	c Amarnath b Venkataraghavan	0	2	5
JB Gannon	not-out	0	2	1
Extras	(lb 25)	25		
Total	(all out; 118.6 overs)	394		

Fall of wickets 1-19 (Serjeant), 2-61 (Ogilvie), 3-65 (Toohey), 4-149 (Dyson), 5-250 (Rixon), 6-321 (Hughes), 7-341 (Mann), 8-388 (Simpson), 9-388 (Thomson), 10-394 (Clark)

Bowling	O	M	R	W	Econ
S Madan Lal	15	1	54	1	2.70
M Amarnath	16	2	57	1	2.67
BS Chandrasekhar	33.6	6	114	1	2.53
BS Bedi	31	6	89	5	2.15
S Venkataraghavan	23	4	55	2	1.79

India 2nd innings		R	M	B
SM Gavaskar	b Clark	127	271	245
CPS Chauhan	c Ogilvie b Thomson	32	56	40
M Amarnath	c †Rixon b Simpson	100	264	175
GR Viswanath	c †Rixon b Clark	1	10	11
DB Vengsarkar	c Hughes b Gannon	9	46	37
BP Patel	b Gannon	27	63	40
SMH Kirmani†	lbw b Gannon	2	1	2
S Venkataraghavan	c Hughes b Gannon	14	46	41
S Madan Lal	b Thomson	3	7	7
BS Bedi*	not-out	0	8	3
BS Chandrasekhar	not-out	0	1	1
Extras	(b 1, lb 4, nb 10)	15		
Total	(9 wickets dec; 73.5 overs)	330		

Fall of wickets 1-47 (Chauhan), 2-240 (Gavaskar), 3-244 (Viswanath), 4-283 (Amarnath), 5-287 (Vengsarkar), 6-289 (Kirmani), 7-327 (Venkataraghavan), 8-328 (Patel), 9-330 (Madan Lal)

Bowling	O	M	R	W	Econ
JR Thomson	21.5	3	65	2	2.25
WM Clark	18	1	83	2	3.45
JB Gannon	18	2	77	4	3.20
AL Mann	8	0	49	0	4.59
RB Simpson	8	2	41	1	3.84

Australia 2nd innings (target: 339 runs)		R	M	B
J Dyson	c Vengsarkar b Bedi	4	24	19
CS Serjeant	c †Kirmani b Madan Lal	12	38	38
AL Mann	c †Kirmani b Bedi	105	183	165
AD Ogilvie	b Bedi	47	208	180
PM Toohey	c Amarnath b Bedi	83	164	140
RB Simpson*	run out	39	95	92
KJ Hughes	lbw b Madan Lal	0	2	1
SJ Rixon†	lbw b Bedi	23	31	34
WM Clark	not-out	5	18	14
JR Thomson	not-out	6	13	15
Extras	(b 8, lb 10)	18		
Total	(8 wickets; 87.2 overs)	342		

Did not bat: JB Gannon

Fall of wickets 1-13 (Dyson), 2-33 (Serjeant), 3-172 (Mann), 4-195 (Ogilvie), 5-295 (Simpson), 6-296 (Hughes), 7-330 (Toohey), 8-330 (Rixon)

Bowling	O	M	R	W	Econ
S Madan Lal	11	0	44	2	3.00
M Amarnath	3	0	22	0	5.50
BS Chandrasekhar	15	0	67	0	3.35
BS Bedi	30.2	6	105	5	2.60
S Venkataraghavan	28	9	86	0	2.30

Match details
Balls per over: 8;
Toss – India, who chose to bat;
Series – Australia led the 5-match series 2-0;
Test debuts – J Dyson and JB Gannon (Australia);
Umpires – RC Bailhache and RA French

3rd Test: Australia v India at Melbourne, Dec 30, 1977 – Jan 4, 1978

India won by 222 runs

India 1st innings		R	M	B
SM Gavaskar	c †Rixon b Thomson	0	12	9
CPS Chauhan	c Mann b Clark	0	9	6
M Amarnath	c Simpson b Clark	72	269	178
GR Viswanath	c †Rixon b Thomson	59	154	95
DB Vengsarkar	c Simpson b Thomson	37	94	88
AV Mankad	c Clark b Gannon	44	119	100
SMH Kirmani†	lbw b Simpson	29	85	62
KD Ghavri	c †Rixon b Gannon	6	26	20
EAS Prasanna	b Clark	0	6	1
BS Bedi*	not-out	2	4	1
BS Chandrasekhar	b Clark	0	2	1
Extras	(lb 3, nb 4)	7		
Total	(all out; 69.2 overs)	256		

Fall of wickets 1-0 (Chauhan), 2-0 (Gavaskar), 3-105 (Viswanath), 4-174 (Vengsarkar), 5-180 (Amarnath), 6-234 (Kirmani), 7-254 (Ghavri), 8-254 (Mankad), 9-256 (Prasanna), 10-256 (Chandrasekhar)

Bowling	O	M	R	W	Econ
JR Thomson	16	2	78	3	3.65
WM Clark	19.2	2	73	4	2.84
JB Gannon	14	2	47	2	2.51
GJ Cosier	12	3	25	0	1.56
RB Simpson	3	1	11	1	2.75
AL Mann	5	1	15	0	2.25

Australia 1st innings		R	M	B
J Dyson	b Ghavri	0	2	2
GJ Cosier	c Chauhan b Chandrasekhar	67	125	101
AD Ogilvie	lbw b Ghavri	6	23	10
CS Serjeant	b Chandrasekhar	85	216	170
RB Simpson*	c Mankad b Chandrasekhar	2	2	3
PM Toohey	c Viswanath b Bedi	14	43	36
AL Mann	c Gavaskar b Bedi	11	9	12
SJ Rixon†	lbw b Chandrasekhar	11	45	49
WM Clark	lbw b Chandrasekhar	3	20	15
JR Thomson	c Ghavri b Chandrasekhar	0	2	2
JB Gannon	not-out	0	5	2
Extras	(b 6, lb 7, nb 1)	14		
Total	(all out; 50.1 overs)	213		

Fall of wickets 1-0 (Dyson), 2-18 (Ogilvie), 3-122 (Cosier), 4-124 (Simpson), 5-166 (Toohey), 6-178 (Mann), 7-202 (Rixon), 8-211 (Serjeant), 9-211 (Clark), 10-213 (Thomson)

Bowling	O	M	R	W	Econ
KD Ghavri	9	0	37	2	3.08
SM Gavaskar	2	0	7	0	2.62
BS Bedi	15	2	71	2	3.55
BS Chandrasekhar	14.1	2	52	6	2.76
EAS Prasanna	10	1	32	0	2.40

India 2nd innings		R	M	B
SM Gavaskar	c Serjeant b Gannon	118	351	285
CPS Chauhan	run out	20	45	27
SMH Kirmani†	c Thomson b Mann	29	82	62
GR Viswanath	lbw b Clark	54	114	94
DB Vengsarkar	c Cosier b Clark	6	18	20
AV Mankad	b Clark	38	130	84
M Amarnath	b Cosier	41	115	100
KD Ghavri	c Simpson b Clark	6	13	10
EAS Prasanna	c †Rixon b Gannon	11	32	23
BS Bedi*	not-out	12	30	13
BS Chandrasekhar	lbw b Cosier	0	2	1
Extras	(lb 1, nb 7)	8		
Total	(all out; 88.7 overs)	343		

Fall of wickets 1-40 (Chauhan), 2-89 (Kirmani), 3-187 (Viswanath), 4-198 (Vengsarkar), 5-265 (Gavaskar), 6-286 (Mankad), 7-294 (Ghavri), 8-315 (Prasanna), 9-343 (Amarnath), 10-343 (Chandrasekhar)

Bowling	O	M	R	W	Econ
JR Thomson	18	4	47	0	1.95
WM Clark	29	3	96	4	2.48
JB Gannon	22	4	88	2	3.00
GJ Cosier	12.7	2	58	2	3.37
RB Simpson	3	0	22	0	5.50
AL Mann	4	0	24	1	4.50

Australia 2nd innings (target: 387 runs)		R	M	B
J Dyson	lbw b Bedi	12	48	31
GJ Cosier	b Chandrasekhar	34	63	55
AD Ogilvie	c Chauhan b Bedi	0	2	4
CS Serjeant	b Chandrasekhar	17	43	41
RB Simpson*	lbw b Chandrasekhar	4	7	7
PM Toohey	c Chauhan b Chandrasekhar	14	52	53
AL Mann	c Gavaskar b Chandrasekhar	18	59	56
SJ Rixon†	c & b Chandrasekhar	12	49	49
WM Clark	c Ghavri b Bedi	33	63	60
JR Thomson	c & b Bedi	7	38	46
JB Gannon	not-out	3	8	8
Extras	(b 6, lb 4)	10		
Total	(all out; 51.1 overs)	164		

Fall of wickets 1-42 (Dyson), 2-42 (Ogilvie), 3-52 (Cosier), 4-60 (Simpson), 5-77 (Serjeant), 6-98 (Toohey), 7-115 (Mann), 8-122 (Rixon), 9-151 (Thomson), 10-164 (Clark)

Bowling	O	M	R	W	Econ
KD Ghavri	4	0	29	0	5.43
BS Bedi	16.1	5	58	4	2.69
BS Chandrasekhar	20	3	52	6	1.95
EAS Prasanna	8	4	5	0	0.46
M Amarnath	3	0	10	0	2.50

Match details
Balls per over: 8;
Toss – India, who chose to bat;
Series – Australia led the 5-match series 2-1;
Umpires – RA French and MG O'Connell

4th Test: Australia v India at Sydney, Jan 7-12, 1978

India won by an innings and 2 runs

Australia 1st innings		R	M	B
J Dyson	lbw b Chandrasekhar	26	136	114
GJ Cosier	b Amarnath	17	46	31
PM Toohey	run out	4	9	9
CS Serjeant	c Ghavri b Bedi	4	41	35
RB Simpson*	c †Kirmani b Chandrasekhar	38	113	99
KJ Hughes	b Bedi	17	22	21
AL Mann	b Bedi	0	1	2
SJ Rixon†	lbw b Chandrasekhar	17	70	68
WM Clark	c Gavaskar b Chandrasekhar	0	1	2
JR Thomson	not-out	1	21	10
JB Gannon	c Amarnath b Prasanna	0	5	6
Extras	(lb 5, nb 2)	7		
Total	(all out; 49.4 overs)	131		

Fall of wickets 1-29 (Cosier), 2-34 (Toohey), 3-46 (Serjeant), 4-61 (Dyson), 5-84 (Hughes), 6-84 (Mann), 7-125 (Simpson), 8-125 (Clark), 9-130 (Rixon), 10-131 (Gannon)

Bowling	O	M	R	W	Econ
KD Ghavri	7	1	25	0	2.67
M Amarnath	7	4	6	1	0.64
BS Bedi	13	3	49	3	2.82
BS Chandrasekhar	15	3	30	4	1.50
EAS Prasanna	7.4	2	14	1	1.40

India 1st innings		R	M	B
SM Gavaskar	c †Rixon b Thomson	49	144	110
CPS Chauhan	c Mann b Clark	42	170	124
M Amarnath	c Gannon b Clark	9	40	37
GR Viswanath	b Thomson	79	202	182
DB Vengsarkar	c †Rixon b Cosier	48	208	121
AV Mankad	b Thomson	16	22	23
SMH Kirmani†	b Cosier	42	95	61
KD Ghavri	c Serjeant b Thomson	64	142	123
EAS Prasanna	not-out	25	56	44
BS Bedi*	not-out	1	1	1
Extras	(lb 9, nb 12)	21		
Total	(8 wickets dec; 101 overs)	396		

Did not bat: BS Chandrasekhar

Fall of wickets 1-97 (Gavaskar), 2-102 (Chauhan), 3-116 (Amarnath), 4-241 (Viswanath), 5-261 (Mankad), 6-263 (Vengsarkar), 7-344 (Kirmani), 8-395 (Ghavri)

Bowling	O	M	R	W	Econ
JR Thomson	27	8	83	4	2.30
WM Clark	21	3	66	2	2.35
JB Gannon	20	4	65	0	2.43
AL Mann	20	0	101	0	3.78
RB Simpson	4	0	34	0	6.37
GJ Cosier	9	1	26	2	2.16

Australia 2nd innings		R	M	B
J Dyson	c & b Chandrasekhar	6	67	51
GJ Cosier	b Bedi	68	193	164
KJ Hughes	c Vengsarkar b Bedi	19	94	81
CS Serjeant	b Prasanna	1	3	6
RB Simpson*	lbw b Prasanna	33	131	126
PM Toohey	c sub (S Madan Lal) b Ghavri	85	231	258
AL Mann	c & b Prasanna	0	1	2
SJ Rixon†	c Viswanath b Chandrasekhar	11	22	27
WM Clark	b Prasanna	10	33	23
JR Thomson	b Ghavri	16	72	55
JB Gannon	not-out	0	4	0
Extras	(b 5, lb 6, nb 3)	14		
Total	(all out; 98.7 overs)	263		

Fall of wickets 1-26 (Dyson), 2-87 (Hughes), 3-88 (Serjeant), 4-106 (Cosier), 5-171 (Simpson), 6-171 (Mann), 7-194 (Rixon), 8-221 (Clark), 9-257 (Toohey), 10-263 (Thomson)

Bowling	O	M	R	W	Econ
KD Ghavri	12.7	3	42	2	2.44
M Amarnath	5	3	9	0	1.35
BS Bedi	28	8	62	2	1.66
BS Chandrasekhar	24	3	85	2	2.65
EAS Prasanna	29	11	51	4	1.31

Match details
Balls per over: 8;
Toss – Australia, who chose to bat;
Series – 5-match series level 2-2;
Umpires – RC Bailhache and TF Brooks

5th Test: Australia v India at Adelaide, Jan 28-Feb 3, 1978

Australia won by 47 runs

Australia 1st innings		R	M	B
GM Wood	st †Kirmani b Chandrasekhar	39	104	
WM Darling	c Vengsarkar b Chandrasekhar	65	125	
GN Yallop	c Gavaskar b Amarnath	121	227	
PM Toohey	c Gavaskar b Chandrasekhar	60	89	
RB Simpson*	c Viswanath b Ghavri	100	264	200
GJ Cosier	b Ghavri	1	7	
SJ Rixon†	b Bedi	32	79	
B Yardley	c & b Ghavri	22	46	
JR Thomson	c Ghavri b Chandrasekhar	24	55	
WM Clark	b Chandrasekhar	0	4	
IW Callen	not-out	22	40	
Extras	(b 4, lb 14, nb 1)	19		
Total	(all out; 112.4 overs)	505		

India 1st innings		R	M	B
SM Gavaskar	c Toohey b Thomson	7	24	18
CPS Chauhan	c Cosier b Clark	15	31	20
M Amarnath	c Cosier b Thomson	0	3	5
GR Viswanath	c †Rixon b Callen	89	195	175
DB Vengsarkar	c †Rixon b Callen	44	214	203
AD Gaekwad	c †Rixon b Callen	27	95	87
SMH Kirmani†	run out	48	117	95
KD Ghavri	c Simpson b Clark	3	15	15
EAS Prasanna	not-out	15	50	40
BS Bedi*	c sub (KJ Hughes) b Clark	6	16	8
BS Chandrasekhar	c & b Clark	2	2	3
Extras	(b 4, lb 1, nb 8)	13		
Total	(all out; 82.2 overs)	269		

Fall of wickets 1-89 (Wood), 2-110 (Darling), 3-230 (Toohey), 4-334 (Yallop), 5-337 (Cosier), 6-406 (Rixon), 7-450 (Yardley), 8-457 (Simpson), 9-458 (Clark), 10-505 (Thomson)

Fall of wickets 1-23 (Gavaskar), 2-23 (Amarnath), 3-23 (Chauhan), 4-159 (Viswanath), 5-166 (Vengsarkar), 6-216 (Gaekwad), 7-226 (Ghavri), 8-249 (Kirmani), 9-263 (Bedi), 10-269 (Chandrasekhar)

Bowling	O	M	R	W	Econ
KD Ghavri	22	2	93	3	3.17
M Amarnath	12	0	45	1	2.81
BS Bedi	34	1	127	1	2.80
EAS Prasanna	10	1	48	0	3.60
BS Chandrasekhar	29.4	0	136	5	3.45
AD Gaekwad	5	0	37	0	5.55

Bowling	O	M	R	W	Econ
JR Thomson	3.3	1	12	2	2.66
WM Clark	20.7	6	62	4	2.22
IW Callen	22	0	83	3	2.82
GJ Cosier	4	3	4	0	0.75
B Yardley	23	6	62	0	2.02
RB Simpson	9	0	33	0	2.75

Australia 2nd innings		R	M	B
GM Wood	c Vengsarkar b Bedi	8	35	24
WM Darling	b Bedi	56	116	122
GN Yallop	b Bedi	24	70	51
PM Toohey	c †Kirmani b Prasanna	10	44	39
RB Simpson*	lbw b Ghavri	51	177	
GJ Cosier	st †Kirmani b Bedi	34	90	105
SJ Rixon†	run out	13	50	
B Yardley	c Vengsarkar b Ghavri	26	48	
WM Clark	lbw b Ghavri	1	23	
IW Callen	not-out	4	26	
JR Thomson	c Amarnath b Ghavri	3	10	
Extras	(b 5, lb 15, w 3, nb 3)	26		
Total	(all out; 82.5 overs)	256		

Fall of wickets 1-17 (Wood), 2-84 (Yallop), 3-95 (Darling), 4-107 (Toohey), 5-172 (Cosier), 6-210 (Rixon), 7-214 (Simpson), 8-240 (Clark), 9-248 (Yardley), 10-256 (Thomson)

Bowling	O	M	R	W	Econ
KD Ghavri	10.5	2	45	4	3.17
M Amarnath	4	0	12	0	2.25
BS Bedi	20	3	53	4	1.98
EAS Prasanna	34	7	68	1	1.50
BS Chandrasekhar	14	0	52	0	2.78

India 2nd innings (target: 493 runs)		R	M	B
SM Gavaskar	c †Rixon b Callen	29	29	54
CPS Chauhan	c Wood b Yardley	32	99	61
M Amarnath	c Callen b Yardley	86	317	
GR Viswanath	c Simpson b Clark	73	188	
DB Vengsarkar	c Toohey b Yardley	78	188	
AD Gaekwad	c & b Yardley	12	99	
SMH Kirmani†	b Clark	51	146	124
KD Ghavri	c sub (KJ Hughes) b Callen	23	109	90
EAS Prasanna	not-out	10	48	33
BS Bedi*	c Cosier b Callen	16	26	21
BS Chandrasekhar	c †Rixon b Simpson	2	4	7
Extras	(b 6, lb 11, nb 16)	33		
Total	(all out; 141.4 overs)	445		

Fall of wickets 1-40 (Gavaskar), 2-79 (Chauhan), 3-210 (Viswanath), 4-256 (Amarnath), 5-323 (Gaekwad), 6-348 (Vengsarkar), 7-415 (Ghavri), 8-417 (Kirmani), 9-442 (Bedi), 10-445 (Chandrasekhar)

Bowling	O	M	R	W	Econ
WM Clark	29	6	79	2	2.04
IW Callen	33	5	108	3	2.45
GJ Cosier	13	6	21	0	1.21
B Yardley	43	6	134	4	2.33
RB Simpson	23.4	6	70	1	2.23

Match details
Balls per over: 8;
Toss – Australia, who chose to bat;
Series – Australia won the 5-match series 3-2;
Test debuts – IW Callen, WM Darling, GM Wood and B Yardley (Australia);
Umpires – RA French and MG O'Connell

Australia tour of West Indies, 1978

1st Test: West Indies v Australia at Port of Spain, Mar 3-5, 1978

West Indies won by an innings and 106 runs

Australia 1st innings		R	M
GM Wood	c Haynes b Croft	2	25
CS Serjeant	c †Murray b Croft	3	64
GN Yallop	c Richards b Croft	2	18
PM Toohey	b Garner	20	66
RB Simpson*	lbw b Garner	0	13
GJ Cosier	c Greenidge b Croft	46	88
SJ Rixon†	run out	1	9
B Yardley	c †Murray b Roberts	2	19
JR Thomson	c Austin b Roberts	0	4
WM Clark	b Garner	0	15
JD Higgs	not-out	0	6
Extras	(b 4, lb 6, nb 4)	14	
Total	(all out; 35.1 overs)	90	

Fall of wickets 1-7 (Wood), 2-10 (Yallop), 3-16 (Serjeant), 4-23 (Simpson), 4-37* (Toohey, retired not-out), 5-45 (Rixon), 6-75 (Yardley), 7-75 (Thomson), 8-84 (Clark), 9-90 (Toohey), 10-90 (Cosier)

Bowling	O	M	R	W	Econ
AME Roberts	12	4	26	2	2.16
CEH Croft	9.1	5	15	4	1.63
J Garner	14	6	35	3	2.50

West Indies 1st innings		R	M
CG Greenidge	b Yardley	43	145
DL Haynes	c †Rixon b Higgs	61	75
IVA Richards	lbw b Thomson	39	64
AI Kallicharran	b Yardley	127	258
CH Lloyd*	b Thomson	86	160
RA Austin	c sub (TJ Laughlin) b Thomson	2	26
DL Murray†	c †Rixon b Higgs	21	70
DR Parry	b Yardley	0	2
AME Roberts	st †Rixon b Higgs	7	39
J Garner	c Cosier b Higgs	0	3
CEH Croft	not-out	4	20
Extras	(lb 9, nb 6)	15	
Total	(all out; 109.5 overs)	405	

Fall of wickets 1-87 (Haynes), 2-143 (Richards), 3-143 (Greenidge), 4-313 (Lloyd), 5-324 (Austin), 6-385 (Kallicharran), 7-385 (Parry), 8-391 (Murray), 9-391 (Garner), 10-405 (Roberts)

Bowling	O	M	R	W	Econ
JR Thomson	21	6	84	3	4.00
WM Clark	16	3	41	0	2.56
JD Higgs	24.5	3	91	4	3.66
RB Simpson	16	2	65	0	4.06
B Yardley	19	1	64	3	3.36
GJ Cosier	13	2	45	0	3.46

Australia 2nd innings		R	M
GM Wood	lbw b Roberts	32	54
CS Serjeant	lbw b Garner	40	79
GN Yallop	b Roberts	81	195
GJ Cosier	lbw b Garner	19	110
RB Simpson*	b Parry	14	68
SJ Rixon†	lbw b Roberts	0	2
B Yardley	not-out	7	18
JR Thomson	b Parry	4	2
WM Clark	b Roberts	0	3
JD Higgs	b Roberts	2	6
PM Toohey	absent hurt	-	
Extras	(b 6, lb 1, w 1, nb 2)	10	
Total	(all out; 63.2 overs)	209	

Fall of wickets 1-59 (Wood), 2-90 (Serjeant), 3-149 (Cosier), 4-194 (Yallop), 5-194 (Rixon), 6-194 (Simpson), 7-200 (Thomson), 8-201 (Clark), 9-209 (Higgs)

Bowling	O	M	R	W	Econ
AME Roberts	16.2	3	56	5	3.42
CEH Croft	13	1	55	0	4.23
J Garner	17	5	39	2	2.29
DR Parry	17	1	49	2	2.88

Match details
Toss – West Indies, who chose to field;
Series – West Indies led the 5-match series 1-0;
Test debuts – JD Higgs (Australia); RA Austin, DL Haynes and DR Parry (West Indies);
Umpires – RG Gosein and D Sang Hue

2nd Test: West Indies v Australia at Bridgetown, Mar 17-19, 1978

West Indies won by 9 wickets

Australia 1st innings		R	M
WM Darling	c Richards b Croft	4	16
GM Wood	lbw b Croft	69	131
GN Yallop	c Austin b Croft	47	152
CS Serjeant	c †Murray b Parry	4	11
RB Simpson*	c †Murray b Croft	9	34
GJ Cosier	c †Murray b Roberts	1	35
SJ Rixon†	lbw b Garner	16	42
B Yardley	b Garner	74	73
JR Thomson	b Garner	12	23
WM Clark	b Garner	0	2
JD Higgs	not-out	4	27
Extras	(b 3, lb 4, nb 3)	10	
Total	(all out; 65.1 overs)	250	

Fall of wickets 1-13 (Darling), 2-105 (Wood), 3-116 (Serjeant), 4-134 (Yallop), 5-135 (Simpson), 6-149 (Cosier), 7-161 (Rixon), 8-216 (Thomson), 9-216 (Clark), 10-250 (Yardley)

Bowling	O	M	R	W	Econ
AME Roberts	18	2	79	1	4.38
CEH Croft	18	3	47	4	2.61
J Garner	16.1	2	65	4	4.02
DR Parry	12	4	44	1	3.66
RA Austin	1	0	5	0	5.00

West Indies 1st innings		R	M
CG Greenidge	c Cosier b Thomson	8	24
DL Haynes	c †Rixon b Higgs	66	163
IVA Richards	c Clark b Thomson	23	23
AI Kallicharran	c Yardley b Thomson	8	18
CH Lloyd*	c Serjeant b Clark	42	114
RA Austin	c Serjeant b Clark	20	50
DL Murray†	c Darling b Thomson	60	107
DR Parry	c Serjeant b Simpson	27	60
AME Roberts	lbw b Thomson	4	3
J Garner	not-out	5	13
CEH Croft	lbw b Thomson	3	3
Extras	(lb 3, nb 19)	22	
Total	(all out; 71 overs)	288	

Fall of wickets 1-16 (Greenidge), 2-56 (Richards), 3-71 (Kallicharran), 4-154 (Haynes), 5-172 (Lloyd), 6-198 (Austin), 7-263 (Parry), 8-269 (Roberts), 9-282 (Murray), 10-288 (Croft)

Bowling	O	M	R	W	Econ
JR Thomson	13	1	77	6	5.92
WM Clark	24	3	77	2	3.20
GJ Cosier	9	4	24	0	2.66
JD Higgs	16	4	46	1	2.87
RB Simpson	7	1	30	1	4.28
B Yardley	2	0	12	0	6.00

Australia 2nd innings		R	M
WM Darling	c †Murray b Croft	8	15
GM Wood	run out	56	140
GN Yallop	c Lloyd b Garner	14	51
CS Serjeant	c †Murray b Roberts	2	13
GJ Cosier	c Croft b Roberts	8	21
SJ Rixon†	c Lloyd b Roberts	0	9
RB Simpson*	c †Murray b Roberts	17	78
B Yardley	b Garner	43	63
JR Thomson	c Richards b Garner	11	27
WM Clark	lbw b Garner	0	11
JD Higgs	not-out	0	6
Extras	(b 1, lb 8, nb 10)	19	
Total	(all out; 48 overs)	178	

Fall of wickets 1-21 (Darling), 2-62 (Yallop), 3-69 (Serjeant), 4-80 (Cosier), 5-95 (Rixon), 6-99 (Wood), 7-154 (Simpson), 8-167 (Yardley), 9-173 (Clark), 10-178 (Thomson).

Bowling	O	M	R	W	Econ
AME Roberts	18	5	50	4	2.77
CEH Croft	15	4	53	1	3.53
J Garner	15	3	56	4	3.73

West Indies 2nd innings (target: 141 runs)		R	M
CG Greenidge	not-out	80	138
DL Haynes	c Yardley b Higgs	55	125
DR Parry	not-out	3	8
Extras	(lb 2, w 1)	3	
Total	(1 wicket; 36.5 overs)	141	

Did not bat: IVA Richards, AI Kallicharran, CH Lloyd*, RA Austin, DL Murray†, AME Roberts, J Garner, CEH Croft

Fall of wickets 1-131 (Haynes)

Bowling	O	M	R	W	Econ
JR Thomson	6	1	22	0	3.66
WM Clark	7	0	27	0	3.85
JD Higgs	13	4	34	1	2.61
B Yardley	10.5	2	55	0	5.07

Match details
Toss – West Indies, who chose to field;
Series – West Indies led the 5-match series 2-0;
Umpires – RG Gosein and SE Parris

3rd Test: West Indies v Australia at Georgetown, Mar 31-Apr 5, 1978

Australia won by 3 wickets

West Indies 1st innings		R	M
AE Greenidge	lbw b Thomson	56	125
AB Williams	lbw b Clark	10	31
HA Gomes	b Clark	4	13
AI Kallicharran*	b Thomson	0	24
IT Shillingford	c Clark b Laughlin	3	23
DA Murray†	c Ogilvie b Clark	21	86
S Shivnarine	c †Rixon b Thomson	53	118
N Phillip	c Yardley b Simpson	15	27
VA Holder	c Laughlin b Clark	1	5
DR Parry	not-out	21	34
ST Clarke	b Thomson	6	5
Extras	(lb 2, nb 13)	15	
Total	(all out; 60.2 overs)	205	

Fall of wickets 1-31 (Williams), 2-36 (Gomes), 3-48 (Kallicharran), 4-77 (Shillingford), 5-84 (Greenidge), 6-130 (Murray), 7-165 (Phillip), 8-166 (Holder), 9-193 (Shivnarine), 10-205 (Clarke)

Bowling	O	M	R	W	Econ
JR Thomson	16.2	1	56	4	3.42
WM Clark	24	6	65	4	2.70
TJ Laughlin	10	4	34	1	3.40
GJ Cosier	2	1	1	0	0.50
RB Simpson	8	1	34	1	4.25

Australia 1st innings		R	M
WM Darling	c Greenidge b Phillip	15	30
GM Wood	lbw b Holder	50	134
AD Ogilvie	c & b Phillip	4	15
GJ Cosier	lbw b Clarke	9	58
CS Serjeant	b Clarke	0	19
RB Simpson*	run out	67	179
TJ Laughlin	c Greenidge b Parry	21	71
SJ Rixon†	c Holder b Phillip	54	118
B Yardley	b Clarke	33	44
JR Thomson	c & b Phillip	3	7
WM Clark	not-out	2	16
Extras	(lb 12, w 1, nb 15)	28	
Total	(all out; 83 overs)	286	

Fall of wickets 1-28 (Darling), 2-36 (Ogilvie), 3-77 (Cosier), 4-85 (Serjeant), 5-90 (Wood), 6-142 (Laughlin), 7-237 (Simpson), 8-256 (Rixon), 9-268 (Thomson), 10-286 (Yardley)

Bowling	O	M	R	W	Econ
N Phillip	18	0	75	4	4.16
VA Holder	17	1	40	1	2.35
ST Clarke	22	3	58	3	2.63
HA Gomes	3	0	8	0	2.66
DR Parry	15	2	39	1	2.60
S Shivnarine	8	0	38	0	4.75

West Indies 2nd innings		R	M	B
AE Greenidge	b Clark	11	22	
AB Williams	c Serjeant b Clark	100	165	118
DA Murray†	lbw b Simpson	16	77	
DR Parry	lbw b Clark	51	104	
HA Gomes	c Simpson b Yardley	101	209	
AI Kallicharran*	b Yardley	22	54	
IT Shillingford	c & b Thomson	16	43	
S Shivnarine	b Cosier	63	147	
N Phillip	st †Rixon b Yardley	4	21	
VA Holder	lbw b Clark	31	62	
ST Clarke	not-out	5	9	
Extras	(b 4, lb 5, nb 10)	19		
Total	(all out; 116.4 overs)	439		

Fall of wickets 1-36 (Greenidge), 2-95 (Murray), 3-172 (Williams), 4-199 (Parry), 5-249 (Kallicharran), 6-285 (Shillingford), 7-355 (Gomes), 8-369 (Phillip), 9-431 (Shivnarine), 10-439 (Holder)

Bowling	O	M	R	W	Econ
JR Thomson	20	2	83	1	4.15
WM Clark	34.4	4	124	4	3.57
TJ Laughlin	7	1	33	0	4.71
GJ Cosier	6	1	14	1	2.33
RB Simpson	19	4	70	1	3.68
B Yardley	30	6	96	3	3.20

Australia 2nd innings (target: 359 runs)		R	M
WM Darling	c Williams b Clarke	0	14
GM Wood	run out	126	335
AD Ogilvie	lbw b Clarke	0	10
RB Simpson*	c †Murray b Clarke	4	14
CS Serjeant	c sub (SFAF Bacchus) b Phillip	124	269
GJ Cosier	b Phillip	0	13
SJ Rixon†	not-out	39	85
TJ Laughlin	c & b Parry	24	55
B Yardley	not-out	15	19
Extras	(b 8, lb 4, w 2, nb 16)	30	
Total	(7 wickets; 101 overs)	362	

Did not bat: JR Thomson, WM Clark

Fall of wickets 1-11 (Darling), 2-13 (Ogilvie), 3-22 (Simpson), 4-273 (Serjeant), 5-279 (Cosier), 6-290 (Wood), 7-338 (Laughlin)

Bowling	O	M	R	W	Econ
N Phillip	19	2	65	2	3.42
VA Holder	20	3	55	0	2.75
ST Clarke	27	5	83	3	3.07
DR Parry	17	1	61	1	3.58
S Shivnarine	18	2	68	0	3.77

Match details

Toss – West Indies, who chose to bat;
Series – West Indies led the 5-match series 2-1;
Test debuts – TJ Laughlin (Australia); ST Clarke, AE Greenidge, DA Murray, N Phillip, S Shivnarine and AB Williams (West Indies);
Umpires – RG Gosein and CF Vyfhuis

4th Test: West Indies v Australia at Port of Spain, Apr 15-18, 1978

West Indies won by 198 runs

West Indies 1st innings		R	M
AE Greenidge	c Wood b Clark	6	11
AB Williams	c Yallop b Higgs	87	223
DA Murray†	c Wood b Yardley	4	28
HA Gomes	c Simpson b Clark	30	127
AI Kallicharran*	c Yallop b Clark	92	163
SFAF Bacchus	b Higgs	9	21
S Shivnarine	c Simpson b Thomson	10	71
DR Parry	st †Rixon b Higgs	22	59
N Phillip	c †Rixon b Thomson	3	7
VA Holder	b Thomson	7	30
RR Jumadeen	not-out	0	4
Extras	(b 7, lb 1, w 2, nb 12)	22	
Total	(all out; 96.5 overs)	292	

Fall of wickets 1-7 (Greenidge), 2-16 (Murray), 3-111 (Gomes), 4-166 (Williams), 5-185 (Bacchus), 6-242 (Shivnarine), 7-258 (Kallicharran), 8-262 (Phillip), 9-291 (Holder), 10-292 (Parry)

Bowling	O	M	R	W	Econ
JR Thomson	23	8	64	3	2.78
WM Clark	24	6	65	3	2.70
B Yardley	18	5	48	1	2.66
JD Higgs	16.5	2	53	3	3.14
RB Simpson	15	4	40	0	2.66

Australia 1st innings		R	M
GM Wood	c †Murray b Phillip	16	53
WM Darling	c Jumadeen b Holder	10	25
PM Toohey	c Williams b Parry	40	83
GN Yallop	c †Murray b Jumadeen	75	189
CS Serjeant	st †Murray b Jumadeen	49	129
RB Simpson*	lbw b Holder	36	53
SJ Rixon†	c †Murray b Holder	21	60
B Yardley	c Williams b Holder	22	38
JR Thomson	b Holder	0	2
WM Clark	b Holder	4	17
JD Higgs	not-out	0	4
Extras	(b 4, lb 2, nb 11)	17	
Total	(all out; 90 overs)	290	

Fall of wickets 1-23 (Darling), 2-43 (Wood), 3-92 (Toohey), 4-193 (Serjeant), 5-204 (Yallop), 6-254 (Simpson), 7-275 (Rixon), 8-275 (Thomson), 9-289 (Yardley), 10-290 (Clark)

Bowling	O	M	R	W	Econ
N Phillip	17	0	73	1	4.29
VA Holder	13	4	28	6	2.15
RR Jumadeen	24	4	83	2	3.45
DR Parry	30	5	77	1	2.56
S Shivnarine	6	1	12	0	2.00

West Indies 2nd innings		R	M
AE Greenidge	c Thomson b Yardley	69	186
AB Williams	c Yallop b Simpson	24	46
DA Murray†	lbw b Clark	4	0
HA Gomes	c Simpson b Higgs	14	23
AI Kallicharran*	c & b Clark	27	109
SFAF Bacchus	c Wood b Yardley	7	24
S Shivnarine	c Serjeant b Simpson	11	74
DR Parry	c Serjeant b Yardley	65	135
N Phillip	c Wood b Yardley	46	101
VA Holder	b Simpson	0	9
RR Jumadeen	not-out	2	15
Extras	(b 1, lb 13, nb 7)	21	
Total	(all out; 101.2 overs)	290	

Fall of wickets 1-36 (Williams), 2-51 (Murray), 3-79 (Gomes), 4-134 (Kallicharran), 5-151 (Greenidge), 6-151 (Bacchus), 7-204 (Shivnarine), 8-273 (Parry), 9-280 (Holder), 10-290 (Phillip)

Bowling	O	M	R	W	Econ
JR Thomson	15	1	76	0	5.06
WM Clark	21	4	62	2	2.95
B Yardley	30.2	15	40	4	1.31
JD Higgs	21	7	46	1	2.19
RB Simpson	14	2	45	3	3.21

Australia 2nd innings (target: 293 runs)		R	M
GM Wood	lbw b Holder	17	73
WM Darling	b Phillip	6	12
PM Toohey	c Bacchus b Jumadeen	17	63
GN Yallop	c Kallicharran b Parry	18	55
CS Serjeant	c Bacchus b Jumadeen	4	24
RB Simpson*	lbw b Jumadeen	6	15
SJ Rixon†	not-out	13	44
B Yardley	b Parry	3	9
JR Thomson	b Parry	1	7
WM Clark	b Parry	0	2
JD Higgs	b Parry	4	12
Extras	(lb 2, nb 3)	5	
Total	(all out; 43.4 overs)	94	

Fall of wickets 1-9 (Darling), 2-42 (Wood), 3-44 (Toohey), 4-60 (Serjeant), 5-72 (Simpson), 6-76 (Yallop), 7-80 (Yardley), 8-86 (Thomson), 9-88 (Clark), 10-94 (Higgs)

Bowling	O	M	R	W	Econ
N Phillip	7	0	24	1	3.42
VA Holder	11	3	16	1	1.45
RR Jumadeen	15	3	34	3	2.26
DR Parry	10.4	4	15	5	1.40

Match details
Toss – Australia, who chose to field;
Series – West Indies led the 5-match series 3-1;
Test debut – SFAF Bacchus (West Indies);
Umpires – RG Gosein and CF Vyfhuis

5th Test: West Indies v Australia at Kingston, Apr 28-May 3, 1978

Match drawn

Australia 1st innings		R	M
GM Wood	c Parry b Phillip	16	46
AD Ogilvie	c Shivnarine b Holder	0	7
PM Toohey	c Williams b Holder	122	316
GN Yallop	c sub (HG Gordon) b Shivnarine	57	196
CS Serjeant	b Holder	26	162
R Simpson*	c †Murray b Foster	46	138
TJ Laughlin	c sub (HG Gordon) b Jumadeen	35	80
SJ Rixon†	not-out	13	52
B Yardley	b Jumadeen	7	12
JR Thomson	c †Murray b Jumadeen	4	12
JD Higgs	c Foster b Jumadeen	0	3
Extras	(lb 5, w 1, nb 11)	17	
Total	(all out; 147.4 overs)	343	

Fall of wickets 1-0 (Ogilvie), 2-38 (Wood), 3-171 (Yallop), 4-217 (Toohey), 5-266 (Serjeant), 6-308 (Simpson), 7-324 (Laughlin), 8-335 (Yardley), 9-343 (Thomson), 10-343 (Higgs)

Bowling	O	M	R	W	Econ
N Phillip	32	5	90	1	2.81
VA Holder	31	8	68	3	2.19
DR Parry	5	0	15	0	3.00
RR Jumadeen	38.4	6	72	4	1.86
MLC Foster	32	10	68	1	2.12
S Shivnarine	9	2	13	1	1.44

West Indies 1st innings		R	M
AB Williams	c Serjeant b Laughlin	17	32
SFAF Bacchus	c Yardley b Thomson	5	17
DA Murray†	c Wood b Laughlin	12	30
HA Gomes	b Thomson	115	324
AI Kallicharran*	c Ogilvie b Laughlin	6	11
MLC Foster	c †Rixon b Laughlin	8	26
S Shivnarine	st †Rixon b Higgs	53	125
DR Parry	lbw b Higgs	4	27
N Phillip	c †Rixon b Simpson	26	49
VA Holder	lbw b Laughlin	24	75
RR Jumadeen	not-out	4	4
Extras	(lb 1, nb 5)	6	
Total	(all out; 90.4 overs)	280	

Fall of wickets 1-13 (Bacchus), 2-28 (Williams), 3-41 (Murray), 4-47 (Kallicharran), 5-63 (Foster), 6-159 (Shivnarine), 7-173 (Parry), 8-219 (Phillip), 9-276 (Gomes), 10-280 (Holder)

Bowling	O	M	R	W	Econ
JR Thomson	22	4	61	2	2.77
TJ Laughlin	25.4	4	101	5	3.93
B Yardley	14	4	27	0	1.92
RB Simpson	10	0	38	1	3.80
JD Higgs	19	3	47	2	2.47

Australia 2nd innings		R	M
GM Wood	c Bacchus b Jumadeen	90	265
AD Ogilvie	st †Murray b Parry	43	90
PM Toohey	st †Murray b Jumadeen	97	179
GN Yallop	not-out	23	49
CS Serjeant	not-out	32	45
Extras	(b 5, lb 8, nb 7)	20	
Total	(3 wickets dec; 86 overs)	305	

Did not bat: RB Simpson*, TJ Laughlin, SJ Rixon†, B Yardley, JR Thomson, JD Higgs

Fall of wickets 1-65 (Ogilvie), 2-245 (Wood), 3-246 (Toohey)

Bowling	O	M	R	W	Econ
N Phillip	17	1	64	0	3.76
VA Holder	18	2	41	0	2.27
DR Parry	18	3	60	1	3.33
RR Jumadeen	23	2	90	2	3.91
MLC Foster	7	1	22	0	3.14
S Shivnarine	3	1	8	0	2.66

West Indies 2nd innings (target: 369 runs)		R	M
AB Williams	c Wood b Yardley	19	65
SFAF Bacchus	c Simpson b Thomson	21	47
HA Gomes	c †Rixon b Higgs	1	23
MLC Foster	run out	5	23
AI Kallicharran*	lbw b Higgs	126	267
DA Murray†	b Yardley	10	58
S Shivnarine	c Yallop b Yardley	27	100
DR Parry	c Serjeant b Yardley	0	7
N Phillip	not-out	26	82
VA Holder	c †Rixon b Higgs	6	13
RR Jumadeen	not-out	0	1
Extras	(b 14, lb 1, nb 2)	17	
Total	(9 wickets; 96.4 overs)	258	

Fall of wickets 1–42 (Bacchus), 2–43 (Williams), 3–43 (Gomes), 4–59 (Foster), 5–88 (Murray), 6–179 (Shivnarine), 7–181 (Parry), 8–242 (Kallicharran), 9–258 (Holder)

Bowling	O	M	R	W	Econ
JR Thomson	15	1	53	1	3.53
TJ Laughlin	10	1	34	0	3.40
B Yardley	29	17	35	4	1.20
RB Simpson	11	4	44	0	4.00
JD Higgs	28.4	10	67	3	2.33
GN Yallop	3	1	8	0	2.66

Match details
Toss – Australia, who chose to bat;
Series – West Indies won the 5-match series 3-1;
Umpires – RG Gosein and W Malcolm

England tour of Australia, 1978–79

1st Test: Australia v England at Brisbane, Dec 1-6, 1978

England won by 7 wickets

Australia 1st innings		R	M	B
GM Wood	c †Taylor b Old	7	45	30
GJ Cosier	run out	1	3	2
PM Toohey	b Willis	1	9	12
GN Yallop*	c Gooch b Willis	7	59	40
KJ Hughes	c †Taylor b Botham	4	34	24
TJ Laughlin	c sub (JK Lever) b Willis	2	8	3
JA Maclean†	not-out	33	135	83
B Yardley	c †Taylor b Willis	17	40	40
RM Hogg	c †Taylor b Botham	36	78	67
AG Hurst	c †Taylor b Botham	0	2	4
JD Higgs	b Old	1	5	5
Extras	(lb 1, nb 6)	7		
Total	(all out; 37.7 overs)	116		

Fall of wickets 1–2 (Cosier), 2–5 (Toohey), 3–14 (Wood), 4–22 (Yallop), 5-24 (Hughes), 6-26 (Laughlin), 7-53 (Yardley), 8-113 (Hogg), 9-113 (Hurst), 10-116 (Higgs)

Bowling	O	M	R	W	Econ
RGD Willis	14	2	44	4	2.35
CM Old	9.7	1	24	2	1.82
IT Botham	12	1	40	3	2.50
GA Gooch	1	0	1	0	0.75
PH Edmonds	1	1	0	0	0.00

England 1st innings		R	M	B
G Boycott	c Hughes b Hogg	13	91	67
GA Gooch	c Laughlin b Hogg	2	18	13
DW Randall	c Laughlin b Hurst	75	223	196
RW Taylor†	lbw b Hurst	20	172	115
JM Brearley*	c †Maclean b Hogg	6	19	13
DI Gower	c †Maclean b Hurst	44	111	90
IT Botham	c †Maclean b Hogg	49	102	73
G Miller	lbw b Hogg	27	93	70
PH Edmonds	c †Maclean b Hogg	1	15	9
CM Old	not-out	29	113	102
RGD Willis	c †Maclean b Hurst	8	44	20
Extras	(b 7, lb 4, nb 1)	12		
Total	(all out; 95.4 overs)	286		

Fall of wickets 1–2 (Gooch), 2–38 (Boycott), 3–111 (Randall), 4–120 (Brearley), 5–120 (Taylor), 6–215 (Botham), 7–219 (Gower), 8–226 (Edmonds), 9–266 (Miller), 10–286 (Willis)

Bowling	O	M	R	W	Econ
AG Hurst	27.4	6	93	4	2.53
RM Hogg	28	8	74	6	1.98
TJ Laughlin	22	6	54	0	1.84
B Yardley	7	1	34	0	3.64
GJ Cosier	5	1	10	0	1.50
JD Higgs	6	2	9	0	1.12

Australia 2nd innings		R	M	B
GM Wood	lbw b Old	19	88	50
GJ Cosier	b Willis	0	1	1
PM Toohey	lbw b Botham	1	7	9
GN Yallop*	c & b Willis	102	347	307
KJ Hughes	c Edmonds b Willis	129	481	411
TJ Laughlin	lbw b Old	5	13	8
JA Maclean†	lbw b Miller	15	63	63
B Yardley	c Brearley b Miller	16	79	70
RM Hogg	b Botham	16	41	35
AG Hurst	b Botham	0	1	2
JD Higgs	not-out	0	4	2
Extras	(b 9, lb 5, nb 22)	36		
Total	(all out; 116.6 overs)	339		

Fall of wickets 1–0 (Cosier), 2–2 (Toohey), 3–49 (Wood), 4-219 (Yallop), 5–228 (Laughlin), 6–261 (Maclean), 7-310 (Yardley), 8-339 (Hogg), 9–339 (Hurst), 10–339 (Hughes)

Bowling	O	M	R	W	Econ
RGD Willis	27.6	3	69	3	1.86
IT Botham	26	5	95	3	2.74
CM Old	17	1	60	2	2.64
G Miller	34	12	52	2	1.14
PH Edmonds	12	1	27	0	1.68

England 2nd innings (target: 170 runs)		R	M	B
G Boycott	run out	16	98	82
GA Gooch	c Yardley b Hogg	2	53	33
DW Randall	not-out	74	210	175
JM Brearley*	c †Maclean b Yardley	13	54	51
DI Gower	not-out	48	109	90
Extras	(b 12, lb 3, nb 2)	17		
Total	(3 wickets; 53.5 overs)	170		

Did not bat: RW Taylor†, IT Botham, G Miller, PH Edmonds, CM Old, RGD Willis

Fall of wickets 1–16 (Gooch), 2–37 (Boycott), 3–74 (Brearley)

Bowling	O	M	R	W	Econ
RM Hogg	12.5	2	35	1	2.07
AG Hurst	10	4	17	0	1.27
B Yardley	13	1	41	1	2.36
TJ Laughlin	3	0	6	0	1.50
JD Higgs	12	1	43	0	2.68
GJ Cosier	3	0	11	0	2.75

Match details
Balls per over: 8;
Toss – Australia, who chose to bat;
Series – England led the 6-match series 1-0;
Test debuts – RM Hogg and JA Maclean (Australia);
Player of the match – DW Randall (England);
Umpires – RA French and MG O'Connell

2nd Test: Australia v England at Perth, Dec 15-20, 1978

England won by 166 runs

England 1st innings		R	M	B
G Boycott	lbw b Hurst	77	454	337
GA Gooch	c †Maclean b Hogg	1	19	10
DW Randall	c Wood b Hogg	0	2	3
JM Brearley*	c †Maclean b Dymock	17	117	104
DI Gower	b Hogg	102	254	221
IT Botham	lbw b Hurst	11	44	28
G Miller	b Hogg	40	145	104
RW Taylor†	c Hurst b Yardley	12	52	59
JK Lever	c Cosier b Hurst	14	60	40
RGD Willis	c Yallop b Hogg	2	41	20
M Hendrick	not-out	7	22	25
Extras	(b 6, lb 9, w 3, nb 8)	26		
Total	(all out; 117.5 overs)	309		

Fall of wickets 1–3 (Gooch), 2–3 (Randall), 3–41 (Brearley), 4–199 (Gower), 5–219 (Botham), 6–224 (Boycott), 7–253 (Taylor), 8–295 (Lever), 9–300 (Miller), 10–309 (Willis)

Bowling	O	M	R	W	Econ
RM Hogg	30.5	9	65	5	1.59
G Dymock	34	4	72	1	1.58
AG Hurst	26	7	70	3	2.01
B Yardley	23	1	62	1	2.02
GJ Cosier	4	2	14	0	2.62

Australia 1st innings		R	M	B
GM Wood	lbw b Lever	5	12	12
WM Darling	run out	25	112	63
KJ Hughes	b Willis	16	43	44
GN Yallop*	b Willis	3	18	17
PM Toohey	not-out	81	272	184
GJ Cosier	c Gooch b Willis	4	33	24
JA Maclean†	c Gooch b Miller	0	2	2
B Yardley	c †Taylor b Hendrick	12	43	44
RM Hogg	c †Taylor b Willis	18	68	67
G Dymock	b Hendrick	11	78	72
AG Hurst	c †Taylor b Willis	5	6	6
Extras	(lb 7, w 1, nb 2)	10		
Total	(all out; 66.5 overs)	190		

Fall of wickets 1–8 (Wood), 2–34 (Hughes), 3–38 (Yallop), 4–60 (Darling), 5–78 (Cosier), 6–79 (Maclean), 7–100 (Yardley), 8–128 (Hogg), 9–185 (Dymock), 10–190 (Hurst)

Bowling	O	M	R	W	Econ
JK Lever	7	0	20	1	2.14
IT Botham	11	2	46	0	3.13
RGD Willis	18.5	5	44	5	1.77
M Hendrick	14	1	39	2	2.08
G Miller	16	6	31	1	1.45

England 2nd innings		R	M	B
G Boycott	lbw b Hogg	23	128	103
GA Gooch	lbw b Hogg	43	174	131
DW Randall	c Cosier b Yardley	45	90	65
JM Brearley*	c †Maclean b Hogg	0	1	1
DI Gower	c †Maclean b Hogg	12	68	47
IT Botham	c Wood b Yardley	30	52	39
G Miller	c Toohey b Yardley	25	79	42
JK Lever	c †Maclean b Hurst	10	45	54
RW Taylor†	c †Maclean b Hogg	2	36	33
RGD Willis	not-out	3	37	21
M Hendrick	b Dymock	1	5	5
Extras	(lb 6, nb 8)	14		
Total	(all out; 66.3 overs)	208		

Fall of wickets 1–58 (Boycott), 2–93 (Gooch), 3–93 (Brearley), 4–135 (Randall), 5–151 (Gower), 6–176 (Botham), 7–201 (Lever), 8–201 (Miller), 9–206 (Taylor), 10–208 (Hendrick)

Bowling	O	M	R	W	Econ
RM Hogg	17	2	57	5	2.51
G Dymock	16.3	2	53	1	2.42
AG Hurst	17	5	43	1	1.89
B Yardley	16	1	41	3	1.92

Australia 2nd innings (target: 328 runs)		R	M	B
GM Wood	c †Taylor b Lever	64	243	168
WM Darling	c Boycott b Lever	5	13	9
KJ Hughes	c Gooch b Willis	12	54	45
GN Yallop*	c †Taylor b Hendrick	3	43	23
PM Toohey	c †Taylor b Hendrick	0	1	1
GJ Cosier	lbw b Miller	47	109	74
JA Maclean†	c Brearley b Miller	1	18	16
B Yardley	c Botham b Lever	7	24	19
RM Hogg	b Miller	0	8	8
G Dymock	not-out	6	14	9
AG Hurst	b Lever	5	6	5
Extras	(lb 3, w 4, nb 4)	11		
Total	(all out; 46.1 overs)	161		

Fall of wickets 1–8 (Darling), 2–36 (Hughes), 3–58 (Yallop), 4–58 (Toohey), 5–141 (Cosier), 6–143 (Wood), 7–143 (Maclean), 8–147 (Hogg), 9–151 (Yardley), 10–161 (Hurst)

Bowling	O	M	R	W	Econ
RGD Willis	12	1	36	1	2.25
JK Lever	8.1	2	28	4	2.58
IT Botham	11	1	54	0	3.68
M Hendrick	8	3	11	2	1.03
G Miller	7	4	21	3	2.25

Match details
Balls per over: 8;
Toss – Australia, who chose to field;
Series – England led the 6-match series 2-0;
Player of the match – RM Hogg (Australia);
Umpires – RC Bailhache and TF Brooks

3rd Test: Australia v England at Melbourne, Dec 29, 1978 – Jan 3, 1979

Australia won by 103 runs

Australia 1st innings		R	M	B
GM Wood	c Emburey b Miller	100	392	283
WM Darling	run out	33	93	71
KJ Hughes	c †Taylor b Botham	0	2	1
GN Yallop*	c Hendrick b Botham	41	83	98
PM Toohey	c Randall b Miller	32	79	70
AR Border	c Brearley b Hendrick	29	105	115
JA Maclean†	b Botham	8	68	47
RM Hogg	c Randall b Miller	0	2	5
G Dymock	b Hendrick	0	13	14
AG Hurst	b Hendrick	0	1	2
JD Higgs	not-out	1	24	15
Extras	(lb 8, nb 6)	14		
Total	(all out; 89.1 overs)	258		

Fall of wickets 1–65 (Darling), 2–65 (Hughes), 3–126 (Yallop), 4–189 (Toohey), 5–247 (Border), 6–250 (Wood), 7–250 (Hogg), 8–251 (Dymock), 9–252 (Hurst), 10–258 (Maclean)

Bowling	O	M	R	W	Econ
RGD Willis	13	2	47	0	2.71
IT Botham	20.1	4	68	3	2.53
M Hendrick	23	3	50	3	1.63
JE Emburey	14	1	44	0	2.35
G Miller	19	6	35	3	1.38

England 1st innings		R	M	B
G Boycott	b Hogg	1	12	13
JM Brearley*	lbw b Hogg	1	16	8
DW Randall	lbw b Hurst	13	88	53
GA Gooch	c Border b Dymock	25	110	91
DI Gower	lbw b Dymock	29	59	48
IT Botham	c Darling b Higgs	22	83	80
G Miller	b Hogg	7	123	101
RW Taylor†	b Hogg	1	3	4
JE Emburey	b Hogg	0	12	14
RGD Willis	c Darling b Dymock	19	87	76
M Hendrick	not-out	6	31	33
Extras	(b 6, lb 4, nb 9)	19		
Total	(all out; 63.6 overs)	143		

Fall of wickets 1–2 (Boycott), 2–3 (Brearley), 3–40 (Randall), 4–52 (Gooch), 5–81 (Gower), 6–100 (Botham), 7–101 (Taylor), 8–101 (Emburey), 9–120 (Miller), 10–143 (Willis)

Bowling	O	M	R	W	Econ
RM Hogg	17	7	30	5	1.32
AG Hurst	12	2	24	1	1.50
G Dymock	15.6	4	38	3	1.80
JD Higgs	19	9	32	1	1.26

Australia 2nd innings		R	M	B
GM Wood	b Botham	34	136	107
WM Darling	c Randall b Miller	21	100	86
KJ Hughes	c Gower b Botham	48	153	142
GN Yallop*	c †Taylor b Miller	16	41	46
PM Toohey	c Botham b Emburey	20	33	30
AR Border	run out	0	9	12
JA Maclean†	c Hendrick b Emburey	10	91	77
RM Hogg	b Botham	1	20	21
G Dymock	c Brearley b Hendrick	6	41	39
JD Higgs	st †Taylor b Emburey	0	10	7
AG Hurst	not-out	0	4	4
Extras	(b 4, lb 6, nb 1)	11		
Total	(all out; 71.2 overs)	167		

Fall of wickets 1–55 (Darling), 2–81 (Wood), 3–101 (Yallop), 4–136 (Toohey), 5–136 (Border), 6–152 (Hughes), 7 157 (Hogg), 8–167 (Maclean), 9–167 (Dymock), 10–167 (Higgs)

Bowling	O	M	R	W	Econ
RGD Willis	7	0	21	0	2.25
IT Botham	15	4	41	3	2.05
M Hendrick	14	4	25	1	1.33
G Miller	14	5	39	2	2.08
JE Emburey	21.2	12	30	3	1.05

England 2nd innings (target: 283 runs)		R	M	B
G Boycott	lbw b Hurst	38	197	155
JM Brearley*	c †Maclean b Dymock	0	7	3
DW Randall	lbw b Hogg	2	5	8
GA Gooch	lbw b Hogg	40	95	87
DI Gower	lbw b Dymock	49	167	128
IT Botham	c †Maclean b Higgs	10	76	62
G Miller	c Hughes b Higgs	1	17	12
RW Taylor†	c †Maclean b Hogg	5	34	40
JE Emburey	not-out	7	44	33
RGD Willis	c Yallop b Hogg	3	20	12
M Hendrick	b Hogg	0	1	2
Extras	(b 10, lb 7, w 1, nb 6)	24		
Total	(all out; 67 overs)	179		

Fall of wickets 1–1 (Brearley), 2–6 (Randall), 3–71 (Gooch), 4–122 (Boycott), 5–163 (Botham), 6–163 (Gower), 7–167 (Miller), 8–171 (Taylor), 9–179 (Willis), 10–179 (Hendrick)

Bowling	O	M	R	W	Econ
RM Hogg	17	5	36	5	1.58
G Dymock	18	4	37	2	1.54
AG Hurst	11	1	39	1	2.65
JD Higgs	16	2	29	2	1.35
AR Border	5	0	14	0	2.10

Match details
Balls per over: 8; **Toss** – Australia, who chose to bat; **Series** – England led the 6-match series 2-1; **Test debut** – AR Border (Australia); **Player of the match** – GM Wood (Australia); **Umpires** – RA French and MG O'Connell

4th Test: Australia v England at Sydney, Jan 6-11, 1979

England won by 93 runs

England 1st innings		R	M	B
G Boycott	c Border b Hurst	8	54	40
JM Brearley*	b Hogg	17	96	80
DW Randall	c Wood b Hurst	0	1	2
GA Gooch	c Toohey b Higgs	18	102	81
DI Gower	c †Maclean b Hurst	7	24	10
IT Botham	c Yallop b Hogg	59	138	108
G Miller	c †Maclean b Hurst	4	4	5
RW Taylor†	c Border b Higgs	10	33	28
JE Emburey	c Wood b Higgs	0	9	11
RGD Willis	not-out	7	62	43
M Hendrick	b Hurst	10	19	24
Extras	(b 1, lb 1, w 2, nb 8)	12		
Total	(all out; 52.6 overs)	152		

Fall of wickets 1–18 (Boycott), 2–18 (Randall), 3–35 (Brearley), 4–51 (Gower), 5–66 (Gooch), 6–70 (Miller), 7–94 (Taylor), 8–98 (Emburey), 9–141 (Botham), 10–152 (Hendrick)

Bowling	O	M	R	W	Econ
RM Hogg	11	3	36	2	2.45
G Dymock	13	1	34	0	1.96
AG Hurst	10.6	2	28	5	1.95
JD Higgs	18	4	42	3	1.75

Australia 1st innings		R	M	B
GM Wood	b Willis	0	3	5
WM Darling	c Botham b Miller	91	276	200
KJ Hughes	c Emburey b Willis	48	184	167
GN Yallop*	c Botham b Hendrick	44	141	136
PM Toohey	c Gooch b Botham	1	5	4
AR Border	not-out	60	245	203
JA Maclean†	lbw b Emburey	12	63	58
RM Hogg	run out	6	13	17
G Dymock	b Botham	5	66	54
JD Higgs	c Botham b Hendrick	11	40	32
AG Hurst	run out	0	5	2
Extras	(b 2, lb 3, nb 11)	16		
Total	(all out; 108 overs)	294		

Fall of wickets 1–1 (Wood), 2–126 (Hughes), 3–178 (Darling), 4–179 (Toohey), 5–210 (Yallop), 6–235 (Maclean), 7–245 (Hogg), 8–276 (Dymock), 9–290 (Higgs), 10–294 (Hurst)

Bowling	O	M	R	W	Econ
RGD Willis	9	2	33	2	2.75
IT Botham	28	3	87	2	2.33
M Hendrick	24	4	50	2	1.56
G Miller	13	2	37	1	2.13
JE Emburey	29	10	57	1	1.47
GA Gooch	5	1	14	0	2.10

England 2nd innings		R	M	B
G Boycott	lbw b Hogg	0	1	1
JM Brearley*	b Border	53	216	195
DW Randall	lbw b Hogg	150	582	498
GA Gooch	c Wood b Higgs	22	128	98
DI Gower	c †Maclean b Hogg	34	98	68
IT Botham	c Wood b Higgs	6	90	88
G Miller	lbw b Hogg	17	96	80
RW Taylor†	not-out	21	110	113
JE Emburey	c Darling b Higgs	14	49	39
RGD Willis	c Toohey b Higgs	0	1	1
M Hendrick	c Toohey b Higgs	7	8	11
Extras	(b 5, lb 3, nb 14)	22		
Total	(all out; 146.6 overs)	346		

Fall of wickets 1–0 (Boycott), 2–111 (Brearley), 3–169 (Gooch), 4–237 (Gower), 5–267 (Botham), 6–292 (Randall), 7–307 (Miller), 8–334 (Emburey), 9–334 (Willis), 10–346 (Hendrick)

Bowling	O	M	R	W	Econ
RM Hogg	28	10	67	4	1.79
G Dymock	17	4	35	0	1.54
AG Hurst	19	3	43	0	1.69
JD Higgs	59.6	15	148	5	1.85
AR Border	23	11	31	1	1.01

Australia 2nd innings (target: 205 runs)		R	M	B
GM Wood	run out	27	75	64
WM Darling	c Gooch b Hendrick	13	51	37
KJ Hughes	c Emburey b Miller	15	55	40
GN Yallop*	c & b Hendrick	1	8	12
PM Toohey	b Miller	5	50	50
AR Border	not-out	45	101	115
JA Maclean†	c Botham b Miller	0	7	11
G Dymock	b Emburey	0	9	12
RM Hogg	c Botham b Emburey	0	5	4
JD Higgs	lbw b Emburey	3	24	29
AG Hurst	b Emburey	0	20	21
Extras	(lb 1, nb 1)	2		
Total	(all out; 49.2 overs)	111		

Fall of wickets 1–38 (Darling), 2–44 (Wood), 3–45 (Yallop), 4–59 (Hughes), 5–74 (Toohey), 6–76 (Maclean), 7–85 (Dymock), 8–85 (Hogg), 9–105 (Higgs), 10–111 (Hurst)

Bowling	O	M	R	W	Econ
RGD Willis	2	0	8	0	3.00
M Hendrick	10	3	17	2	1.27
JE Emburey	17.2	7	46	4	2.00
G Miller	20	7	38	3	1.42

Match details
Balls per over: 8;
Toss – England, who chose to bat;
Series – England led the 6-match series 3-1;
Player of the match – DW Randall (England);
Umpires – RC Bailhache and RA French

5th Test: Australia v England at Adelaide, Jan 27 – Feb 1, 1979

England won by 205 runs

England 1st innings		R	M	B
G Boycott	c †Wright b Hurst	6	22	21
JM Brearley*	c †Wright b Hogg	2	28	14
DW Randall	c Carlson b Hurst	4	25	13
GA Gooch	c Hughes b Hogg	1	10	10
DI Gower	lbw b Hurst	9	18	13
IT Botham	c †Wright b Higgs	74	158	97
G Miller	lbw b Hogg	31	80	89
RW Taylor†	run out	4	28	21
JE Emburey	b Higgs	4	25	21
RGD Willis	c Darling b Hogg	24	25	20
M Hendrick	not-out	0	13	9
Extras	(b 1, lb 4, w 3, nb 2)	10		
Total	(all out; 40.4 overs)	169		

Fall of wickets 1–10 (Boycott), 2–12 (Brearley), 3–16 (Gooch), 4–18 (Randall), 5–27 (Gower), 6–80 (Miller), 7–113 (Taylor), 8–136 (Emburey), 9–147 (Botham), 10–169 (Willis)

Bowling	O	M	R	W	Econ
RM Hogg	10.4	1	26	4	1.85
AG Hurst	14	1	65	3	3.48
PH Carlson	9	1	34	0	2.83
B Yardley	4	0	25	0	4.68
JD Higgs	3	1	9	2	2.25

Australia 1st innings		R	M	B
WM Darling	c Willis b Botham	15	35	33
GM Wood	c Randall b Emburey	35	210	117
KJ Hughes	c Emburey b Hendrick	4	7	10
GN Yallop*	b Hendrick	0	9	4
AR Border	c †Taylor b Botham	11	20	18
PH Carlson	c †Taylor b Botham	0	8	5
B Yardley	b Botham	28	79	75
KJ Wright†	lbw b Emburey	29	76	69
RM Hogg	b Willis	0	2	1
JD Higgs	run out	16	79	63
AG Hurst	not-out	17	47	39
Extras	(b 1, lb 3, nb 5)	9		
Total	(all out; 53.4 overs)	164		

Fall of wickets 0–0* (Darling, retired not-out), 1–5 (Hughes), 2–10 (Yallop), 3–22 (Border), 4–24 (Carlson), 5–72 (Yardley), 6–94 (Darling), 7–114 (Wood), 8–116 (Hogg), 9–133 (Wright), 10–164 (Higgs)

Bowling	O	M	R	W	Econ
RGD Willis	11	1	55	1	3.75
M Hendrick	19	1	45	2	1.77
IT Botham	11.4	0	42	4	2.73
JE Emburey	12	7	13	2	0.81

England 2nd innings		R	M	B
G Boycott	c Hughes b Hurst	49	265	212
JM Brearley*	lbw b Carlson	9	82	65
DW Randall	c Yardley b Hurst	15	57	50
GA Gooch	b Carlson	18	85	74
DI Gower	lbw b Higgs	21	72	54
IT Botham	c Yardley b Hurst	7	30	29
G Miller	c †Wright b Hurst	64	235	203
RW Taylor†	c †Wright b Hogg	97	361	300
JE Emburey	b Hogg	42	147	132
RGD Willis	c †Wright b Hogg	12	35	18
M Hendrick	not-out	3	16	10
Extras	(b 1, lb 16, w 2, nb 4)	23		
Total	(all out; 142.6 overs)	360		

Fall of wickets 1–31 (Brearley), 2–57 (Randall), 3–97 (Gooch), 4–106 (Boycott), 5–130 (Botham), 6–132 (Gower), 7–267 (Miller), 8–336 (Taylor), 9–347 (Emburey), 10–360 (Willis)

Bowling	O	M	R	W	Econ
RM Hogg	27.6	7	59	3	1.59
AG Hurst	37	9	97	4	1.96
PH Carlson	27	8	41	2	1.13
B Yardley	20	6	60	0	2.25
JD Higgs	28	4	75	1	2.00
AR Border	3	2	5	0	1.25

Australia 2nd innings (target: 366 runs)		R	M	B
WM Darling	b Botham	18	49	37
GM Wood	run out	9	63	41
KJ Hughes	c Gower b Hendrick	46	208	176
GN Yallop*	b Hendrick	36	182	176
AR Border	b Willis	1	30	19
PH Carlson	c Gower b Hendrick	21	74	51
B Yardley	c Brearley b Willis	0	1	2
KJ Wright†	c Emburey b Miller	0	16	16
RM Hogg	b Miller	2	10	7
JD Higgs	not-out	3	30	10
AG Hurst	b Willis	13	9	13
Extras	(lb 1, nb 10)	11		
Total	(all out; 67 overs)	160		

Fall of wickets 1–31 (Darling), 2–36 (Wood), 3–115 (Yallop), 4–120 (Hughes), 5–121 (Border), 6–121 (Yardley), 7–124 (Wright), 8–130 (Hogg), 9–147 (Carlson), 10–160 (Hurst)

Bowling	O	M	R	W	Econ
RGD Willis	12	3	41	3	2.56
M Hendrick	14	6	19	3	1.01
IT Botham	14	4	37	1	1.98
G Miller	18	3	36	2	1.50
JE Emburey	9	5	16	0	1.33

Match details
Balls per over: 8; **Toss** – Australia, who chose to field; **Series** – England led the 6-match series 4-1; **Test debuts** – PH Carlson and KJ Wright (Australia); **Player of the match** – IT Botham (England); **Umpires** – RC Bailhache and MG O'Connell

6th Test: Australia v England at Sydney, Feb 10-14, 1979

England won by 9 wickets

Australia 1st innings		R	M	B
GM Wood	c Botham b Hendrick	15	30	25
AMJ Hilditch	run out	3	18	8
KJ Hughes	c Botham b Willis	16	99	86
GN Yallop*	c Gower b Botham	121	267	212
PM Toohey	c †Taylor b Botham	8	46	37
PH Carlson	c Gooch b Botham	2	6	5
B Yardley	b Emburey	7	14	15
KJ Wright†	st †Taylor b Emburey	3	9	11
RM Hogg	c Emburey b Miller	9	47	46
JD Higgs	not-out	9	52	45
AG Hurst	b Botham	0	1	1
Extras	(lb 3, nb 2)	5		
Total	(all out; 60.7 overs)	198		

Fall of wickets 1–18 (Hilditch), 2–19 (Wood), 3–67 (Hughes), 4–101 (Toohey), 5–109 (Carlson), 6–116 (Yardley), 7–124 (Wright), 8–159 (Hogg), 9–198 (Yallop), 10–198 (Hurst)

Bowling	O	M	R	W	Econ
RGD Willis	11	4	48	1	3.27
M Hendrick	12	2	21	1	1.31
IT Botham	9.7	1	57	4	4.32
JE Emburey	18	3	48	2	2.00
G Miller	9	3	13	1	1.08
G Boycott	1	0	6	0	4.50

England 1st innings		R	M	B
G Boycott	c Hilditch b Hurst	19	91	80
JM Brearley*	c Toohey b Higgs	46	200	148
DW Randall	lbw b Hogg	7	14	9
GA Gooch	st †Wright b Higgs	74	148	136
DI Gower	c †Wright b Higgs	65	141	111
IT Botham	c Carlson b Yardley	23	54	53
G Miller	lbw b Hurst	18	89	84
RW Taylor†	not-out	36	160	118
JE Emburey	c Hilditch b Hurst	0	20	18
RGD Willis	b Higgs	10	70	63
M Hendrick	c & b Yardley	0	3	7
Extras	(b 3, lb 5, nb 2)	10		
Total	(all out; 103 overs)	308		

Fall of wickets 1–37 (Boycott), 2–46 (Randall), 3–115 (Brearley), 4–182 (Gooch), 5–233 (Botham), 6–247 (Gower), 7–270 (Miller), 8–280 (Emburey), 9–306 (Willis), 10–308 (Hendrick)

Bowling	O	M	R	W	Econ
RM Hogg	18	6	42	1	1.75
AG Hurst	20	4	58	3	2.17
B Yardley	25	2	105	2	3.15
PH Carlson	10	1	24	0	1.80
JD Higgs	30	8	69	4	1.72

Australia 2nd innings		R	M	B
GM Wood	c Willis b Miller	29	96	78
AMJ Hilditch	c †Taylor b Hendrick	1	19	17
KJ Hughes	c Gooch b Emburey	7	26	16
GN Yallop*	c †Taylor b Miller	17	107	120
PM Toohey	c Gooch b Emburey	0	3	2
PH Carlson	c Botham b Emburey	0	1	2
B Yardley	not-out	61	160	147
KJ Wright†	c Boycott b Miller	5	55	62
RM Hogg	b Miller	7	24	25
JD Higgs	c Botham b Emburey	2	5	4
AG Hurst	c & b Miller	4	16	17
Extras	(b 3, lb 6, nb 1)	10		
Total	(all out; 61.1 overs)	143		

Fall of wickets 1–8 (Hilditch), 2–28 (Hughes), 3–48 (Wood), 4–48 (Toohey), 5–48 (Carlson), 6–82 (Yallop), 7–114 (Wright), 8–130 (Hogg), 9–136 (Higgs), 10–143 (Hurst)

Bowling	O	M	R	W	Econ
RGD Willis	3	0	15	0	3.75
M Hendrick	7	3	22	1	2.35
JE Emburey	24	4	52	4	1.62
G Miller	27.1	6	44	5	1.21

England 2nd innings (target: 34 runs)		R	M	B
G Boycott	c Hughes b Higgs	13	35	52
JM Brearley*	not-out	20	39	30
DW Randall	not-out	0	2	2
Extras	(nb 2)	2		
Total	(1 wicket; 10.2 overs)	35		

Did not bat: GA Gooch, DI Gower, IT Botham, G Miller, RW Taylor†, JE Emburey, RGD Willis, M Hendrick

Fall of wickets 1-31 (Boycott)

Bowling	O	M	R	W	Econ
B Yardley	5.2	0	21	0	3.00
JD Higgs	5	1	12	1	1.80

Match details
Balls per over: 8;
Toss – Australia, who chose to bat;
Series – England won the 6-match series 5-1;
Test debut – AMJ Hilditch (Australia);
Player of the match – GN Yallop (Australia);
Umpires – AR Crafter and DG Weser

Pakistan tour of Australia, 1979

Australia v Pakistan: 1st Test, at Melbourne, 10-15 March, 1979

Pakistan won by 71 runs

Pakistan 1st innings		R	M	B
Majid Khan	c †Wright b Hogg	1	5	3
Mohsin Khan	c Hilditch b Hogg	14	39	30
Zaheer Abbas	b Hogg	11	49	27
Javed Miandad	b Hogg	19	131	95
Asif Iqbal	c †Wright b Clark	9	26	14
Mushtaq Mohammad*	c †Wright b Hurst	36	152	121
Wasim Raja	b Hurst	13	26	16
Imran Khan	c †Wright b Hurst	33	107	90
Sarfraz Nawaz	c †Wright b Sleep	35	105	82
Wasim Bari†	run out	0	9	4
Sikander Bakht	not out	5	24	23
Extras	(b 2, lb 7, w 1, nb 10)	20		
Total	(all out; 61.7	196		

Fall of wickets 1-2 (Majid Khan), 2-22 (Mohsin Khan), 3-28 (Zaheer Abbas), 4-40 (Asif Iqbal), 5-83 (Javed Miandad), 6-99 (Wasim Raja), 7-122 (Mushtaq Mohammad), 8-173 (Imran Khan), 9-177 (Wasim Bari), 10-196 (Sarfraz Nawaz)

Bowling	O	M	R	W	Econ
RM Hogg	17	4	49	4	2.16
AG Hurst	20	4	55	3	2.06
WM Clark	17	4	56	1	2.47
PR Sleep	7.7	2	16	1	1.52

Australia 1st innings		R	M	B
GM Wood	not out	5	39	23
AMJ Hilditch	c Javed Miandad b Imran Khan	3	42	17
AR Border	b Imran Khan	20	110	85
GN Yallop*	b Imran Khan	25	114	79
KJ Hughes	run out	19	88	54
DF Whatmore	lbw b Sarfraz Nawaz	43	206	147
PR Sleep	c †Wasim Bari b Imran Khan	10	35	30
KJ Wright†	c Imran Khan b Wasim Raja	9	43	33
WM Clark	c Mushtaq Mohammad b Wasim Raja	9	21	21
RM Hogg	run out	9	19	13
AG Hurst	c & b Sarfraz Nawaz	0	2	1
Extras	(b 1, lb 5, w 2, nb 8)	16		
Total	(all out; 61.6	168		

Fall of wickets 0-10* (Wood, retired not out), 1-11 (Hilditch), 2-53 (Border), 3-63 (Yallop), 4-97 (Hughes), 5-109 (Sleep), 6-140 (Wright), 7-152 (Clark), 8-167 (Hogg), 9-167 (Hurst), 10-168 (Whatmore)

Bowling	O	M	R	W	Econ
Imran Khan	18	8	26	4	1.08
Sarfraz Nawaz	21.6	6	39	2	1.34
Sikander Bakht	10	1	29	0	2.17
Mushtaq Mohammad	7	0	35	0	3.75
Wasim Raja	5	0	23	2	3.45

Pakistan 2nd innings		R	M	B
Majid Khan	b Border	108	219	157
Mohsin Khan	c & b Hogg	14	28	21
Zaheer Abbas	b Hogg	59	149	105
Javed Miandad	c †Wright b Border	16	65	57
Asif Iqbal	lbw b Hogg	44	153	119
Mushtaq Mohammad*	c sub (JD Higgs) b Sleep	28	93	75
Wasim Raja	c †Wright b Hurst	28	73	53
Imran Khan	c Clark b Hurst	28	71	54
Sarfraz Nawaz	lbw b Hurst	1	8	3
Wasim Bari†	not out	8	26	20
Extras	(b 4, lb 6, nb 9)	19		
Total	(9 wickets dec; 81.5	353		

Did not bat: Sikander Bakht
Fall of wickets 1-30 (Mohsin Khan), 2-165 (Zaheer Abbas), 3-204 (Majid Khan), 4-209 (Javed Miandad), 5-261 (Mushtaq Mohammad), 6-299 (Asif Iqbal), 7-330 (Wasim Raja), 8-332 (Sarfraz Nawaz), 9-353 (Imran Khan)

Bowling	O	M	R	W	Econ
RM Hogg	19	2	75	3	2.96
AG Hurst	19.5	1	115	3	4.39
WM Clark	21	6	47	0	1.67
PR Sleep	8	0	62	1	5.81
AR Border	14	5	35	2	1.87

Australia 2nd innings (target: 382 runs)		R	M	B
DF Whatmore	b Sarfraz Nawaz	15	78	48
AMJ Hilditch	b Sarfraz Nawaz	62	159	132
AR Border	b Sarfraz Nawaz	105	378	275
GN Yallop*	run out	8	55	36
KJ Hughes	c Mohsin Khan b Sarfraz Nawaz	84	267	209
GM Wood	c †Wasim Bari b Sarfraz Nawaz	0	2	1
PR Sleep	b Sarfraz Nawaz	0	10	5
KJ Wright†	not out	1	40	26
WM Clark	b Sarfraz Nawaz	0	2	1
RM Hogg	lbw b Sarfraz Nawaz	0	22	14
AG Hurst	c †Wasim Bari b Sarfraz Nawaz	0	2	2
Extras	(b 13, lb 13, nb 9)	35		
Total	(all out; 92.4	310		

Fall of wickets 1-49 (Whatmore), 2-109 (Hilditch), 3-128 (Yallop), 4-305 (Border), 5-305 (Wood), 6-306 (Sleep), 7-308 (Hughes), 8-309 (Clark), 9-310 (Hogg), 10-310 (Hurst)

Bowling	O	M	R	W	Econ
Imran Khan	27	9	73	0	2.02
Sarfraz Nawaz	35.4	7	86	9	1.81
Sikander Bakht	7	0	29	0	3.10
Mushtaq Mohammad	11	0	42	0	2.86
Wasim Raja	3	0	11	0	2.75
Majid Khan	9	1	34	0	2.83

Match details: Balls per over 6; **Toss –** Australia, who chose to field; **Series –** Pakistan led the 2-match series 1-0; **Test debuts –** PR Sleep and DF Whatmore (Australia); **Umpires –** RC Bailhache and CE Harvey

Australia v Pakistan: 2nd Test, at Perth, 24-29 March, 1979

Australia won by 7 wickets

Pakistan 1st innings		R	M	B
Majid Khan	c Hilditch b Hogg	0	1	2
Mudassar Nazar	c †Wright b Hurst	5	43	38
Zaheer Abbas	c †Wright b Hurst	29	60	33
Javed Miandad	not out	129	390	276
Haroon Rasheed	c Border b Hurst	4	9	4
Asif Iqbal	run out	35	44	46
Mushtaq Mohammad*	run out	23	140	109
Imran Khan	c †Wright b Dymock	14	51	32
Sarfraz Nawaz	c †Wright b Hurst	27	110	81
Wasim Bari†	c Hilditch b Dymock	0	6	6
Sikander Bakht	b Dymock	0	2	1
Extras	(lb 3, w 3, nb 5)	11		
Total	(all out; 77.6	277		

Fall of wickets 1-0 (Majid Khan), 2-27 (Mudassar Nazar), 3-41 (Zaheer Abbas), 4-49 (Haroon Rasheed), 5-90 (Asif Iqbal), 6-176 (Mushtaq Mohammad), 7-224 (Imran Khan), 8-276 (Sarfraz Nawaz), 9-277 (Wasim Bari), 10-277 (Sikander Bakht)

Bowling	O	M	R	W	Econ
RM Hogg	19	2	88	1	3.47
AG Hurst	23	4	61	4	1.98
G Dymock	21.6	4	65	3	2.24
B Yardley	14	2	52	0	2.78

Australia 1st innings		R	M	B
WM Darling	lbw b Mudassar Nazar	75	205	131
AMJ Hilditch	c Zaheer Abbas b Imran Khan	41	147	107
AR Border	c Majid Khan b Javed Miandad	85	347	250
KJ Hughes*	lbw b Sikander Bakht	9	23	28
JK Moss	c †Wasim Bari b Mudassar Nazar	22	121	79
DF Whatmore	c Asif Iqbal b Imran Khan	15	64	51
KJ Wright†	c †Wasim Bari b Mudassar Nazar	16	46	29
B Yardley	b Sarfraz Nawaz	19	38	29
G Dymock	not out	5	72	39
RM Hogg	b Imran Khan	3	18	15
AG Hurst	c †Wasim Bari b Sarfraz Nawaz	16	45	24
Extras	(b 3, lb 4, w 1, nb 13)	21		
Total	(all out; 95.6	327		

Fall of wickets 1-96 (Hilditch), 2-143 (Darling), 3-161 (Hughes), 4-219 (Moss), 5-246 (Whatmore), 6-273 (Wright), 7-297 (Border), 8-301 (Yardley), 9-304 (Hogg), 10-327 (Hurst)

Bowling	O	M	R	W	Econ
Imran Khan	32	5	105	3	2.46
Sarfraz Nawaz	35.1	7	112	2	2.39
Sikander Bakht	10.5	1	33	1	2.32
Mudassar Nazar	16	2	48	3	2.25
Javed Miandad	2	0	8	1	3.00

Pakistan 2nd innings		R	M	B
Majid Khan	c sub (TJ Laughlin) b Hogg	0	5	8
Mudassar Nazar	c Hilditch b Hurst	25	125	73
Zaheer Abbas	c †Wright b Hogg	18	63	49
Javed Miandad	c †Wright b Hurst	19	94	78
Haroon Rasheed	c Yardley b Dymock	47	153	117
Asif Iqbal	not out	134	304	280
Mushtaq Mohammad*	lbw b Yardley	1	6	7
Imran Khan	c †Wright b Hurst	15	115	56
Sarfraz Nawaz	c Yardley b Hurst	3	41	17
Wasim Bari†	c Whatmore b Hurst	0	4	3
Sikander Bakht	run out	0	37	3
Extras	(b 3, lb 8, nb 12)	23		
Total	(all out; 85.7	285		

Fall of wickets 1-0 (Majid Khan), 2-35 (Zaheer Abbas), 3-68 (Mudassar Nazar), 4-86 (Javed Miandad), 5-152 (Haroon Rasheed), 6-153 (Mushtaq Mohammad), 7-245 (Imran Khan), 8-263 (Sarfraz Nawaz), 9-263 (Wasim Bari), 10-285 (Sikander Bakht)

Bowling	O	M	R	W	Econ
RM Hogg	20	5	45	2	1.68
AG Hurst	24.7	2	94	5	2.83
G Dymock	23	5	72	1	2.34
B Yardley	14	3	42	1	2.25
AR Border	4	0	9	0	1.68

Australia 2nd innings (target: 236 runs)		R	M	B
WM Darling	run out	79	189	140
AMJ Hilditch	handled the ball	29	122	85
AR Border	not out	66	155	115
B Yardley	run out	1	4	2
JK Moss	not out	38	83	57
Extras	(lb 13, nb 10)	23		
Total	(3 wickets; 48.1	236		

Did not bat: KJ Hughes*, DF Whatmore, KJ Wright†, G Dymock, RM Hogg, AG Hurst
Fall of wickets 1-87 (Hilditch), 2-153 (Darling), 3-155 (Yardley)

Bowling	O	M	R	W	Econ
Imran Khan	17	1	81	0	3.57
Sarfraz Nawaz	19	1	85	0	3.35
Mudassar Nazar	10.1	2	35	0	2.59
Javed Miandad	2	0	12	0	4.50

Match details: Balls per over 6;
Toss – Australia, who chose to field;
Series – 2-match series drawn 1-1;
Test debut – JK Moss (Australia);
Umpires – AR Crafter and MG O'Connell

1979 Prudential World Cup

SATURDAY 9 JUNE 1979
ROUND ONE, GROUP B: ENGLAND vs
AUSTRALIA
LORD'S: ENGLAND WON BY 6 WICKETS

AUSTRALIA

A. M. J. Hilditch b Boycott	47
W. M. Darling lbw b Willis	25
A. R. Border c Taylor b Edmonds	34
K. J. Hughes (capt) c Hendrick b Boycott	6
G. N. Yallop run out	10
G. J. Cosier run out	6
T. J. Laughlin run out	8
K. J. Wright (wk) lbw b Old	6
R. M. Hogg run out	0
A. G. Hurst not-out	3
G. Dymock not-out	4
Extras b4 lb5 w1	10
(60 overs)	9-159

1/56 2/97 3/111 4/131 5/132 6/137 7/150 8/153
9/153
Bowling: Willis 11-2-20-1; Hendrick 12-2-24-0;
Old 12-2-33-1; Botham 8-0-32-0; Edmonds 11-1-
25-1; Boycott 6-0-15-2

ENGLAND

J. M. Brearley (capt) c Wright b Laughlin	44
G. Boycott lbw b Hogg	1
D. W. Randall c Wright b Hurst	1
G. A. Gooch lbw b Laughlin	53
D. I. Gower not-out	22
I. T. Botham not-out	18
Extras lb10 nb11	21
(47.1 overs)	4-160

Did not bat: P. H. Edmonds, R. W. Taylor (wk), C.
M. Old, M. Hendrick, R. G. D. Willis
1/4 2/5 3/113 4/124
Bowling: Hogg 9-1-25-1; Hurst 10-3-33-1; Dymock
11-2-19-0; Cosier 8-1-24-0; Laughlin 9.1-0-38-2

Umpires: D.J. Constant B.J. Meyer
Toss: England Points: England 4 Australia 0

THURSDAY 14 JUNE 1979
ROUND TWO, GROUP B: AUSTRALIA vs
PAKISTAN
TRENT BRIDGE: PAKISTAN WON BY 89 RUNS

PAKISTAN

Sadiq Mohammad c Moss b Porter	27
Majid Khan b Dymock	61
Zaheer Abbas c & b Cosier	16
Haroon Rashid c Wright b Cosier	16
Javed Miandad c Border b Cosier	46
Asif Iqbal (capt) c sub (D. F. Whatmore) b Hurst	61
Wasim Raja c Moss b Border	18
Imran Khan not-out	15
Mudassar Nazar not-out	1
Extras b6 lb4 w5 nb10	25
(60 overs)	7-286

Did not bat: Wasim Bari (wk), Sikander Bakht
1/99 2/99 3/133 4/152/5/239 6/268 7/274
Bowling: Porter 12-3-20-1; Dymock 12-3-28-1;
Cosier 12-1-54-3; Hurst 12-0-65-1; Yallop 8-0-56-0;
Border 4-0-38-1

AUSTRALIA

W. M. Darling c Wasim Bari b Imran Khan	13
A. M. J. Hilditch c Sadiq Mohammad b Mudassar Nazar	72
A. R. Border b Sikander Bakht	0
K. J. Hughes (capt) lbw b Sikander Bakht	16
G. N. Yallop b Majid Khan	37
J. K. Moss run out	7
G. J. Cosier c & b Majid Khan	0
K. J. Wright (wk) c Wasim Bari b Imran Khan	23
G. D. Porter c Sadiq Mohammad b Majid Khan	3
G. Dymock lbw b Sikander Bakht	10
A. G. Hurst not-out	3
Extras b1 lb5 w8	14
(57.1 overs)	197

1/22 2/24 3/46 4/117 5/136 6/137 7/172 8/175
9/193 10/197
Bowling: Asif Iqbal 12-0-36-0; Majid Khan 12-0-53-3;

Mudassar Nazar12-0-31-1; Imran Khan10.1-2-29-2;
Sikander Bakht 11-1-34-3

Umpires: H.D. Bird K.E. Palmer
Toss: Australia Points: Pakistan 4 Australia 0

SATURDAY 16 JUNE 1979
ROUND THREE, GROUP B: AUSTRALIA vs
CANADA
EDGBASTON: AUSTRALIA WON BY 7 WICKETS

CANADA

G. R. Sealy c Porter b Dymock	25
C. J. D. Chappell lbw b Hurst	19
F. A. Dennis lbw b Hurst	1
Tariq Javed c Wright b Porter	8
S. Baksh b Hurst	0
J. C. B. Vaughan b Porter	29
B. M. Mauricette (capt/wk) c Hilditch b Cosier	5
J. M. Patel b Cosier	2
R. G. Callender c Wright b Hurst	0
C. C. Henry c Hughes b Hurst	5
J. N. Valentine not-out	0
Extras b4 lb5 w1 nb1	11
(33.2 overs)	105

1/44 2/50 3/51 4/51 5/78 6/97 7/97 8/98 9/104
10/105
Bowling: Hogg 2-0-26-0; Hurst 10-3-21-5; Dymock
8-2-17-1; Porter 6-2-13-2; Cosier 7.2-2-17-2

AUSTRALIA

A. M. J. Hilditch c Valentine b Henry	24
W. M. Darling lbw b Valentine	13
A. R. Border b Henry	25
K. J. Hughes (capt) not-out	27
G. N. Yallop not-out	13
Extras lb1 nb3	4
(26 overs)	3-106

Did not bat: G. J. Cosier, K. J. Wright (wk),
G. D. Porter, R. M. Hogg, G. Dymock, A. G. Hurst
1/23 2/53 3/72
Bowling: Valentine 3-0-28-1; Callender 3-0-12-0;
Henry 10-0-27-2; Vaughan 6-0-15-0; Patel 4-0-20-0

Umpires: D.J. Constant J.G. Langridge
Toss: Australia Points: Australia 4 Canada 0

Australia in India, 1979

India v Australia, 1st Test at Chennai, 11-16 September, 1979

Match drawn

Australia 1st innings		R	M	B
AMJ Hilditch	c Venkataraghavan b Kapil Dev	4	12	8
GM Wood	lbw b Doshi	33	124	83
AR Border	run out	162	416	360
KJ Hughes*	c Venkataraghavan b Doshi	100	276	204
GN Yallop	c Yajurvindra Singh b Doshi	18	55	53
DF Whatmore	c Venkataraghavan b Doshi	20	36	44
KJ Wright†	b Venkataraghavan	20	32	36
G Dymock	lbw b Kapil Dev	16	62	58
RM Hogg	c Kapil Dev b Doshi	3	6	4
AG Hurst	c †Kirmani b Doshi	0	1	1
JD Higgs	not out	1	26	21
Extras	(b 1, lb 7, w 1, nb 4)	13		
Total	(all out; 143.4	390		

Fall of wickets 1-8 (Hilditch), 2-75 (Wood), 3-297 (Hughes), 4-318 (Border), 5-339 (Yallop), 6-352 (Whatmore), 7-369 (Wright), 8-375 (Hogg), 9-376 (Hurst), 10-390 (Dymock)

Bowling	O	M	R	W	Econ
N Kapil Dev	25.4	3	95	2	3.70
KD Ghavri	20	4	49	0	2.45
Yajurvindra Singh	9	1	29	0	3.22
S Venkataraghavan	46	16	101	1	2.19
DR Doshi	43	10	103	6	2.39

India 1st innings		R	M	B
SM Gavaskar*	c Wood b Hogg	50	130	80
CPS Chauhan	c †Wright b Higgs	26	115	91
SMH Kirmani†	c Border b Hogg	57	235	206
GR Viswanath	c Hughes b Higgs	17	65	45
DB Vengsarkar	c Whatmore b Higgs	65	111	77
Yashpal Sharma	lbw b Higgs	52	204	150
Yajurvindra Singh	c †Wright b Yallop	15	72	47
N Kapil Dev	c Hurst b Higgs	83	104	74
KD Ghavri	not out	23	49	38
S Venkataraghavan	lbw b Higgs	4	26	19
DR Doshi	c Hogg b Higgs	3	5	4
Extras	(b 2, lb 5, nb 23)	30		
Total	(all out; 130.3	425		

Fall of wickets 1-80 (Chauhan), 2-89 (Gavaskar), 3-122 (Viswanath), 4-221 (Vengsarkar), 5-240 (Kirmani), 6-281 (Yajurvindra Singh), 7-371 (Yashpal Sharma), 8-394 (Kapil Dev), 9-417 (Venkataraghavan), 10-425 (Doshi)

Bowling	O	M	R	W	Econ
RM Hogg	22	1	85	2	3.86
AG Hurst	23	8	51	0	2.21
JD Higgs	41.3	12	143	7	3.44
G Dymock	24	6	65	0	2.70
AR Border	14	4	30	0	2.14
GN Yallop	6	1	21	1	3.50

Australia 2nd innings		R	M	B
AMJ Hilditch	lbw b Doshi	55	211	188
GM Wood	c Chauhan b Kapil Dev	2	3	4
AR Border	b Venkataraghavan	50	174	138
KJ Hughes*	lbw b Venkataraghavan	36	135	125
GN Yallop	run out	2	25	23
DF Whatmore	c Chauhan b Doshi	8	26	28
KJ Wright†	b Venkataraghavan	5	25	24
G Dymock	not out	28	85	69
RM Hogg	not out	8	60	58
Extras	(b 11, lb 4, nh 3)	18		
Total	(7 wickets; 113.4	212		

Did not bat: AG Hurst, JD Higgs
Fall of wickets 1-2 (Wood), 2-103 (Border),
3-123 (Hilditch), 4-127 (Yallop), 5-146
(Whatmore), 6-156 (Wright), 7-175 (Hughes)

Bowling	O	M	R	W	Econ
N Kapil Dev	9	3	30	1	3.33
KD Ghavri	17.4	8	23	0	1.30
S Venkataraghavan	45	10	77	3	1.71
DR Doshi	42	15	64	2	1.52

Match details: 8 ball overs;
Toss – Australia, who chose to bat;
Series – 6-match series level 0-0;
Test debut – DR Doshi (India);
Umpires – MV Gothoskar and S Kishen

India v Australia: 2nd Test, at Bangalore, 19-24 September, 1979

Match drawn

Australia 1st innings	R	M	B
AMJ Hilditch c sub (J Arun Lal) b Yadav	62	182	154
WM Darling b Kapil Dev	7	31	17
AR Border c Yadav b Doshi	44	97	68
KJ Hughes* c Ghavri b Kapil Dev	86	261	195
GN Yallop c Viswanath b Yadav	12	34	21
B Yardley c & b Ghavri	47	118	107
GM Wood c †Kirmani b Ghavri	18	43	32
KJ Wright† not out	16	77	48
RM Hogg lbw b Venkataraghavan	19	63	52
JD Higgs lbw b Yadav	1	2	3
AG Hurst b Yadav	0	3	4
Extras (b 5, lb 6, nb 10)	21		
Total (all out; 114.5	333		

Fall of wickets 1-21 (Darling), 2-99 (Border), 3-137 (Hilditch), 4-159 (Yallop), 5-258 (Yardley), 6-294 (Wood), 7-294 (Hughes), 8-332 (Hogg), 9-333 (Higgs), 10-333 (Hurst)

Bowling	O	M	R	W	Econ
N Kapil Dev	25	4	89	2	3.56
KD Ghavri	19	5	68	2	3.57
DR Doshi	28	6	63	1	2.25
S Venkataraghavan	20	6	43	1	2.15
NS Yadav	22.5	6	49	4	2.14

India 1st innings	R	M	B
SM Gavaskar* c Hilditch b Yardley	10	45	22
CPS Chauhan c Hilditch b Yardley	31	100	77
DB Vengsarkar lbw b Yardley	112	366	283
SMH Kirmani† st †Wright b Higgs	30	96	81
GR Viswanath not out	161	405	297
Yashpal Sharma c Border b Yardley	37	121	88
N Kapil Dev not out	38	67	40
Extras (b 12, lb 8, w 1, nb 17)	38		
Total (5 wickets dec; 144	457		

Did not bat: KD Ghavri, NS Yadav, S Venkataraghavan, DR Doshi
Fall of wickets 1-22 (Gavaskar), 2-61 (Chauhan), 3-120 (Kirmani), 4-279 (Vengsarkar), 5-372 (Yashpal Sharma)

Bowling	O	M	R	W	Econ
RM Hogg	32	6	118	0	3.68
AG Hurst	29	3	93	0	3.20
B Yardley	44	16	107	4	2.43
JD Higgs	37	9	95	1	2.56
GN Yallop	2	0	6	0	3.00

Australia 2nd innings		R	M	B
AMJ Hilditch	lbw b Yadav	3	31	25
GM Wood	c Viswanath b Yadav	30	103	88
AR Border	b Yadav	19	47	55
KJ Hughes*	not out	13	44	42
GN Yallop	not out	6	20	17
Extras	(lb 5, nb 1)	6		
Total	(3 wickets; 37.4	77		

Did not bat: WM Darling, B Yardley,
KJ Wright†, RM Hogg, JD Higgs, AG Hurst
Fall of wickets 1-13 (Hilditch), 2-53 (Border),
3-62 (Wood)

Bowling	O	M	R	W	Econ
N Kapil Dev	3	2	1	0	0.33
KD Ghavri	3	1	9	0	3.00
DR Doshi	8	4	11	0	1.37
S Venkataraghavan	8	2	18	0	2.25
NS Yadav	15.4	4	32	3	2.04

Match details: 8 ball overs;
Toss – Australia, who chose to bat;
Series – 6-match series level 0-0;
Test debut – NS Yadav (India);
Umpires – PR Punjabi and KB Ramaswami

India v Australia: 3rd Test, at Green Park, Kanpur 2-7 October 1979

India won by 153 runs

India 1st innings		R	M
SM Gavaskar*	lbw b Dymock	76	175
CPS Chauhan	c & b Hogg	58	303
DB Vengsarkar	lbw b Hogg	52	115
GR Viswanath	c sub (PR Sleep) b Dymock	44	115
Yashpal Sharma	b Hogg	0	6
N Kapil Dev	c Hughes b Border	5	
SMH Kirmani†	c Whatmore b Hogg	4	
KD Ghavri	c Whatmore b Dymock	5	
NS Yadav	lbw b Dymock	0	
S Venkataraghavan	c Border b Dymock	1	
DR Doshi	not out	0	
Extras	(b 5, lb 6, nb 15)	26	
Total	(all out; 91	271	

Fall of wickets 1-114 (Gavaskar), 2-201 (Vengsarkar), 3-206 (Chauhan), 4-214 (Yashpal Sharma), 5-231 (Kapil Dev), 6-239 (Kirmani), 7-246 (Ghavri), 8-246 (Yadav), 9-256 (Venkataraghavan), 10-271 (Viswanath)

Australia 1st innings		R	M
AMJ Hilditch	c Chauhan b Ghavri	1	6
B Yardley	c Yashpal Sharma b Ghavri	29	98
AR Border	c Viswanath b Venkataraghavan	24	128
KJ Hughes*	b Yadav	50	135
GN Yallop	hit wicket b Kapil Dev	89	198
KJ Wright†	lbw b Kapil Dev	6	7
DF Whatmore	c Gavaskar b Doshi	14	29
WM Darling	c †Kirmani b Ghavri	59	186
G Dymock	run out	11	20
RM Hogg	b Yadav	10	79
JD Higgs	not out	3	21
Extras	(lb 2, nb 6)	8	
Total	(all out; 109.3	304	

Fall of wickets 1-1 (Hilditch), 2-51 (Yardley), 3-75 (Border), 4-168 (Hughes), 5-175 (Wright), 6-192 (Whatmore), 7-246 (Yallop), 8-263 (Dymock), 9-294 (Hogg), 10-304 (Darling)

Bowling	O	M	R	W	Econ
G Dymock	35	7	99	5	2.82
RM Hogg	26	3	66	4	2.53
B Yardley	20	6	54	0	2.70
JD Higgs	7	4	23	0	3.28
AR Border	3	2	3	1	1.00

Bowling	O	M	R	W	Econ
N Kapil Dev	27	5	78	2	2.88
KD Ghavri	23.3	5	65	3	2.76
S Venkataraghavan	18	6	56	1	3.11
DR Doshi	16	5	32	1	2.00
NS Yadav	25	3	65	2	2.60

India 2nd innings		R	M
SM Gavaskar*	c Whatmore b Yardley	12	30
CPS Chauhan	c Yardley b Dymock	84	368
DB Vengsarkar	c Whatmore b Dymock	20	44
GR Viswanath	c Whatmore b Yardley	52	140
Yashpal Sharma	c †Wright b Dymock	0	15
N Kapil Dev	b Dymock	10	24
SMH Kirmani†	b Dymock	45	90
KD Ghavri	c sub (PR Sleep) b Hogg	25	70
NS Yadav	c Whatmore b Dymock	18	75
S Venkataraghavan	not out	4	26
DR Doshi	b Dymock	0	2
Extras	(b 11, lb 9, nb 21)	41	
Total	(all out; 111.4	311	

Fall of wickets 1-24 (Gavaskar), 2-48 (Vengsarkar), 3-161 (Viswanath), 4-163 (Yashpal Sharma), 5-177 (Kapil Dev), 6-256 (Kirmani), 7-261 (Chauhan), 8-302 (Ghavri), 9-311 (Yadav), 10-31(Doshi)

Bowling	O	M	R	W	Econ
G Dymock	28.4	5	67	7	2.33
RM Hogg	19	4	49	1	2.57
B Yardley	40	15	82	2	2.05
JD Higgs	22	7	68	0	3.09
AR Border	2	1	4	0	2.00

Australia 2nd innings (target: 279 runs)		R	M
WM Darling	lbw b Kapil Dev	4	28
AMJ Hilditch	b Doshi	23	97
GN Yallop	c †Kirmani b Ghavri	15	25
KJ Hughes*	lbw b Kapil Dev	1	14
DF Whatmore	b Yadav	33	125
AR Border	b Yadav	8	68
KJ Wright†	b Yadav	11	49
B Yardley	lbw b Kapil Dev	5	15
G Dymock	st †Kirmani b Yadav	6	10
RM Hogg	lbw b Kapil Dev	6	18
JD Higgs	not out	8	9
Extras	(b 1, lb 2, nb 2)	5	
Total	(all out; 60.2	125	

Fall of wickets 1-13 (Darling), 2-32 (Yallop), 3-37 (Hughes), 4-49 (Hilditch), 5-74 (Border), 6-93 (Whatmore), 7-104 (Wright), 8-106 (Yardley), 9-113 (Dymock), 10-125 (Hogg)

Bowling	O	M	R	W	Econ
N Kapil Dev	16.2	5	30	4	1.83
KD Ghavri	11	0	28	1	2.54
S Venkataraghavan	9	4	13	0	1.44
DR Doshi	12	5	14	1	1.16
NS Yadav	12	0	35	4	2.91

Match details: 8 ball overs;
Toss – India, who chose to bat;
Series – India led the 6-match series 1-0;
Umpires – SN Hanumantha Rao and Mohammad Ghouse

India v Australia - 4th Test at Feroz Shah Kotla, Delhi, 13-18 October

Match drawn

India 1st innings		R	M	B
SM Gavaskar*	lbw b Higgs	115	329	238
CPS Chauhan	c Whatmore b Dymock	19	45	40
DB Vengsarkar	st †Wright b Higgs	26	103	73
GR Viswanath	st †Wright b Higgs	131	274	207
Yashpal Sharma	not out	100	280	239
N Kapil Dev	c Whatmore b Dymock	29	72	47
MV Narasimha Rao	c †Wright b Dymock	5	32	26
SMH Kirmani†	b Dymock	35	46	39
KD Ghavri	not out	8	29	23
Extras	(b 6, lb 12, nb 24)	42		
Total	(7 wickets dec; 144.2	510		

Did not bat: NS Yadav, DR Doshi
Fall of wickets 1-38 (Chauhan), 2-108 (Vengsarkar), 3-267 (Gavaskar), 4-338 (Viswanath), 5-395 (Kapil Dev), 6-415 (Narasimha Rao), 7-467 (Kirmani)

Bowling	O	M	R	W	Econ
G Dymock	42.2	8	135	4	3.18
RM Hogg	33	8	91	0	2.75
GN Yallop	5	0	21	0	4.20
AR Border	4	2	5	0	1.25
JD Higgs	47	11	150	3	3.19
PR Sleep	13	1	66	0	5.07

Australia 1st innings		R	M	B
AMJ Hilditch	c †Kirmani b Yadav	29	134	101
WM Darling	c †Kirmani b Kapil Dev	19	62	46
AR Border	c Narasimha Rao b Kapil Dev	24	131	119
KJ Hughes*	c †Kirmani b Kapil Dev	18	29	32
DF Whatmore	lbw b Yadav	77	119	91
PR Sleep	c Chauhan b Narasimha Rao	17	51	37
GN Yallop	c Chauhan b Narasimha Rao	21	61	36
KJ Wright†	not out	55	139	92
G Dymock	c †Kirmani b Kapil Dev	0	24	16
RM Hogg	b Kapil Dev	0	15	10
JD Higgs	lbw b Doshi	11	89	48
Extras	(b 4, lb 4, nb 19)	27		
Total	(all out; 106.3	298		

Fall of wickets 1-32 (Darling), 2-72 (Hilditch), 3-93 (Hughes), 4-116 (Border), 5-160 (Sleep), 6-225 (Whatmore), 7-228 (Yallop), 8-242 (Dymock), 9-246 (Hogg), 10-298 (Higgs)

Bowling	O	M	R	W	Econ
KD Ghavri	22	8	58	0	2.63
N Kapil Dev	32	7	82	5	2.56
DR Doshi	13.3	5	29	1	2.14
NS Yadav	27	10	56	2	2.07
MV Narasimha Rao	12	1	46	2	3.83

Australia 2nd innings (following on)		R	M	B
AMJ Hilditch	c †Kirmani b Ghavri	85	182	162
WM Darling	c †Kirmani b Kapil Dev	7	20	12
AR Border	c Narasimha Rao b Ghavri	46	168	120
KJ Hughes*	c & b Ghavri	40	145	125
GN Yallop	b Doshi	25	89	77
DF Whatmore	lbw b Kapil Dev	54	146	110
PR Sleep	c sub (J Arun Lal) b Chauhan	64	224	195
KJ Wright†	b Yadav	15	46	35
G Dymock	not out	31	89	66
RM Hogg	run out	0	4	1
JD Higgs	c Vengsarkar b Viswanath	7	20	17
Extras	(b 13, lb 9, w 1, nb 16)	39		
Total	(all out; 151.3	413		

Fall of wickets 1-20 (Darling), 2-147 (Hilditch),
3-156 (Border), 4-205 (Yallop), 5-241
(Hughes), 6-318 (Whatmore), 7-344 (Wright),
8-395 (Sleep), 9-395 (Hogg), 10-413 (Higgs)

Bowling	O	M	R	W	Econ
KD Ghavri	30	8	74	3	2.46
N Kapil Dev	20	7	48	2	2.40
DR Doshi	34	11	69	1	2.02
NS Yadav	36	10	101	1	2.80
MV Narasimha Rao	19	3	50	0	2.63
SM Gavaskar	4	1	10	0	2.50
CPS Chauhan	5	1	11	1	2.20
GR Viswanath	3.3	0	11	1	3.14

Match details: 8 ball overs; **Toss** – India, who
chose to bat; **Series** – India led the 6-match
series 1-0; **Umpires** – PR Punjabi and KB
Ramaswami

India v Australia: 5th Test at Kolkata, 26-31 Oct, 1979

Match drawn

Australia 1st innings		R	M	B
AMJ Hilditch	c †Kirmani b Kapil Dev	0	3	4
GN Yallop	c Gavaskar b Yadav	167	520	392
AR Border	lbw b Kapil Dev	54	133	101
KJ Hughes*	lbw b Kapil Dev	92	301	240
DF Whatmore	b Kapil Dev	4	15	12
WM Darling	st †Kirmani b Doshi	39	106	73
B Yardley	not out	61	96	70
KJ Wright†	lbw b Doshi	0	2	1
G Dymock	lbw b Doshi	3	22	10
RM Hogg	c Yashpal Sharma b Doshi	0	7	8
JD Higgs	lbw b Kapil Dev	1	14	11
Extras	(b 7, lb 7, nb 7)	21		
Total	(all out; 153	442		

Fall of wickets 1-0 (Hilditch), 2-97 (Border), 3-303 (Hughes), 4-311 (Whatmore), 5-347 (Yallop), 6-396 (Darling), 7-396 (Wright), 8-418 (Dymock), 9-426 (Hogg), 10-442 (Higgs)

Bowling	O	M	R	W	Econ
N Kapil Dev	32	9	74	5	2.31
KD Ghavri	24	3	85	0	3.54
NS Yadav	42	8	135	1	3.21
MV Narasimha Rao	8	0	24	0	3.00
DR Doshi	43	10	92	4	2.13
CPS Chauhan	4	0	11	0	2.75

India 1st innings		R	M	B
SM Gavaskar*	lbw b Hogg	14	10	9
CPS Chauhan	c Border b Higgs	39	232	160
DB Vengsarkar	c Hughes b Yardley	89	262	228
GR Viswanath	c †Wright b Yardley	96	247	177
Yashpal Sharma	c †Wright b Hogg	22	128	92
MV Narasimha Rao	run out	10	56	33
N Kapil Dev	c Hughes b Dymock	30	49	40
SMH Kirmani†	not out	13	51	31
KD Ghavri	c †Wright b Yardley	1	7	9
NS Yadav	c †Wright b Yardley	0	7	4
DR Doshi	b Dymock	0	5	4
Extras	(b 12, lb 9, w 4, nb 8)	33		
Total	(all out; 125.4	347		

Fall of wickets 1-15 (Gavaskar), 2-132 (Chauhan), 2-169* (Vengsarkar, retired not out), 3-256 (Yashpal Sharma), 4-290 (Narasimha Rao), 5-290 (Vengsarkar), 6-305 (Viswanath), 7-341 (Kapil Dev), 8-342 (Ghavri), 9-346 (Yadav), 10-347 (Doshi)

Bowling	O	M	R	W	Econ
G Dymock	26.4	8	56	2	2.10
RM Hogg	26	2	103	2	3.96
B Yardley	42	11	91	4	2.16
JD Higgs	28	12	56	1	2.00
AR Border	2	0	8	0	4.00
GN Yallop	1	1	0	0	0.00

Australia 2nd innings		R	M	B
AMJ Hilditch	b Ghavri	29	88	69
GN Yallop	lbw b Kapil Dev	4	30	24
AR Border	st †Kirmani b Doshi	6	26	28
KJ Hughes*	not out	64	137	120
DF Whatmore	c Vengsarkar b Doshi	4	22	28
WM Darling	c Gavaskar b Yadav	7	21	15
B Yardley	c Narasimha Rao b Yadav	12	29	28
KJ Wright†	not out	12	41	32
Extras	(b 9, lb 4)	13		
Total	(6 wickets dec; 57.3)	151		

Did not bat: G Dymock, RM Hogg, JD Higgs
Fall of wickets 1-21 (Yallop), 2-39 (Border),
3-53 (Hilditch), 4-62 (Whatmore), 5-81
(Darling), 6-115 (Yardley)

Bowling	O	M	R	W	Econ
N Kapil Dev	11	3	33	1	3.00
KD Ghavri	13.3	5	39	1	2.88
NS Yadav	11	6	16	2	1.45
DR Doshi	22	6	50	2	2.27

India 2nd innings (target: 247 runs)		R	M	B
SM Gavaskar*	c Hilditch b Dymock	25	73	62
CPS Chauhan	c †Wright b Dymock	50	180	130
DB Vengsarkar	c †Wright b Dymock	2	6	9
GR Viswanath	lbw b Dymock	7	22	17
Yashpal Sharma	not out	85	145	117
MV Narasimha Rao	not out	20	75	52
Extras	(b 4, lb 7)	11		
Total	(4 wickets; 63.2)	200		

Did not bat: N Kapil Dev, SMH Kirmani†, KD
Ghavri, NS Yadav, DR Doshi
Fall of wickets 1-52 (Gavaskar), 2-54
(Vengsarkar), 3-70 (Viswanath), 4-123
(Chauhan)

Bowling	O	M	R	W	Econ
G Dymock	25	7	63	4	2.52
RM Hogg	8.2	1	26	0	3.12
B Yardley	13	1	47	0	3.61
JD Higgs	16	3	51	0	3.18
GN Yallop	1	0	2	0	2.00

Match details: 8 ball overs;
Toss – Australia, who chose to bat;
Series – India led the 6-match series 1-0;
Umpires – SN Hanumantha Rao and S Kishen

India v Australia: 6th Test, at Mumbai, 3-7 November, 1979

India won by an innings and 100 runs

India 1st innings		R	M	B
SM Gavaskar*	c Hughes b Border	123	303	239
CPS Chauhan	b Dymock	73	228	178
DB Vengsarkar	c Whatmore b Border	6	77	64
GR Viswanath	c & b Higgs	10	56	40
SMH Kirmani†	not out	101	306	206
Yashpal Sharma	c Whatmore b Hogg	8	55	47
M Amarnath	hit wicket b Hogg	2	9	7
N Kapil Dev	c Whatmore b Higgs	17	39	29
KD Ghavri	c sub (GD Porter) b Dymock	86	153	99
NS Yadav	not out	0	6	6
Extras	(b 3, lb 12, nb 17)	32		
Total	(8 wickets dec; 149	458		

Did not bat: DR Doshi
Fall of wickets 1-192 (Chauhan), 2-222
(Vengsarkar), 3-231 (Gavaskar), 4-240
(Viswanath), 5-272 (Yashpal Sharma), 6-281
(Amarnath), 7-327 (Kapil Dev), 8-454 (Ghavri)

Bowling	O	M	R	W	Econ
G Dymock	31	5	95	2	3.06
RM Hogg	28	14	53	2	1.89
JD Higgs	29	4	116	2	4.00
AR Border	27	7	60	2	2.22
PR Sleep	28	7	79	0	2.82
DF Whatmore	5	2	11	0	2.20
GN Yallop	1	0	12	0	12.00

Australia 1st innings		R	M	B
AMJ Hilditch	run out	13	30	28
GN Yallop	c Kapil Dev b Yadav	60	180	125
AR Border	c Vengsarkar b Yadav	23	78	48
KJ Hughes*	c Vengsarkar b Doshi	14	41	42
DF Whatmore	lbw b Doshi	6	19	22
WM Darling	c sub (RMH Binny) b Yadav	16	40	35
PR Sleep	b Yadav	1	5	2
KJ Wright†	not out	11	60	41
G Dymock	c Chauhan b Doshi	1	6	5
RM Hogg	c Amarnath b Doshi	5	30	24
JD Higgs	b Doshi	0	6	7
Extras	(b 1, lb 2, nb 7)	10		
Total	(all out; 61.5	160		

Fall of wickets 1-28 (Hilditch), 2-77 (Border),
3-110 (Hughes), 4-118 (Whatmore), 5-124
(Yallop), 6-125 (Sleep), 7-144 (Darling), 8-145
(Dymock), 9-158 (Hogg), 10-160 (Higgs)

Bowling	O	M	R	W	Econ
N Kapil Dev	8	0	26	0	3.25
KD Ghavri	8	1	30	0	3.75
DR Doshi	19.5	4	43	5	2.16
NS Yadav	21	7	40	4	1.90
M Amarnath	5	1	11	0	2.20

Australia 2nd innings (following on)		R	M	B
AMJ Hilditch	b Kapil Dev	9	16	14
GN Yallop	c Amarnath b Ghavri	4	26	12
AR Border	b Doshi	61	257	182
KJ Hughes*	c Ghavri b Kapil Dev	80	168	144
DF Whatmore	lbw b Kapil Dev	0	7	2
WM Darling	retired hurt	0	3	2
PR Sleep	c Kapil Dev b Doshi	3	7	10
KJ Wright†	lbw b Doshi	5	35	31
G Dymock	c Viswanath b Yadav	7	8	9
RM Hogg	not out	3	30	22
JD Higgs	b Kapil Dev	4	20	22
Extras	(lb 12, nb 10)	22		
Total	(all out; 73.1)	198		

Fall of wickets 1-11 (Hilditch), 2-17 (Yallop),
3-149 (Hughes), 4-154 (Whatmore), 4-154*
(Darling, retired not out), 5-159 (Sleep), 6-176
(Wright), 7-183 (Dymock), 8-187 (Border),
9-198 (Higgs)

Bowling	O	M	R	W	Econ
N Kapil Dev	14.1	5	39	4	2.75
KD Ghavri	10	0	28	1	2.80
DR Doshi	25	6	60	3	2.40
NS Yadav	22	9	48	1	2.18
M Amarnath	2	1	1	0	0.50

Match details: 8 ball overs;
Toss – India, who chose to bat;
Series – India won the 6-match series 2-0;
Umpires – JD Ghosh and Mohammad Ghouse

All statistics courtesy www.cricinfo.com

Photo Credits

Front Cover and Back Cover background – Shutterstock

Back Cover images: Australian Cricket team, Sydney Test 1979; Kerry Packer – New Holland Publishers

Front Cover Flap: Australian batsman, Peter Toohey felled by a bouncer during the West Indies Tour, 1978 – Ken Piesse Collection

Back Cover Flap: Author Barry Nicholls – ABC

Internal image section

P. 1: Top image: Bob Simpson – New Holland Publishers; Bottom: Paul Hibbert – Ken Piesse Collection

P. 2: Top image: Phil Carlson, John Mclean and Gary Cosier; Bottom image: Gary Cosier – New Holland Publishers

P. 3 Top image: Craig Serjeant; Bottom image: Tony Mann – Patrick Eagar

P. 4 Top image: Randall not out; Bottom image: Alan Hurst – New Holland Publishers

P. 5 Top image: Phil Carlson – New Holland Publishers; Bottom image: Jeff Moss – Ken Piesse Collection

P. 6 Top image: Phil Carlson picks up Mushtaq; Bottom image: Steve Rixon – New Holland Publishers

P. 7 Top image: Bishan Bedi; Bottom image: Bruce Yardley – New Holland Publishers

P. 8 Top image: Wayne Clark; Bottom image: Peter Toohey and Wayne Clark – New Holland Publishers

P. 9 Top image: Wayne Clark strikes; Bottom image: Kim Hughes – New Holland Publishers

P. 10 Top image: Viv Richards; Bottom image: Andy Roberts – New Holland Publishers

P. 11 Top image: England team – New Holland Publishers; Bottom image: Rick Darling – Ken Piesse Collection

P. 12 Top image: Boycott and Hogg; Bottom image: Kevin Wright – New Holland Publishers

P. 13 Top image: Australian Test team, 1979; Bottom image: Mike Brearley – New Holland Publishers

P. 14 Top image: Rod Hogg and Graham Yallop; Bottom image: Derek Randall – New Holland Publishers

P. 15 Top image: Allan Border; Bottom image: Rick Darling – New Holland Publishers

P. 16 Top image: Rod Hogg – Patrick Eagar; Bottom image: Graham Yallop – New Holland Publishers